Game of My Life
KANSAS

STEVE BUCKNER

FOREWORD BY BILL SELF

SportsPublishingLLC.com

ISBN-10: 1-58261-971-9
ISBN-13: 978-1-58261-971-2

© 2007 by Steve Buckner

Publishers: Peter L. Bannon and Joseph J. Bannon Sr.
Senior managing editor: Susan M. Moyer
Acquisitions editor: Mike Pearson
Developmental editor: Doug Hoepker
Art director: K. Jeffrey Higgerson
Dust jacket design: Joseph Brumleve
Interior layout: Dustin J. Hubbart
Photo editor: Erin Linden-Levy

Printed in the United States of America

Sports Publishing L.L.C.
804 North Neil Street
Champaign, IL 61820
Phone: 1-877-424-2665
Fax: 217-363-2073
SportsPublishingLLC.com

CIP data available upon request

For my good friend and former classmate, Col. Gary Patton (M.S. Journalism 1990), and all the Jayhawks—KU graduates and native Kansans—serving in the U.S. military.

CONTENTS

FOREWORD
By Bill Self

One thing I have learned as a coach at the University of Kansas, first as a graduate assistant in 1985-86 and currently in the four years as head coach, is that Kansas basketball isn't a typical program. Instead, it's a way of life.

And when basketball is a way of life, the players become part of something much bigger than themselves. They learn that the game is not about "me" or "you," it's about "us." They gain this awareness through sacrifice, discipline, and unselfishness. When the team gets "it," they reap the rewards of success.

This success extends beyond wins and losses. One of the great traits of a great program is how much the ex-players care about having played at Kansas and how much they care for the current team. In turn, the current players are made aware of who came before them, and they realize they are the caretakers of the program while they are here, and that the responsibility will go to someone else when they depart.

When you read about the different games detailed in *Game of My Life: Kansas,* you'll gain an insight into the selfless efforts expended by Kansas players over the past 20 years. You'll see how much Kansas basketball, their teammates, coaches, and the fans mean to them. You'll understand how much they rely on their teammates for their success, how no shot is taken without first a rebound or steal by a teammate, a pass from a teammate, and the right positioning on offense by their teammates.

From arriving on campus to joining pick-up games at Robinson Gymnasium to participating in full-scale practices to playing games, the continuum repeats itself year after year. It's a continuum that becomes a part of our lives as coaches, players, administrators, and fans. It's important, and we all care deeply.

So sit back with this book and enjoy the heroics and fun of select games from the past 20 years. Re-live some memories and learn new stories about young men overcoming hardship and demonstrating perseverance. And always remember that *Game of My Life* represents the games of our lives.

Bill Self
Men's Head Basketball Coach, University of Kansas
"Rock, Chalk Jayhawk!"

INTRODUCTION
By Steve Buckner

U pon starting this book, I was informed by Brent Zwerneman (author of the first book in this series on Texas A&M football) and my editor at Sports Publishing that I'd be surprised by the games selected by the former University of Kansas Jayhawk basketball players.

They were right. The choices were surprising—at first. I mean, why wouldn't former Jayhawks from the past 20 seasons all pick a Missouri game at Allen Fieldhouse? But only two players chose games involving the Tigers.

Or what about a bunch of Oklahoma games, given the heated nature of that rivalry dating to the early 1980s? But only one game versus the Sooners was selected (and I bet you know which one that was).

Or what about a complete slate of NCAA tournament games? Well, eight players did choose memorable games from March and April, yet three of those contests ended in defeat. Surprising, huh?

As you read further into *Game of My Life: Kansas,* however, you'll see why each player selected the game he did. More importantly, you'll get to know the players better than before. They have had their share of doubts, just like the rest of us. They have wondered about their places in life. And, they have faced significant obstacles off and on the court, no matter how easy they have made the game of basketball appear in person and on television.

Regardless of the situation, these players never lost heart and always kept trying. They listened to their coaches, trusted in their teammates, and did everything in their powers to make Jayhawk fans cheer even louder and feel even prouder about them.

After interviewing these former players, I can assure you that Jayhawk fans have plenty to feel proud about. The players featured in this book are good people. They get it. To a person they treasure their time at the University of Kansas, and they love their teammates and coaches. And believe me, they hear us fans. The only thing matching the players' love of the game is the passion of the fans who root them on, and that relationship is not a surprise.

Enjoy the games!

Steve Buckner
Lawrence, Kansas

I

MARK TURGEON

The Life of Young Mark Turgeon

A common theme runs through Mark Turgeon's life and basketball career. "I'm very fortunate," Turgeon says.

He says those words, or something similar, frequently. Not to the point to make you doubt his sincerity, but enough to convince you. Besides, his story speaks for itself, and it is indeed one of good fortune buttressed by hard work, intelligence, and pure determination.

Mark's father, Robert Turgeon, introduced basketball to Mark when he was three years old.

"I fell in love with the game real early, as far back as I can remember," Turgeon says. "I loved dribbling, passing, and shooting. I just loved it."

Robert Turgeon noted his son's passion for the game and decided to act upon it. With Phil Reilly, the father of Turgeon's friend Rob Reilly, the two men started the Capital City Youth Basketball League for their third-grade sons and other boys to play in. Some 30-plus years later, the league still exists.

"I was always fortunate enough to be around good players and play ball," Turgeon says. "I wasn't the best player in the world, but I had enough knowledge of it to be successful."

Another attribute Turgeon brought to his game was a highly competitive drive to succeed.

"I've always been determined," he says. "I've always been little. A lot of people have told me, 'You can't do this; you can't do that.' I can remember that as far back as second and third grade with sports or different things. It's always driven me."

Turgeon kept playing basketball and improving. His Hayden High School team won the Kansas state 4A championship his junior and senior years and went 47-3 in those two seasons. Turgeon averaged 11.5 points and 6.8 assists during his senior season.

"I've been very fortunate my whole life—I've always been surrounded by great people," Turgeon says. "I had a good coach in Ben Meseke and great teammates. We were really good."

But being good on the court didn't translate to scholarship offers from top-notch colleges. Turgeon's offers came from hometown Washburn (then an NAIA school) and a handful of Kansas junior colleges. However, changes were underway in Lawrence in the spring of 1983. The University of Kansas fired longtime coach Ted Owens and his staff. KU then hired Larry Brown from the New Jersey Nets. Most of Brown's coaching success had occurred in the ABA and NBA, but he had led UCLA to the 1980 NCAA championship game during his two seasons in Westwood.

Brown liked smart, determined guards, players who reminded Brown of himself.

"Coach Brown being short—5-foot-10—really helped me," Turgeon says with a knowing laugh.

College Life

Chris Piper knows the following story may cause him physical harm or worse, but he tells it anyway. As freshmen, Piper and Turgeon met with KU's weight coordinator to learn about working out. Piper said he noticed the coordinator was talking to him rather than Turgeon, but thought nothing about it until the meeting wrapped up. As they were walking out, the coordinator told Piper, "Yeah, come over Monday to get started. And if you want, you can bring your little friend with you," Piper recalls while laughing heartily. "Mark got so mad."

It wasn't the last of the indignities Turgeon endured as a freshman. He still wore braces, adding to his youthful appearance. Given his looks and slight build, Turgeon was mistaken for a team manager, trainer, and even Coach Brown's son during the 1983-84 season. But Turgeon had the last

Notes on Mark Turgeon

Years lettered:	1983-84 to 1986-87
Position:	Guard
Height:	5-foot-10
Playing weight:	150 pounds
Hometown:	Topeka, Kansas
Current residence:	Wichita, Kansas
Occupation:	Head Coach, men's basketball, Wichita State University
Accomplishments:	Set team record for most assists by a freshman (138); named Academic All-Big Eight first team as a junior.
Nicknames:	"Turg" and "The Surgeon"
The game:	Kansas vs. Duke in Dallas, Texas, March 29, 1986

laugh. He was named a starter when conference play began, and became the team's sparkplug and an Allen Fieldhouse favorite. The Jayhawks went 13-5 in games Turgeon started, and he set a team record for freshmen with 138 assists while averaging 4.3 points.

Turgeon averaged 15 minutes per game and 2.3 points as a sophomore, starting eight games (KU won seven of those contests). The team, bolstered by heralded freshman Danny Manning, improved from 22-10 to 26-8. Despite the setback in his own career that season, big things lay ahead for Turgeon and the 1985-86 Jayhawks. KU returned seniors Greg Dreiling, Ron Kellogg, and Calvin Thompson. Cedric Hunter and Turgeon (who averaged 2.4 points) were juniors. Manning showed constant improvement as a sophomore, and redshirt sophomore Piper was part of the team's rotation off the bench. Kansas finished the regular season at 28-3 and won the Big Eight title with a 13-1 record. The No. 2 Jayhawks then won the Big Eight tournament at Kemper Arena in Kansas City, Missouri, defeating Oklahoma in the semifinals and Iowa State in the finals by two points each.

As the No. 1 seed in the Midwest Regional, the 'Hawks easily defeated North Carolina A&T and Temple in Dayton, Ohio, before returning to Kemper Arena to face Michigan State in a Sweet 16 match-up. Kansas outlasted the Spartans 96-86 in an overtime game marred by a malfunctioning game clock toward the end of regulation. Two days later, the Jayhawks defeated coach Jim Valvano's North Carolina State Wolfpack 75-67 with Manning and Dreiling keying a pair of second-half surges.

For the first time in 12 years, Kansas was Final Four bound.

The Setting

The NCAA Tournament had changed drastically since Kansas had last appeared in the Final Four in 1974. The tournament field had expanded from 25 to 64 teams. The increase in teams meant more games, and more games meant more television exposure. The extra exposure brought new fans to college basketball. Households around the country tuned in, drawn to the drama that accompanied early-round upsets and last-second buzzer-beaters.

The debut of ESPN (1979), CNN (1980), and *USA Today* (1982) had already made a significant impact on sports coverage. In most metropolitan areas, sports talk radio was limited to a couple of hours in the afternoon on AM news stations (many of which had been playing music just a few years earlier), but it was a start. Al McGuire had gone from the coach who directed Marquette over KU in the 1974 Final Four to a renowned television broadcaster who sometimes spoke in his own language. McGuire and ESPN's Dick Vitale broadened the vocabulary of the sports world with terms like "March Madness," "mid-majors," and "brackets."

In short, the heavy attention transformed the tournament from "just" a high-level competition to an omnipresent "event." The Kansas Jayhawks found themselves in the middle of "an event" soon after defeating N.C. State on Sunday, March 23, 1986.

The fans followed the team's every move. So did the national media, including the *New York Times,* which ran a story headlined, "A triumphant heritage rebounds with Jayhawks." The story recounted the university's basketball history and included a quote from Turgeon, who said, "I just wanted to be on the team. Even if I could only be that guy on the end of the bench. I just wanted to be him."

The team paid homage to the 1952 national champion Jayhawk team by shaving their heads, and would even wear red uniforms (as did the KU team 34 years earlier) versus Duke in the semifinals.

"The event" continued. Large groups of fans saw the Jayhawks off to Dallas, where another crowd greeted the team upon its arrival.

"I think we were the first team to get in, and our fans were so excited," Turgeon recalls. "There were fans all over our hotel. You'd go out to dinner and there'd be KU fans everywhere. It was a very special time."

In Duke, Kansas would face the top-ranked, 36-2 Blue Devils, a team that had defeated the Jayhawks 92-86 in the finals of the Preseason NIT tournament that season in New York. Writing for *USA Today*, Valvano picked Duke to defeat Kansas 72-70. "The crucial element in this game will be fouls," wrote the North Carolina State coach. "Take 7-foot-1 Greg Dreiling out, and Kansas loses its inside advantage."

On the last Friday of March 1986, no one had any idea just how good a prognosticator "Jimmy V" really was.

The Game of My Life

BY MARK TURGEON
KANSAS VS. DUKE, MARCH 29, 1986

When I ran out on the court, I said a little prayer thanking God for letting me be a part of [this game]. I still feel that way today, every time I go to a Final Four. I still can't believe I got to play in a game like this.

We were prepared. Our game prep went well. And we played well considering all the tough breaks that we had during the game. [Duke led 36-33 at halftime. Though the score was close and would remain so, Kansas was in foul trouble: Hunter had three and Manning had picked up two early fouls that limited him to only seven minutes in the first half. Four other players also had two fouls. Mark, who had just hoped to play a minute in the game, already had logged 10 minutes by intermission. By game's end, Manning, Dreiling, and Hunter had fouled out. Kansas was called for 33 fouls compared with Duke's 14, and the Blue Devils shot 30 free throws to the Jayhawks' 12.]

As players, we knew we had one of the best coaches of all time in Larry Brown. He has a knack for figuring out how to win games, no matter if he's playing [me] 20 minutes or playing Danny Manning for 40 minutes. He figures it out.

It was unfortunate the way the foul trouble happened—how many free throws they shot compared to ours. And then Archie [Marshall] getting hurt when we were up four [with 8:10 left in the game].

I remember the game was tied at 67 in the last minute. They're holding the ball. Mark Alarie goes up and takes a shot, and we're playing pretty good defense. The ball bounces right to Danny Ferry, and he lays it in with 22 seconds to go. They made the play and we didn't is what it came down to.

Ronnie and Calvin were the two guys you wanted to take the shot late with who we had out on the court. Ronnie had a good look to tie it and send it into overtime. [Kellogg missed a six-foot left-side jumper with 11 seconds left, and then a 16-foot jump shot from the right side with four seconds remaining.] That's all you can ask.

Because of the foul trouble, we finished the game with a funny lineup on the court that we had never practiced: Cedric was at the one; I was at the two; Ronnie was at the three; Calvin was playing the four; and Piper was at the five.

I was so proud of our guys because we had so much go wrong. Altonio Campbell got in the game because even I got into foul trouble at one point, and Altonio *never* played. We overcame a lot and gave ourselves a chance. It was a tremendous experience, one that we'll never forget.

I'm a big believer that some things are meant to be and some aren't, and that year wasn't meant to be for the Jayhawks.

Game and Season Results

Duke's Tommy Amaker sank two free throws with two seconds to play to ice the Blue Devils' 71-67 victory over Kansas. The Jayhawks ended the season at 35-4, the best record in school history (since matched by the 1997-98 team).

"We played well in almost every game that year," Turgeon says. "Our losses were all close losses. We had a chance to win every game.

"We had a group of different personalities, but we had one common goal and that was to win. We stayed out of trouble and we did what we had to do. To this day, I'm proud to be associated with that team and the kind of year we had, win the Big Eight championship and play in the Final Four."

BOX SCORE
Kansas vs. Duke, March 29, 1986

Kansas	33 34	– 67
Duke	36 35	– 71

Kansas (67)

	Min	FG	FT	Reb	PF	TP
Manning	23	2-9	0-0	5	5	4
Kellogg	33	11-15	0-0	3	4	22
Dreiling	30	1-7	4-4	6	5	6
Hunter	22	2-5	1-4	8	5	5
Thompson	39	5-12	3-3	5	1	13
Turgeon	19	1-1	0-0	0	3	2
Marshall	19	6-10	1-1	2	3	13
Piper	13	1-1	0-0	1	0	2
Campbell	1	0-0	0-0	0	0	0
Hull	1	0-0	0-0	0	0	0
(team)				3		
TOTALS	**200**	**29-60**	**9-12**	**33**	**26**	**67**

Assists: 18 (Turgeon 5, Kellogg 3, Hunter 3, Thompson 3, Dreiling 2, Manning, Campbell); Turnovers: 21 (Hunter 4, Turgeon 4, Kellogg 3, Dreiling 3, Thompson 3, Marshall 2, Manning , Campbell); Blocked shots: 4 (Dreiling 3, Manning); Steals: 4 (Kellogg 2, Manning, Thompson).

Duke (71)

	Min	FG	FT	Reb	PF	TP
Henderson	33	3-12	7-8	4	1	13
Alarie	35	4-13	4-6	8	3	12
Bilas	29	1-2	5-7	5	2	7
Amaker	37	2-5	3-4	2	1	7
Dawkins	38	11-17	2-4	3	3	24
Strickland	4	0-1	0-0	0	0	0
Ferry	15	4-5	0-1	3	1	8
King	9	0-0	0-0	3	3	0
(team)				6		
TOTALS	**200**	**25-55**	**21-30**	**34**	**14**	**71**

Assists: 12 (Amaker 6, Henderson 3, Alarie, Bilas, King); Turnovers: 17 (Henderson 6, Alarie 3, Amaker 3, Strickland 2, Bilas, Dawkins, Ferry); Blocked shots: 1 (Alarie); Steals: 10 (Alarie 4, Amaker 3, Henderson 2, Bilas).

Officials: Paul Galvan, John Clougherty, Tom Finchen. Attendance: 16,493.

Piper says the 'Hawks made some mistakes down the stretch that cost KU the game. Still, had Kansas defeated Duke and then Louisville—who they had beaten earlier in the season—would the future of Jayhawk basketball have been altered?

"This team was so much better than '88 from a talent standpoint," Piper says. "People will say in '86 if you had played the way you should have, you would have two national championships. And I always say, well, if we had won in '86, Danny probably would not have been there in '88."

What Became of Mark Turgeon?

Turgeon returned for his senior season in 1987-88 to a team that missed its stars from the previous year. Gone were Dreiling, Kellogg, and Thompson, plus Marshall missed the season recovering from the knee injury he suffered against Duke. The team slipped to 25-11 and 9-5 in the Big Eight. Kansas' season—and Turgeon's playing career—ended in a 70-59 second-round loss to Georgetown in the NCAA tournament. For the season, Turgeon averaged a career-best 5.0 points.

After graduating with a bachelor's degree in personnel administration, Turgeon joined Brown's coaching staff as a student assistant and junior varsity coach.

"I learned a lot about teaching the game of basketball from Coach Brown," he says.

When Roy Williams took over for Brown in the summer of 1998, the new coach retained Turgeon as part of his new staff.

"He helped me grow up and showed me how hard you had to work to be successful in this business—how to run an office, how to be organized, and how to treat people," Turgeon says.

In 1992, Turgeon left Kansas when Jayhawk assistant head coach Jerry Green became head coach at the University of Oregon.

"It was a big risk," Turgeon says. "I tell people all the time the biggest mistake I ever made was leaving KU to go to Oregon as an assistant. But one of the best things I ever did in my life also was leaving KU to go to Oregon.

"I really had to grow up and learn how to really work and sell. It was hard, but it was paramount in the development of me as a coach and a person."

When Green took the head coaching job at Tennessee in 1996, Turgeon opted to go to Philadelphia to again work with Brown as an assistant with the NBA's '76ers. Turgeon stayed there a season and then re-entered college basketball as a head coach at Jacksonville State University of the Trans America Conference. In two seasons in Jacksonville, Alabama, Turgeon improved the Gamecocks from 8-18 in 1998-99 to 17-11 in 1999-2000.

"Jacksonville State was a huge risk, but they were the first ones to say 'Yes,'" Turgeon says about fulfilling his dreams to be a college head coach.

In March 2000, Wichita State hired Turgeon as its 25th head basketball coach.

"I've been in a lot of places in the country," he says. "I've been in Kansas, Oregon, Philadelphia, and Alabama, so I've learned how different parts of the country act. We're one great country, but we're all different. It's been a good learning experience for me, and Coach Green taught me how to build programs that weren't very good."

In each of Turgeon's six seasons in Wichita, the Shockers have improved their win total from nine to 15 to 18 to 21 to 22 to 26. The Shockers defeated Seton Hall and Tennessee to advance to the Sweet 16 of the 2006 tournament. In doing so, Wichita State was one of several "Cinderella teams" to become one of America's favorites during the tournament.

"I had a great group of kids," Turgeon says of his 2005-06 Shockers team. "Going to practice every day was fun. If I could coach that team for the rest of my life, I would be the happiest guy in the world. They always did what I asked."

Turgeon also appreciated how the community fell in love with Shockers basketball again.

"The support has been great, selling out games and all," he says. "Cutting down the nets in front of our people that night was remarkable."

And it all began in a Topeka basketball league that led Turgeon to Kansas as a college player.

"You have to understand, I grew up dreaming about playing for KU," he says. "It was probably more special to me than for a lot of kids. Then to play on a Final Four team, play for a great coach like Larry Brown, and be with a championship team—to be doing what I'm doing, I would not be where I am today without Kansas basketball."

"Kansas basketball has put me in a position to be successful in this game. I don't think anyone will know how grateful I was to be a part of that."

Actually, we do, Mark. It goes with the good fortune of knowing how fortunate you are.

2

MILT NEWTON

The Life of Young Milt Newton

That basketball meant the world to Milt Newton as he grew up is hardly surprising.

That Newton spent the first 12 years of his life living on the Virgin Islands and still loved the game is more surprising, except that the game is quite popular on the U.S. territory.

"We'd catch [NBA] games on CBS," Newton says. "I was a big 'Dr. J' fan. Being young, I had idols, but really I was just concerned with playing basketball."

Which Newton did almost all of the time. Sometimes as a sixth grader, he sneaked out of his home to play until 10 p.m. at a nearby playground with older boys.

"My mom would lock the door, so I'd have to knock and wake her up to get in," he says, adding he was punished for his transgressions.

Newton moved to New Jersey as a seventh grader and fit in with his classmates in part because he had "game." As a ninth grader, his team won the county championship by defeating the high school's junior varsity team.

"I remember playing on the playground all day in the summer by myself, shooting or whatever," Newton says. "It was a lot of fun."

For high school, Newton moved to Washington, D.C., where he also adjusted quickly and easily to his new surroundings thanks in part to his talent on the court. Newton played for coach Frank Williams—whom he holds in high esteem—at Coolidge High School. Williams protected his players—especially sophomores and juniors—from college recruiting lest they get "big headed." The coach stored college letters for his underclassmen in a big, locked cabinet.

"We spent three years trying to find that key so we could see what letters were in there," Newton says.

The first recruiting letter Newton saw with his name on it came from Nebraska. Although he knew of interest from local programs, Newton was so inspired by the Nebraska letter that he decided to visit Lincoln on the spot.

"Worst visit I ever had," he says with a big laugh.

Newton became acquainted with Kansas through assistant coach John Calipari at the Five-Star Basketball Camp in Pennsylvania's Pocono Mountains the summer before his senior year. Newton recalls fellow camper Rod Strickland telling him to "run the floor and I'll get you the ball." Strickland delivered, and Newton made the camp's all-tournament team.

Recruiting interest picked up after Newton's strong showing at the camp. He also visited New Mexico, and he was interested in Kansas because of Larry Brown's pro experience and Danny Manning's commitment to the Jayhawks. But geography served as another factor in Newton's decision. In his case, Newton wanted to get away from the D.C. area, figuring it would help him grow up.

When Newton returned home from "a really good visit at New Mexico, I think even better than Kansas," he sat down with the man he calls "Dad" (guardian Kent Amos) to determine his college choice. The two rated New Mexico and Kansas regarding the arenas, the area of the country, the coaching staff, and the ability to play right away, among other factors. The following will come as a big shock to Kansas fans, but Newton says New Mexico "came out on top, every time … but only by a hair."

But Newton kept "having a feeling about Kansas," so he chose the Jayhawks.

College Life

Initially, Newton experienced some adjustment issues with KU in the classic case of "big city comes to smaller town." His new college teammates helped him make the adjustment.

Notes on Milt Newton

Years lettered:	1984-85; 1986-87 through 1988-89
Position:	Forward
Height:	6-foot-4 ½
Playing weight:	180 pounds
Hometown:	Washington, D.C.
Current Residence:	Washington, D.C.
Occupation:	Director of player personnel and assistant general manager of the Washington Wizards
Accomplishments:	Named team's MVP in 1989; named All-Big Eight Conference second team in '89 by Associated Press and United Press International; named one of the five most underrated players in the nation by *USA Today* in '89; selected to the NCAA All-Tournament teams for the Midwest sub-regional, Midwest Regional, and NCAA Final Four in 1988.
Nickname:	"Alfreaka"
The game:	Kansas State vs. Kansas in Pontiac, Michigan, March 27, 1988

"Coming from D.C., you got to have a little edge on you," Newton says. "I remember walking down campus one day with Scooter Barry and Mark Turgeon. People were really friendly, but at first I had this guard up. I remember Scooter, Mark, and even Chris Piper saying one time, 'Milt, you're not in D.C. anymore. People don't want anything from you. You don't have to be on guard. ... It's all right to smile every now and then.'"

Turgeon, now the head coach for men's basketball at Wichita State, remembers the time well.

"The thing I appreciate about Milt is that he was an East Coast kid who came in and had to adapt to another part of the country," Turgeon says. "It was hard on him at first. Milt's maturity level over five years was remarkable—how much he matured. He became a leader, an all-around great guy. His playing ability got better and better and his confidence grew."

But first Newton had to learn how to play basketball as a team sport. When he began playing pick-up games with the team, Newton's style of play was to embarrass his defender with a spectacular play. The other Jayhawks quickly noticed this tendency, and Cedric Hunter nicknamed Newton "Alfreaka." When Newton asked why, Hunter replied, "Because if you guard me, I'll freak ya!"

Just as his teammates had told Newton to lighten up around his fellow students, so, too, did Hunter inform him to stop trying to embarrass people on the court and just play and have fun. Newton took the lesson to heart, later sporting "Alfreaka" on a vanity license plate and his letter jacket.

In his freshman season, Newton played in 30 of 36 games and averaged 3.2 points. The low scoring average was due in part by limited playing time, which was mostly by design. Brown emphasized to Newton to shoot only when he was open. Otherwise, he was to pass the ball.

Newton continued to learn more lessons. Upset by a lack of playing time, he gave Brown an ultimatum: "Play me more or I'll transfer." Brown answered, "Really? Give me a list of schools you want to transfer to, and I'll try to help get you there." That wasn't the response Newton wanted to hear, so he decided to earn his minutes.

Newton also struggled with his free time as a freshman. After practice, he preferred "going out, partying, or hanging out with girls" to doing his homework. Newton's first-semester grades reflected his misplaced priorities.

"My dad said, 'If you don't shape up pretty soon, I will pull you out of school and I will send you to Delaware State where I went,'" Newton recalls. "That was a wake-up call. So I shaped up and my dad said he was proud of me doing my schoolwork."

In 1985-86, Newton made the difficult but mature decision to redshirt. He knew minutes would remain scarce playing behind Ron Kellogg and junior college transfer Archie Marshall. The Jayhawks, one of the best teams in school history, advanced to the Final Four in Dallas before losing to Duke in the national semifinals.

Newton returned to the court in 1986-87 as a redshirt sophomore. He averaged 3.7 points while playing slightly more minutes than he did as a freshman. In the summer of 1987, Newton showed a portent of things to

AP Images

come, averaging 20 points a game for the U.S. Virgin Island team at the Pan Am Games.

No one could possibly know it at the time, but Newton's transformation would prove vital to Kansas' 1987-88 season. In the Jayhawks' 11th game that year, Marshall re-injured his knee and essentially was lost for the season. Newton started in Marshall's place and began asserting himself more. Still, the Jayhawk team struggled to find its identity. On January 30, 1988, Kansas State came to Lawrence and ended the 'Hawks 55-game win streak at Allen Fieldhouse. Worse for Newton, the Wildcat player he defended, Mitch Richmond, scored 35 points in the 72-61 loss.

"I knew I couldn't let that happen again," Newton says. So, he cut out the box score from the game and taped it to his locker as a reminder and a motivational tool.

Despite the loss, Brown told the team they were improving. Newton says he thought the coach "was crazy at the time, telling us we were getting better," but Brown was right. The Jayhawks went 8-3 during the remainder of the regular season. One of those victories was a 64-63 win over K-State. Newton scored 14 points and grabbed six rebounds in the game, compared with Richmond's totals of 11 and one.

Newton lit up Oklahoma State in the first round of the Big Eight tournament, scoring a career-high 29 points in the 74-58 victory. But the next day, Richmond scored a game-high 21 points to lead Kansas State past KU, 69-54, much to Newton's chagrin.

Kansas entered the NCAA tournament with a 21-11 record and a six seed in the Midwest Regional. The Jayhawks had made "The Dance," but few people—if any—viewed them as the Cinderella they were in the midst of becoming.

The Setting

Ironically for Newton, the Jayhawks' first two tournament games were played in Lincoln, Nebraska, site of his worst recruiting trip as a high schooler. In the first-round game, Kansas led the entire contest and defeated Xavier 85-72. Manning scored 24 points for KU, and Newton added 21. Both players grabbed a game-best 12 rebounds. In the second round, Kansas escaped Murray State's upset bid, 61-58. Newton hit a key jumper in the final minute and scored 11 points, third best on the team behind Manning's 25 and Kevin Pritchard's 16.

Earlier that afternoon, Vanderbilt had upset Pittsburgh in overtime. That outcome meant KU would face the Commodores instead of the rugged Panthers in the "Sweet 16" game at the Pontiac Silverdome in Pontiac, Michigan.

"We thought, 'Wow, their big fellow, Will Perdue versus Danny—no contest. We got this game," Newton recalls.

The Jayhawks' overconfidence didn't matter. Manning turned Perdue inside out, outscoring him 38 to 16 in KU's 77-64 victory. In the late game, Kansas State stunned Purdue 73-70 behind Richmond's 27-point, 11-rebound performance. The Wildcats' upset spurred many feel-good stories about KU fans cheering for K-State and vice versa on that Friday night in suburban Detroit. The local media also wrote about how great it was that two Kansas schools would play each other for the right to go to the Final Four at Kemper Arena in Kansas City, Missouri.

All of these accounts were as true as they were "well and good." But on Sunday, March 27, 1988, all of those positive feelings evaporated as two in-state and conference rivals squared off with an invaluable Final Four berth at stake.

The Game of My Life

BY MILT NEWTON
KANSAS STATE VS. KANSAS, MARCH 27, 1988

These tournament games give you such a short time to prepare, but we knew them and they knew us. We were so familiar with them that there was no "fear factor" there.

We knew we had to stick to our game plan and utilize Danny. Kansas State had no one who could guard him. Likewise, we knew Mitch was the key for them, and I decided if we were to lose, it would not be because Mitch Richmond had a big day for them.

We played a little tentatively in the first half. All of a sudden, we said to ourselves, "If we win this game, we're in the Final Four," which is added pressure. We started playing like there was something at stake, whereas before we were just playing.

But Mitch wasn't having a good game, either. Will Scott was playing well and some other guys were stepping up for them. [Kansas State led 29-27 at halftime. Manning had 10 points for KU, Barry added seven, and Newton scored six on three-for-five shooting from the field.]

In the second half, we settled down and came out more focused. We did not want to have a team beat us three times in a season. [Keith Harris, Barry, and I] continued doing a good job on Mitch, and we started pulling away. I remember face-guarding him at times, but mainly we just made it really tough for him to catch the ball. That's because once he caught the ball, he was pretty good because he was bigger and stronger than I was.

So we denied him the ball as much as we could. When he got the ball, we got some help on him. When Mitch drove, our best defender—Chris Piper—would show and make him slow up a little bit. We just did a really good job on Mitch defensively.

I think I had my best game of the tournament all the way around. I got it going in the second half. I remember Coach calling a play for me. I got the ball and started making a move. But then I noticed Keith Harris was wide open. I went up to shoot and I dumped it down to Keith and he made the shot. I remember looking over at Coach and he had this big smile on his face, like he was thinking, "That's good basketball right there."

Game and Season Results

Kansas pulled away from K-State as the second half wound down and captured a 71-58 victory. Manning played his typical, impeccable game and scored a game-high 20 points. Newton scored 18, grabbed a team-high nine rebounds, and dished seven assists. Most impressively, he held Richmond to 11 points and four boards.

"Milt was great and extremely focused," Piper said. "It was a great atmosphere. We were in control. K-State seemed tight."

Kansas continued exacting its revenge during the 1988 Final Four. As detailed in the next chapter, the Jayhawks jumped out to an early 14-0 lead and tenaciously held on to defeat Duke 66-59 in the national semifinal game. Newton scored 20 points and grabbed seven rebounds against the Blue Devils.

Kansas State vs. Kansas, March 27, 1988

Kansas	27 44	– 71
Kansas State	29 29	– 58

Kansas (71)

	Min	FG	FT	Reb	PF	Pts
Newton	29	7-10	2-2	9	3	18
Piper	36	3-6	0-2	4	2	6
Manning	39	10-18	0-1	6	3	20
Pritchard	38	2-7	3-4	3	3	8
Gueldner	11	0-3	0-0	0	1	0
Barry	25	5-6	4-4	5	1	15
Harris	15	2-3	0-0	1	0	4
Minor	4	0-1	0-0	0	0	0
Maddox	1	0-0	0-0	0	0	0
Normore	1	0-0	0-0	0	0	0
Mattox	1	0-0	0-1	0	0	0
(team)				4		
TOTALS	**200**	**29-54**	**9-14**	**32**	**13**	**71**

Three-point goals: 4-11 (Newton 2-3, Pritchard 1-4, Barry 1-1, Piper 0-1, Manning 0-1, Gueldner 0-1); Assists: 22 (Newton 7, Pritchard 7, Barry 3, Gueldner 2, Piper, Manning, Minor); Turnovers: 10 (Barry 3, Newton 2, Pritchard 2, Piper, Gueldner, Minor); Blocked shots: 1 (Manning); Steals: 6 (Pritchard 2, Harris 2, Newton, Barry).

Kansas State (58)

	Min	FG	FT	Reb	PF	TP
Richmond	37	4-14	2-4	4	3	11
Bledsoe	33	5-6	0-4	9	4	10
Meyer	26	1-3	0-0	2	0	2
Henson	40	2-8	0-0	3	4	6
Scott	30	6-15	2-2	0	0	18
McCoy	18	3-5	3-4	5	2	9
Glover	9	1-3	0-0	1	0	2
Diggins	3	0-0	0-0	0	1	0
Dobbins	3	0-0	0-0	1	0	0
Stanfield	1	0-0	0-0	1	0	0
(team)				3		
TOTALS	**200**	**22-54**	**7-14**	**29**	**14**	**58**

Three-point goals: 7-22 (Scott 4-10, Henson 2-6, Richmond 1-5, Glover 0-1); Assists: 15 (Richmond 5, Henson 5, Meyer 2, Bledsoe, Scott, Glover); Turnovers: 12 (Richmond 6, Bledsoe 4, Henson 2); Blocked shots 3 (Bledsoe, Henson, Scott); Steals: 4 (Scott 2, Meyer, Henson).

Officials: Booker Turner, Dick Poparo, Wally Tanner. Attendance: 31,632.

"The way Duke plays was good for us," Newton explains. "When they overplay you on defense, [you] go back door, and that's what we did. The way we played on offense fit with the way they played on defense."

The victory pitted Kansas against Big Eight rival Oklahoma, which had defeated KU twice in the regular season.

"Once again, we said to ourselves that we could not let a team beat us three times in a row," Newton says.

Two days later, Kansas earned its second national championship by defeating the favored Sooners 83-79. Newton scored 15 points on perfect six-for-six shooting from the field, including two baskets from beyond the arc. He joined MVP Danny Manning on the All-Tournament team.

"What can I say? We had Danny, we had Clint Normore coming off the bench and hitting a three, and we had Coach Brown, which we always thought was worth five to 10 points," Newton says.

Newton also recalls the team's bus driver in Detroit, Jimmy Dunlop, and how the ultra-superstitious Brown brought him to the Final Four to drive the Jayhawks to and from Kemper Arena the following weekend.

"He became part of our family," Newton says.

But one important person in Newton's life didn't live to see the championship season. His high school coach, Frank Williams, died May 24, 1987. Newton dedicated the season in his coach's memory, a memory that involved teaching, concern for others, and an emphasis on discipline.

As a champion who stepped up when he was needed the most by his team, Newton's fine junior season did his late coach proud.

What Became of Milt Newton?

A Hollywood producer reviewing a script about Kansas' improbable ride to the 1988 national championship probably would reject the story as too preposterous. The same likely could be said about the events of the next 11 months after the Jayhawks cut down the Kemper Arena nets. A breathtaking series of "good news, bad news" events awaited Kansas that would test the souls of players, coaches, administrators, and fans.

Good news: KU coach Larry Brown turned down an opportunity to return to UCLA as basketball coach.

Bad news: Brown left Kansas a few weeks later for the San Antonio Spurs head coaching job.

More bad news: With Kansas facing possible NCAA sanctions, the open coaching job didn't draw the interest of "big-name, established" candidates.

Good news: Kansas hired Roy Williams, an assistant coach at North Carolina, in early July 1988. The new coach said all the right things about the challenge before him at his introductory press conference and immediately began working to put his words into action.

Bad news: Two weeks into practice, the NCAA placed Kansas on probation, including banning KU from postseason play in the 1988-89 season. The Jayhawks could not defend their national championship.

Good news: The Jayhawks race to a 13-1 start and a No. 16 national ranking.

Bad news: KU loses 10 of its next 13 games, including eight in a row.

Good news: The Jayhawks never lost heart and played as hard during the losing streak as they did all season.

Bad news: The Jayhawks season ended again at Kemper Arena, this time in a 73-65 loss to Kansas State in the first round of the Big Eight Conference Tournament. KU's final record was 19-12 including 6-8 in league play.

Playing a larger role in the offense, Newton led the Jayhawks in scoring with 17.7 points per game, which ranked him seventh in the Big Eight. He was second among conference shooters with 45.5 percent accuracy from three-point range. In the final game of his career, Newton scored a season-high 28 points and snared seven rebounds in the loss to K-State.

After the season, Newton worked hard to stay in shape and further improve his conditioning. He signed with the Los Angeles Lakers and impressed the team at its summer camp. But in a pick-up game back in Lawrence, Kirk Wagner fell on Newton's ankle and injured him rather severely.

"I thought my foot came off," Newton says. "The doctor said the tendon that connects my calf muscles behind my ankle bone had slipped from behind to up front. I was in excruciating pain."

Newton returned to the Lakers camp "at about 70 percent." The second day of camp, he made a cut and the tendon slipped again. Newton's NBA dreams were over. Still, he persevered and played in the Continental Basketball Association and in Australia for a couple of seasons before retiring and entering the business world. His first job was working in community relations with the Denver Nuggets. Then came a five-year stint as assistant director with U.S.A. Basketball, followed by a year and a half with the Philadelphia 76ers during Brown's tenure as coach. Newton then moved to the NBA office and helped set up the Development League.

"It was a very good experience for me to be around some very, very smart people," he says.

Today, Newton works as director of player personnel and assistant general manager for the Washington Wizards. Former teammate and roommate Mark Turgeon isn't the least bit surprised by Newton's ascension through the NBA front-office ranks.

"Milt's got a presence about him, and that's why he is successful in today's world, too," Turgeon says. "I'm really proud of him with what he's doing in the basketball world, climbing the ladder in the right way."

3

CHRIS PIPER

The Life of Young Chris Piper

Recreationally, basketball played a big role in Chris Piper's life as he grew up in Lawrence. Piper and his buddies—including Rod Zinn, Jamie Steinhauser, Paul Johnson, and Eric Lienhard—usually played basketball together wherever and whenever they could.

"We'd sneak into Robinson Gymnasium [on KU's campus] and invariably get kicked out every day," Piper says. "We just played pick-up basketball all the time—that's all we really did."

Competitively, however, Piper came *this* close to having basketball remain as only a recreational part of his life. When he entered South Junior High School, Piper tried out for the seventh grade basketball team. He says he did so to be with his friends more than to play on the team. Problem was, the coach cut him. Ditto for eighth grade.

By his freshman year, Piper stood 6-foot-3 and had improved his game just enough to be the last player to make the team. That's how close the University of Kansas came to perhaps missing out on its headiest role player ever. His close call as a freshman notwithstanding, Piper continued improving as a basketball player. He started for the Lawrence High School sophomore team. As a junior, he played well enough on the Lawrence High junior varsity that he was promoted to the Lions varsity team. The promotion didn't overly impress the unassuming Piper.

23

"This shows my mentality: I wasn't really thrilled about going up to varsity, because all my friends were on jayvee," he says.

Piper quickly learned, however, about the benefits of varsity-level play. New head coach Ted Juneau gave the Lions and Piper more direction that season. Piper and his friends continued playing ball between their junior and senior years to elevate their game, and the Lions won the state 6A championship and finished with a 20-4 record in 1983. Piper shot 12-for-13 from the floor in the title game, and averaged 14.4 points and 8.1 rebounds for the season.

Despite the good stats, success, and height that now measured 6-foot-8, Piper received little attention from college scouts. Once during the season, KU assistants Bob Hill and Dolph Carroll attended Lawrence High's practice. Piper made a mistake toward the end of practice, and Juneau jokingly got in his face and yelled, "They're not here to see you, why are you so nervous?" True enough. The Jayhawk coaches had dropped by to ask the team about working weekends at KU's summer basketball camp for younger kids.

Piper's best offers came from state schools such as Washburn and Emporia State (then NAIA members) and Kansas junior colleges in Hutchinson and Dodge City. But then KU fired Ted Owens and his staff after the '83 season and hired Larry Brown. Piper, whose basketball fandom began and ended with KU hoops, had never heard of Coach Brown. His friends clued him in, telling Piper that Brown was "the great coach" from the New Jersey Nets of the NBA.

Soon after Brown arrived in Lawrence, Juneau advised Piper that the new KU coach wanted to talk with him. An extremely nervous Piper met with Brown in his office. Brown told him that he had some open scholarships and was looking for players such as Piper. The only stipulation was that Piper would have to redshirt as a freshman.

Piper says he thought to himself, "Hey, great, whatever," and returned to class at Lawrence High. Juneau approached him and asked about the meeting. Piper said he wasn't sure if Brown wanted him to "walk on or what." So Juneau called the basketball office for a definitive answer. He got one. Juneau then pulled Piper out of his calculus class, and said, "They are offering you a full ride. Are you interested?"

In one of the greatest understatements in Kansas basketball history, Piper says now, "That fell into place extremely well for me."

Notes on Chris Piper

Name:	Chris Piper
Years lettered:	1984-85 to 1987-88
Position:	Forward
Height:	6-foot-8
Playing weight:	195 pounds
Hometown:	Lawrence, Kansas
Current Residence:	Lawrence, Kansas
Occupation:	President of Grandstand Sportswear & Glassware, Lawrence; basketball analyst with the Jayhawk radio network
Accomplishments:	Lee Jeans Academic All-Big Eight team (1988); All-Big Eight "surprise" team (1987) for starting all 36 games as a junior after playing limited minutes as a sophomore; made game-winning free throw versus Missouri at Allen Fieldhouse on January 20, 1987.
Nickname:	"Pipe"
The Game:	Kansas vs. Oklahoma, NCAA championship game in Kansas City, Missouri, April 4, 1988

College Life

When you can see Allen Fieldhouse from a window in your home one block away, transitioning to college at KU is not that big of a deal, and it wasn't for Piper. In the summer of 1983, he moved out of his house and in with a fellow "skinny Kansas kid" named Mark Turgeon, another of Brown's freshman recruits. Brown liked his players to play basketball all of the time, so, other than adjusting to Calvin Thompson's trash talk and a higher level of play, Piper was in his element.

The freshman was okay with redshirting when school started. Doing so helped him realize how much he needed to improve his game, he notes, especially on defense.

"The great thing about my first year was that I guarded Carl Henry and Kelly Knight every day in practice," Piper says. "Guarding Carl made me a much better player because he worked so hard and sprinted up-and-down the floor. That established for me how you play the game from a hustle standpoint."

KU improved from 13-16 in 1982-83 to 22-10 in Brown's first season. As a redshirt freshman in 1984-85, Piper mopped up in 20 games and averaged just less than a point a game while the Jayhawks further improved to 26-8.

"It was nerve-wracking to finally be out there," Piper recalls. "I was nervous and happy to be there, I think. So I didn't put that much emphasis on being out on the floor and getting better once I was in the game. I think that held me back a little bit, but I did start to get a little 'hunger' towards the end of the year."

What whetted Piper's appetite for more playing time was the Jayhawks' season-ending upset loss to Auburn in the NCAA tournament. Piper played more than usual in the 66-64 setback to the Tigers in South Bend, Indiana, due to KU's foul trouble.

"They threw a junk defense at us, a triangle-and-two, and they left me wide open," he says. "I made some shots (three-for-four from the field for six points) and had some impact on the game. That started me thinking, 'Hey, I can play at this level, and I want to play at this level.'"

Kansas enjoyed one of its finest seasons in school history in 1985-86, going 35-4 and reaching the Final Four in Dallas. Piper, along with Archie Marshall and Turgeon, became part of the team's rotation of players. Piper averaged 2.0 points and 2.3 rebounds while playing in all 39 games that season.

"That was an unbelievably talented team," Piper says of the Jayhawk squad that lost to Duke in the national semifinals.

Minus the seniors from that season—Thompson, Greg Dreiling, and Ron Kellogg, plus the injured Archie Marshall—Kansas slipped to 25-11 in 1986-87. Piper started all season but played out of position as a small forward instead of his typical power forward.

"I wasn't a scorer, but I was playing a scoring position," Piper says. "It was a tough year. We didn't seem to click on all cylinders. Cedric [Hunter] was still there and he was fantastic. But we really missed somebody— probably at the three-spot [small forward]—who could take the pressure off Danny [Manning] and Cedric. That season was a struggle."

So, too, would be most of the 1987-88 season.

Piper pulled a groin muscle during the summer of 1987 but passed on surgery so he could play. But in November he was forced to undergo arthroscopic surgery on his strained right knee and miss KU's first four games. On the court, the Jayhawks started 8-2 but lost to St. John's 70-58 on December 30 in the championship game of the ECAC Holiday Festival in New York's Madison Square Garden. Worse, the Jayhawks lost senior forward Marshall essentially for the season with another knee injury.

"That was devastating," Piper says. "We were done in that game. I remember Coach Brown breaking down on the bench when he returned from the floor being with Archie."

The Jayhawks lost another player before the second semester began when starting center Marvin Branch was declared academically ineligible. KU then lost five of its next six games and stood 12-8 (1-4 in the Big Eight) after a 73-65 home loss to Oklahoma in early February. In the previous game, Kansas State had ended the Jayhawks' 55-game home-court win streak behind Mitch Richmond's 35 points.

The Jayhawks rebounded, however, to win eight of their final 10 regular-season games. The two losses came against Duke and Oklahoma, teams that Kansas would see again before the season concluded. Kansas finished 9-5 in conference play, good for third place. Heading into the Big Eight tournament, Kansas was 20-10.

At this point, Kansas would suffer two more off-the-court losses and only one more on-court defeat. Brown suspended guard Otis Livingston for the season before the conference tournament. KU defeated Oklahoma State in the tournament's opening round before losing to Kansas State in the semi-finals. A day before the unranked, sixth-seeded 'Hawks' first-round NCAA game against Xavier, Brown suspended freshman center Mike Masucci for the season. This move would be Kansas' last "loss" of the year.

The Setting

Kansas returned to the Final Four for the second time in three seasons after two triumphs in the Midwest sub-regional in Lincoln, Nebraska, and two decisive victories in the Midwest regional in Pontiac, Michigan. The

Final Four would be held in Kansas City, Missouri's Kemper Arena, site of the annual Big Eight tournament and a 40-minute drive from Lawrence.

Although the Jayhawks could enjoy the familiar surroundings of Kemper and Kansas City, the team drew an extremely difficult semifinal opponent in Duke. The two schools had a short and bitter (for KU) history in basketball. The Blue Devils defeated Kansas 74-70 in February at Allen Fieldhouse after KU blew a six-point lead in overtime. In 1985-86, Duke beat the Jayhawks twice, including a heartbreaking 71-67 defeat in the Final Four that ended KU's marvelous 35-4 season.

This time Kansas overwhelmed Duke at the outset, racing to leads of 14-0 and 24-6 before the Blue Devils returned somewhat to form to trim the Jayhawks advantage at halftime to 38-27.

"We knew they were going to come back," Piper says, which Duke did, of course. The Blue Devils twice cut the Jayhawks' lead to three points late in the second half. When the two teams met in February, KU had led Duke 23-8 in the first half before losing in overtime. Forty days later, Kansas had come too far to fold again. Manning stuck back a rebound to give KU a five-point lead with 2:08 left. Forced to foul the Jayhawks in the final two minutes, Kansas converted seven of nine free throws down the stretch to seal the victory, 66-59.

"I felt so absolutely drained after that game," says Piper, who scored 10 points. "You go back and look at old videos, and it doesn't seem that you're playing that hard, but I remember every possession meant something in that game to both sides. We were wiped out."

It showed. Piper's face remained beet red for an hour after the game. But he wasn't the only exhausted player. Coach Brown told the team the next day that he saw some Duke players at dinner that night and they remarked they had never been so tired, too.

While Piper and the Jayhawks were recovering in Kansas City, KU fans in Lawrence reveled in the team's first championship game appearance since 1957. Students and fans—on foot and in packed cars—swarmed Jayhawk Boulevard on campus and Mass Street in downtown. Strangers hugged and high-fived, and students were sprayed with champagne in front of Strong Hall while basketballs flew over the crowd.

About three hours into the celebration, Kansas and its fans learned the Jayhawks' opponent for the championship would be Oklahoma. The

Sooners defeated Arizona 86-78 to set up the title game between two Big Eight foes and recent archrivals.

Oklahoma hired coach Billy Tubbs in 1980, and he brought the Sooners to national prominence in short order. In Brown's first season in Lawrence, Oklahoma clinched the Big Eight regular-season championship in Lawrence. The Sooners' overexuberant postgame celebration on the Allen Fieldhouse floor rubbed KU and its fans the wrong way, thus stoking the rivalry's intensity from red- to white-hot.

"I could not stand them," Piper says of the Sooners with a laugh. "They were brash, they would do whatever it took. But that's how sports should be, I think. You don't like the other team that you play. They liked to rub your nose in it, and I think that's what made people mad."

Heading into the championship game, Kansas held a 7-6 advantage over Oklahoma in the five seasons Brown had directed the Jayhawks, but the last nine of those games had been decided by an average of five points. In 1988, Oklahoma twice defeated Kansas by eight points in games that were closer than the final score might indicate. Oddsmakers stuck with that margin and made Oklahoma an eight-point favorite to defeat Kansas.

The Jayhawks practiced well on Sunday, Piper recalls, adding the familiarity with their opponent was to KU's advantage. "We felt confident, strong, and everybody felt good," he says. "What really helped us in the last three games [Kansas State, Duke, and Oklahoma] was that we already had played the teams we faced. Coach Brown knew these teams' weaknesses and how we could exploit them."

Monday, April 4, 1988, represents one of the biggest sports days in the history of Kansas City. The Royals lost their baseball season opener to Toronto 5-3 that afternoon on the city's east side in front of more than 40,000 fans at the Truman Sports Complex. Meanwhile, ticket prices for the championship game turned the basketball buzz into a roar around the West Bottoms area, where Kemper Arena is located, and at downtown hotels. Scalping is illegal in Missouri, as some wannabe entrepreneurs learned that day. Still, market forces (a supply of 16,392 seats versus a demand of four to five times that amount) prevailed in many instances, and suddenly $50 tickets were being offered from $600 to $1,250. In Lawrence, merchants selling Jayhawk memorabilia ran out of stock. Local T-shirt vendors even sold out of extra shirts printed after the Duke game on Saturday.

Fortunately for the Jayhawks, the team had been shielded from most of the madness that had spilled over from March and inundated early April. Their focus remained on the task at hand: beating the Sooners. Piper drew Oklahoma's much-improved center Stacey King as his defensive assignment, but would switch with Manning as needed and also guard forward Harvey Grant.

"I don't know that we still felt like we were going to win a national championship, but I felt like we belonged," Piper says.

While he felt fairly self-assured, apparently Piper's facial expression told a different story. "Somebody remarked to me after the game that they were real confident until they saw me walk through the hotel on the way to the bus," he says. "I guess the look on my face must have been petrified."

Piper's internal confidence and concerned countenance likely paralleled how Jayhawk fans felt about the game. Victory was imaginable, even possible, but would they experience a national championship for the first time since 1952? As the bus rumbled toward Kemper Arena in the fading daylight, the Kansas Jayhawks were in the midst of taking themselves on the final leg of an improbable ride to the game of their lives.

The Game of My Life

BY CHRIS PIPER
KANSAS VS. OKLAHOMA, APRIL 4, 1988

Coach did not want us to get into an up-and-down game [with Oklahoma]. That's just the way it opened up for us. Our philosophy was always to attack full-court pressure and beat it. When we beat it, though, we had an avenue. But if you look at some of the shots that our guys like Milt [Newton] and Kevin [Pritchard] made in transition, those were some really unbelievable shots. If they hadn't dropped for us, it would really have put us in a bind. I watched the game a while ago, and I just loved Billy Packer talking: "Kansas can run with them, but they can't beat them."

Having Coach and Danny on our side, those are really two big keys in any game. But everybody stepped up, as they had all during the tournament. Danny was having a great first half (14 points and seven rebounds), but he got in foul trouble and came out for a while.

I remember them going zone against us, unbelievably, when Danny left, which played right into our hands. Clint Normore had some big shots there, including his three-pointer to put us ahead 36-33 with 7:40 to go in the half. Later in the half, I was down in the post and Clint would look at me inside, and I'd say, "Uh-uh, don't even throw the ball in here. Let's keep working the clock." We were milking that clock toward the end, which made the 50-50 halftime score even more remarkable, because I think we ran the last three minutes out pretty much.

In the second half, Oklahoma took a 65-60 lead around the 12-minute mark. That's when I took the only shot I purposely knew I was going to take. They were not guarding me at the high post. They hadn't guarded me all night. I just knew coming down the floor that I was going to swing up and take that shot because we needed it—I was wide open and had been wide open—and they were really collapsing on Danny. I knew I was going to come off the set we had called and take that jumper from the high post.

Around this time, Oklahoma stopped hitting its shots. Our defense was much better in the second half, but we also did not give them as many opportunities at the offensive end as well. When I watched the game most recently, I noticed that Stacey King wasn't as active moving for the ball in the second half as he was in the first half.

Anyway, OU was stuck on 68 points for more than four minutes. I hit a 16-foot jumper from the right side to make it 71-68 with 7:38 left. [Oklahoma also went another four minutes without scoring after tying the game at 71.] Later, I made an eight-footer from the baseline to make it 77-71 in our favor.

In both of those cases we were running the shot clock down. A couple of times Clint or Kevin would drive, and I moved with the angle because everyone collapsed on them or Danny. When they passed to me at those times, I had no choice but to go up and shoot. Thankfully, they went in.

Look at the substitution patterns in that game [Kansas had five players come off the bench to total 49 minutes, while Oklahoma only used one sub for seven minutes]. I think Oklahoma was tired at the end, no question. We helped them a bit. We were tired, too, holding the ball. But it's a lot easier to hold it on offense than to go after it on defense. I think that wore them down even more.

Game and Season Results

As with Duke in the semifinals, Oklahoma would not go down without a fight. Sooner guards Ricky Grace and Mookie Blaylock scored 18 seconds apart to cut Kansas' lead to one, 78-77, with 41 seconds to go. Scooter Barry hit the front end of a one-and-one with 16 seconds left to give KU a two-point lead. Manning grabbed the rebound from the missed second shot and was fouled. He hit both free throws to put the 'Hawks ahead 81-77.

Grace drove in for a finger roll, making the score 81-79 with nine seconds on the clock. The Jayhawks and their fans held their collective breath as the ball was in-bounded to Manning, whom the Sooners had to foul. With five seconds left, the National Player of the Year thought to himself, "It's over," and made both free throws. At 10:09 p.m., Kansas captured the 1988 NCAA championship, 83-79.

"I didn't think it was over 'til Danny hit the free throws at the end," Piper says. "I didn't feel confident until we had a four-point lead, and they didn't have time to get two possessions. They just scored too fast."

The Jayhawks believed their defense had carried them to the Final Four, and the championship game made a believer out of the Sooners' King.

"Kansas surprised us with their defense," he said. "I think Piper played the best defense against me that I've seen all year. He was really working hard denying me the ball."

Manning was named the tournament's MVP. Newton, who shot six-for-six from the field—including two treys—in the championship game, joined Manning on the all-Final Four team.

"This is something that about two months ago was totally unexpected," Brown said afterward. "When it was 50-50 at halftime, and we were shooting about 70 percent, we were concerned because we couldn't get ourselves slowed down. We didn't panic when we were five down. We were just hoping to get it to the last five minutes."

The Jayhawks wore ear-splitting grins and donned "national champion" T-shirts to whoop it up on the Kemper Arena floor before an exultant, partisan crowd. Meanwhile in Lawrence, a crowd estimated at more than 30,000 people basked in the championship and unseasonable 68-degree weather on Jayhawk Boulevard until 3 a.m. Bars downtown were jam-packed

BOX SCORE
KANSAS VS. OKLAHOMA, APRIL 4, 1988

Kansas	50 33	– 83
Oklahoma	50 29	– 79

Kansas (83)

	Min	FG	FT	Reb	PF	Pts
Newton	32	6-6	1-2	4	1	15
Piper	37	4-6	0-0	7	3	8
Manning	36	13-24	5-7	18	3	31
Pritchard	31	6-7	0-0	1	1	13
Gueldner	15	1-2	0-0	2	0	2
Barry	9	0-2	1-2	0	1	1
Normore	16	3-3	0-1	1	3	7
Harris	13	1-1	0-0	1	2	2
Minor	11	1-4	2-2	1	1	4
Maddox	1	0-0	0-0	0	1	0
(team)				1		
TOTALS	**200**	**35-55**	**9-14**	**36**	**16**	**83**

Three-point shots: 4-6 (Newton 2-2, Pritchard 1-1, Normore 1-1, Manning 0-1, Gueldner 0-1); Assists: 17 (Pritchard 4, Normore 4, Piper 2, Manning 2, Barry 2, Newton, Gueldner, Minor); Steals: 11 (Manning 5, Piper 3, Pritchard, Gueldner, Minor); Blocked shots: 4 (Newton 2, Manning 2); Turnovers: 23 (Piper 5, Pritchard 5, Manning 4, Harris 4, Barry 2, Normore 2, Minor).

Oklahoma (79)

	Min	FG	FT	Reb	PF	Pts
Grant	40	6-14	2-3	5	4	14
Sieger	40	7-15	1-2	5	2	22
King	39	7-14	3-3	7	3	17
Blaylock	40	6-13	0-1	5	4	14
Grace	34	4-14	3-4	7	4	12
Mullins	7	0-0	0-0	1	1	0
(team)				1		
TOTALS	**200**	**30-70**	**9-13**	**31**	**18**	**79**

Three-point shots: 10-24 (Sieger 7-13, Blaylock 2-4, Grace 1-7); Assists: 19 (Grace 7, Sieger 7, Blaylock 4, Grant); Steals 13: (Blaylock 7, Sieger 3, Grant, King, Grace); Blocked shots: 3 (King 2, Grant); Turnovers: 15 (Sieger 6, King 3, Grace 3, Blaylock 2, Mullins).

Officials: John Clougherty, Tim Higgins, Ed Hightower. Attendance: 16,392.

as well. For those fans who stayed home, fireworks rang out in neighborhoods all over town.

Kansas chancellor Gene Budig cancelled classes on Tuesday. The team returned to Lawrence that afternoon and addressed 30,000 still-celebrating fans at Memorial Stadium.

"One of the greatest things was driving down I-70 the next day and cars were pulled over," Piper says. "That's a pretty good feeling when you stop traffic. And pulling into the stadium was a culmination. To come home and see what it meant to the community was pretty special."

Piper, whom Manning had called "the heart and soul of our team," told the fans they had been the team's "sixth man" all season.

"You don't know what kind of support and confidence that gives us," he said. "One thing—never give up on the Jayhawks."

The next three months turned into another blur for the Kansas basketball program. The team visited the White House and President Reagan. Brown turned down a chance to return to UCLA, where he had coached from 1979-81. But a few weeks later, he accepted the head-coaching job of the NBA's San Antonio Spurs and took his staff with him. In early July, Kansas hired a relatively unheralded assistant coach from the University of North Carolina named Roy Williams.

One extraordinary five-year era in Kansas basketball history had ended. Another extraordinary 15-year era was about to begin.

What Became of Chris Piper?

The 1988 national championship game was the last competitive basketball Piper played. The groin injury he suffered in the summer of 1987 bothered him throughout the season, and he was disinclined to keep playing in the summer of 1988. Piper turned down an offer from the New Jersey team of the USBL and an Australian team to instead jump into the business world.

"In retrospect I really regret not going overseas to play," he says. "The process then was not as sophisticated as it is now. I definitely would have (gone) if it was later."

Piper bought into a local T-shirt company and succeeded to the point where he was able to buy another related company called Grandstand

Sportswear & Glassware. Piper serves as president of the Lawrence-based company, which has "8888," not so surprisingly the last four digits in its telephone number.

In the summer of 2006, Chris was selected to replace 60-year veteran broadcaster Max Falkenstien as an analyst on Jayhawk radio broadcasts beginning with the 2006-07 basketball season. Previously, he worked as a television broadcaster of KU games for the Jayhawk Network, called Big XII games during conference play, and was a part of the "Studio 66" crew for the Saturday pre-game, halftime, and post-game segments of the broadcasts.

Between those two jobs, Piper also makes time for his family. He and his wife, Kristin, have three children: daughters Madison and Kate, and son Andrew.

Listening to Piper recount his nearly accidental career, its struggles and triumphs leave one knowing he fully realizes how fortunate and blessed he's been.

"[Basketball] kept me here in Lawrence to meet my wife and have the family that we have," he says. "You look back and the changing point for me was that day in calculus class when I found out that KU was offering me a full ride."

A full ride lived by Piper, shared by the 1988 national champion Jayhawks, and enjoyed by Kansas fans everywhere.

4

MIKE MADDOX

The Life of Young Mike Maddox

Mike Maddox was always on the move.

First, with his family: the Maddoxes lived in Wichita, Kansas City, Vermont, and Colorado while Maddox was growing up before relocating to Oklahoma City for his high school years. On the basketball court, Maddox traveled with the Oklahoma Rams AAU team and teamed with future college stars Brent Price, Byron Houston, Richard Dumas, and Kermit Holmes. The team stayed on the move by playing up-tempo basketball and continually pressing the opposition. In the summer of 1986, the Rams won the national championship against a South Carolina team led by Stanley Roberts, and Maddox was named tournament most valuable player. When he wasn't on the road for an AAU tournament, Maddox attended various summer camps around the United States.

"I was basically traveling or playing somewhere all summer long," he says. "There wasn't a lot of down time. I don't know how many games I played in the summer, but it was a lot."

During those rare occasions when he found himself home, Maddox took his basketball and boom box to the gymnasium at Putnam City North High School in Oklahoma City. There his regimen included ball-handling drills, weights, jumping rope, and shooting 300 shots per day, varying his routine to keep it interesting.

"I pretty much had all access at the gym," Maddox says. "I had a great experience at Putnam City North. I had a very good coach in Bill Robertson, and we had a successful team. The school prepared me well for college from an academic standpoint and an athletic standpoint."

Maddox's basketball accomplishments, skills and work ethic, combined with his 6-foot-7 height and strong academic performance, steered his future college career on the fast track. He heard from 150 colleges (starting in ninth grade with a letter from the University of Utah) and eventually narrowed his choices to Arizona and Kansas.

His family took a keen interest in his recruiting. His father, Jim, knew the recruiting ropes having played football and basketball at Wichita State University. Jim was the sixth man on Ralph Miller's Shocker basketball teams, and he roomed with a football player named Bill Parcells.

"My dad was a coach and he had been through recruiting," Maddox says. "It was helpful to have that experience. That process gets pretty crazy, but everybody had fun with it."

Though Maddox was well traveled, he chose Kansas for its Midwest location and strong basketball program.

"Larry Brown is a great coach and had a very good reputation," Maddox says. "KU had a great group of guys on the team and had just been to the Final Four the year before. I had some good choices [for college], it just came down to where I was most comfortable."

College Life

As with most college freshmen, Maddox found the adjustment to Kansas tough in some ways, especially when adding basketball on top of academics. He joined the Phi Delta Theta fraternity to help him connect with other students, and settled in on basketball and his studies. Immediately, Maddox knew he had to work on his strength as a 185-pound player who was going up against Danny Manning, Chris Piper, Mark Randall, and Keith Harris in practice. Maddox also worked with assistant coach R.C. Buford on facing the basket, going out on the perimeter, putting the ball on the floor, and creating shots as he transitioned from a high school center to a college power forward.

Maddox spent most of the 1987-88 season on the bench behind Manning and Piper. He understood his place behind two seniors, one of whom would become national player of the year and a future No. 1 draft pick. The 1987-88 season would be as trying for the Jayhawks as it was

Notes on Mike Maddox

Years lettered:	1987-88 to 1990-91
Position:	Forward
Height:	6-foot-7
Playing weight:	200
Hometown:	Oklahoma City, Oklahoma
Current Residence:	Lawrence, Kansas
Occupation:	Regional president, northeast Kansas region, Intrust Bank
Accomplishments:	Chosen as captain of the Big Eight All-Bench team (UPI) in 1989-90; member of the gold-medal basketball team at the 1987 U.S. Olympic Sports Festival before entering college; All-America selection senior year of high school.
The Game:	Kansas vs. UNLV in New York, New York, November 22, 1989

eventually rewarding when the team rallied late in the season to win the national championship.

"We went through a lot of struggles," Maddox recalls. "It was a long season. It wasn't until right before the tournament that we started coming together.

"Probably the game that changed the season was when we lost at home against Kansas State [on January 30]. It was a loss, but we played well. You could see our confidence starting to turn there. We lost to Oklahoma and Duke after that, but we were competitive. Even though our record wasn't great, we went into the tournament with confidence."

Maddox played in all six NCAA tournament games and even saw some "decent" minutes in the first three games against Xavier, Murray State, and Vanderbilt. Though his minutes were limited during the finish of the tourney, the experience of playing in the '88 Final Four was something that Maddox will never forget.

"It was a once-in-a-lifetime experience, different from 1991," Maddox says. "Kansas City was special, and not just because we won. We were close to a lot of friends and family, and it really was like playing home games."

Two months after the Jayhawks defeated Oklahoma for the championship, Brown left Lawrence for the San Antonio Spurs. After a few uncertain weeks following Brown's departure, Kansas hired North Carolina assistant coach Roy Williams as its new coach. Then, shortly after fall practice began for the 1988-89 season, the NCAA put Kansas on probation for violations that occurred during Brown's tenure. One stipulation of the probation was that the Jayhawks were barred from the 1989 NCAA tournament, meaning the Jayhawks would not be allowed to defend their national championship. Still, the team shook off its misfortune by opening the season with a 16-3 record before losing eight games.

"We had a tough year," Maddox says. "We had nine players. It was a learning year, a transition year. But I think it did a lot to set Roy's career moving upward at Kansas. We built a foundation that year that I think catapulted the next generation of KU basketball."

The Setting

Every college basketball season is unique, but for the Kansas Jayhawks, few have started as oddly as the 1989-90 campaign. The Jayhawks were coming off a down year by KU standards, as Maddox noted. The 1988-89 team finished 19-12, and NCAA sanctions regarding off-campus recruiting still hovered above the program in the fall of '89. Coach Williams had earned respect for handling the team as well as he did under difficult circumstances, but few people outside of the KU program could have predicted how successful he would become. Count the editors at *Inside Sports* magazine among the unimpressed. The magazine picked KU to finish eighth in the Big Eight in the coming season.

With that less-than-pretty backdrop, Kansas opened the season on November 15 at home in a first-round preseason NIT game against the University of Alabama-Birmingham. The game was not included in the KU season-ticket package, and only 7,025 fans showed up at Allen Fieldhouse to see the 'Hawks rout the Blazers 59-30 in the first half en route to a 109-83 decision. Kevin Pritchard led KU with 22 points while Maddox scored 21 points in 27 minutes off the bench.

NIT officials then set the pairings for the next round, keeping in mind travel distance and, above all, games that *should* ensure that the "best" teams

would win and advance to New York for the Thanksgiving holiday tournament. To that end, unranked Kansas was sent packing to Baton Rouge, Louisiana, to face second-ranked Louisiana State. The Tigers justified their ranking with a lineup featuring three of the best young players in college hoops. Sophomore guard Chris Jackson (now Mahmoud Abdul-Rauf) had averaged 30.2 points as a freshman. Freshmen Shaquille O'Neal, 7-foot-1 and 286 pounds, and Stanley Roberts, 7 feet tall and 288 pounds, represented one of the biggest and strongest frontcourts to ever play at the college level.

But KU didn't blink. The Jayhawks led by two at halftime and stayed ahead for most of the second half. Still, it took free throws by Pritchard and Jeff Gueldner in the final 22 seconds to clinch the victory. Mark Randall, who was at least three inches shorter and 50 pounds lighter than O'Neal and Roberts, impressively hit 12-for-15 from the field and led KU with 26 points.

"Our system was hard for them," Maddox says. "We played well, moved the ball, and made them play defense. In all fairness, Shaq then was not the Shaq of today. At that point, if you could make him catch the ball six or seven feet from the basket, he couldn't score."

Then confusion took over. ESPN reported shortly after the LSU game that KU would face DePaul in the tournament semifinals in New York City. Williams saw that report and studied DePaul game film the next evening after returning from Louisiana. However, NIT officials said they never released that scheduling information. By Saturday night, reports circulated that Kansas would play No. 1-ranked University of Nevada-Las Vegas instead. KU assistant coaches noticed the discrepancy Sunday morning and a call to NIT officials confirmed the Jayhawks-Running Rebels matchup. This pairing enabled the NIT to pit DePaul against hometown St. John's in the other semifinal game.

Williams said he understood the NIT wanting the best matchups for the tournament, but also quipped, "I don't think any wino in Kansas City can explain the pairings."

Williams knew UNLV would present an even tougher test than LSU because of the Rebels experience. UNLV's starting line-up included Big West Conference player of the year Stacey Augmon, junior college player of the year Larry Johnson, and guard Greg Anthony. All three players would go on to enjoy NBA careers lasting at least 10 seasons.

"They are more athletic. They run faster, jump higher," Williams said of UNLV, which employed a full-court, pressure defense.

KU athletics director Bob Frederick joked in a staff meeting that week that the NIT had again changed schedules on the Jayhawks, and now KU would be playing the New York Knicks.

For what KU had in store for UNLV, a Knicks-Jayhawks game may have been an even better test of KU's mettle.

The Game of My Life

BY MIKE MADDOX
KANSAS VS. UNLV, NOVEMBER 22, 1989

A few of us had played at Madison Square Garden before, the other time being when Archie Marshall re-injured his knee [against St. John's in 1987] when I was a freshman. Still, it was always exciting to go to New York.

Coach Williams had preached the lack of respect we got and played a lot on how they kept changing the schedule because they didn't want us there. And he probably mentioned to us a few times how they had called him 'Ron' Williams at a banquet.

We were not in awe of Las Vegas. We had just beaten LSU, and that game gave us confidence. We knew all of the UNLV players, and I had played against Johnson and Augmon in AAU basketball. You had to keep them from catching the ball, deny them as much as you could, which was about the only way to slow them down.

UNLV's pressure was tough, but we did a real good job spreading the floor and getting a lot of backdoor cuts. We had a lot of layups. They got ahead of us by eight points late in the first half. But we went on a nice run [14-2] and I had a couple of lay-ups [including one with 0.9 seconds left in the half to give KU a 42-38 lead].

We basically ran our motion offense, spread the floor and got a lot of easy shots. We also did well on the defensive end. I don't know what they averaged scoring that year, but holding them to 77 points is probably a pretty good number.

I don't remember the New York crowd being an issue. There weren't a lot of people cheering for anybody other than St. John's. We were probably being supported because St. John's probably rather would play us in the finals.

Game and Season Results

Kansas outscored UNLV 21-13 in the first eight minutes of the second half and cruised to a 91-77 victory. Maddox scored eight points in the second half and a team-high 17 in the game. All five Kansas starters also scored in double figures.

The next day, Williams woke the team early so they could watch the Macy's Day parade, which passed just outside of their hotel. All four of the tournament teams later dined together to celebrate Thanksgiving.

In the championship game, Kansas defeated No. 25 St. John's 66-57. In nine days, Kansas had gone from a non-entity to preseason NIT champion, knocking off nationally ranked powerhouses in the process. Yet the feat marked just the beginning for the Jayhawks. KU won its next 15 games before No. 4 Missouri ended the streak with a 95-87 defeat of the No. 1-ranked Jayhawks on January 20, 1990, in Columbia. Kansas then won its next five games in a row before No. 2 Missouri paid a mid-February visit to Lawrence. The Tigers again defeated the No. 1 Jayhawks, this time 77-71. Oklahoma later defeated KU twice, once in conference play and the other time in the Big Eight Tournament.

Kansas entered the NCAA tournament ranked fifth with a 29-4 record. The Jayhawks were seeded second in the Southeast Region and outlasted Robert Morris 79-71 in the first-round game in Atlanta. Next up came UCLA. Although KU was favored, the Bruins abruptly ended Kansas' season in a 71-70 upset.

Despite the early exit, the 1989-90 season put Kansas back on the college basketball map after a brief hiatus, and established Williams as a coach to be reckoned with.

Oh, and what team won the 1990 national championship? UNLV.

What Became of Mike Maddox?

Maddox returned for a bittersweet senior year in 1990-91. The sweetness came from a return to the Final Four and appearance in the national championship game against Duke. The bitter part stemmed from a back injury that refused to improve.

BOX SCORE
KANSAS VS. UNLV, NOVEMBER 22, 1989

UNLV	38	39 –	77
Kansas	42	49 –	91

UNLV (77)

	Min	FG	FT	Reb	PF	TP
Augmon	37	7-12	2-2	9	4	17
Johnson	37	5-11	3-4	9	4	13
Jones	21	2-2	1-2	3	5	5
Anthony	37	4-10	2-2	2	5	11
Hunt	36	9-21	1-1	1	3	21
Young	23	2-7	0-0	0	1	5
Bice	8	1-4	2-2	1	1	5
Jeter	1	0-0	0-0	0	0	0
(team)				2		
TOTALS	**200**	**30-67**	**11-13**	**27**	**23**	**77**

Three-point goals: 6-23 (Hunt 2-10, Young 1-6, Augmon 1-3, Anthony 1-2, Bice 1-2); Assists: 19 (Anthony 9, Young 3, Augmon 2, Hunt 2, Johnson, Jones, Bice); Turnovers: 15 (Augmon 4, Johnson 4, Hunt 3, Marshall 2, Jones, Anthony, Young); Blocked shots: 1 (Jones); Steals: 8 (Augmon 5, Hunt 2, Johnson).

Kansas (91)

	Min	FG	FT	Reb	PF	TP
Calloway	23	4-6	5-6	5	2	13
Randall	31	5-10	6-6	7	2	16
Markkanen	26	7-9	0-1	4	1	14
Gueldner	32	4-5	1-2	5	2	10
Pritchard	31	4-10	2-2	3	3	12
Maddox	19	7-11	3-5	7	1	17
West	16	0-1	0-0	0	0	0
Brown	10	1-2	1-3	1	0	4
Jordan	9	2-2	0-1	1	0	5
Nash	1	0-0	0-0	0	0	0
Wagner	1	0-0	0-0	0	0	0
Alexander	1	0-0	0-0	0	0	0
(team)				9		
TOTALS	**200**	**34-56**	**18-26**	**42**	**11**	**91**

Three-point goals: 5-8 (Pritchard 2-3, Brown 1-2, Gueldner 1-1, Jordan 1-1, Randall 0-1); Assists: 25 (Pritchard 7, Maddox 5, Calloway 4, Randall 3, Gueldner 3, Markkanen, West, Jordan); Turnovers: 18 (Pritchard 5, Gueldner 4, Randall 2, West 2, Jordan 2, Calloway, Markkanen, Maddox); Blocked shots 0; Steals: 4 (Pritchard 2, Markkanen, Wagner).

Officials: Larry Lembo, Jim Burr, Joe Mingle. Attendance: 10,546.

"I was getting epidural steroid shots in my back my senior year," Maddox says. "When I was finished playing at KU, physically I was done."

Maddox played the most minutes of his career as a senior, but his productivity slipped slightly because he took less shots than he had in either his sophomore or junior season. His scoring average dipped from 8.7 points as a junior to 7.4 points as a senior. Still, Kansas basketball has always been more about teamwork than individual statistics, and Maddox contributed senior leadership for the 27-8 Jayhawks, along with Randall, Terry Brown, and Kirk Wagner.

With pro basketball not an option, Maddox entered law school at KU and completed his juris doctorate degree in 1994. He practiced law in Lawrence for six years before joining Intrust Bank in 2000. Today, Maddox is regional president of Intrust's northeast Kansas region. He commutes to his Prairie Village office from his Lawrence home that he shares with his wife, Bonnie, and their three children: Jamie, Sarah, and Anderson.

Through his collegiate basketball experiences, Maddox says he learned the value of hard work, determination, preparation, and organization.

"The experience from playing at that level under that kind of pressure, there are not a lot of situations in life that duplicate that," he says. "It sounds silly, but once you've shot a free throw in front of 45 million people, speaking publicly in front of 100 people is not that big of a deal."

Maddox considers himself very fortunate to have played in two national championship games, winning one.

"Winning a national championship changes your life," he says. "You're forever tied to that team. It gives you a lot of opportunities.

"I've been very lucky. And one of the fun things I get to do is attend events with the other former players. I always enjoy getting to know the players who played before and after me. It's a great fraternity with a strong, strong group of people. There are many people who have done a lot of impressive things outside of basketball."

5

ALONZO JAMISON

The Life of Young Alonzo Jamison

Only one person prevented Alonzo Jamison from playing quarterback for Valley High School in Santa Ana, California. The person wasn't another player, coach, or even an opponent. Instead, it was Jamison's mother, Theadie Sue Jamison, who refused to sign the insurance papers that would have allowed her son to call signals for the Falcons as a senior.

"It was a funny thing. I wanted to play, but my mom told me, 'No,'" Jamison says. "She saw the opportunity for me to play basketball and get an education out of that. Actually, it would have been pretty funny because they wanted me to play quarterback at 6-foot-4. It means I would have been hovering over my linemen who were 5-foot-11, 6 foot and 6-foot-1."

Jamison grew up in Santa Ana, and as he got older began playing basketball "anywhere and everywhere" he could.

"I played a lot in Newport Beach in suburban Orange County and a lot on the beach, which is probably where I get most of my shin splints from," he says.

The constant playing paid dividends by the time Jamison entered high school. He was the leading scorer on the freshman team and then grew four to five inches going into his sophomore year, when he became a 6-foot-4 center and the team's third-leading scorer.

As a junior, Jamison played football, basketball, and baseball for Valley High. He suffered a broken leg playing as a wide receiver in his second game of the football season (an event that no doubt influenced his mother's decision a year later) and missed the rest of that season. He recovered to play well during basketball season, earning all-league honors.

"People knew who I was in basketball circles in Orange County," Jamison says.

Basketball recruiters recognized Jamison, too. After a successful senior season, he signed with Oregon State and headed to Corvallis, Oregon, to take on Pacific 10 Conference hoops. The 1986-87 academic year marked the first year of "Proposition 48," the NCAA's new admission guidelines for student-athletes. These more stringent guidelines—and various colleges' reactions to them—affected some prospective freshman student-athletes that year, including Jamison.

"Not all of the universities had matched their requirements to Prop 48. Some colleges' requirements to get in were higher [than the NCAA's new rules]," he explains. "I was right on the borderline. I had passed Prop 48, but I was in that 'gray area' with Oregon State, and they made the decision that they didn't want to take a chance on me."

So Jamison returned home to Southern California. He sat out the 1986-87 academic year and worked for his father, Lee, at a Chevrolet dealership in Costa Mesa. After a year out of school, Jamison enrolled at Rancho Santiago Junior College in his hometown. He averaged 19.5 points and 12 rebounds in the 1987-88 season, earning team and league MVP honors, and was named co-player of the year in the California junior college system and a third-team junior college All-American.

Now more colleges pursued Jamison. Almost all of the Pac-10 schools were interested in him, including Oregon State. Indiana wanted Jamison to replace transfer Rick Calloway, who eventually settled on Kansas as the place to finish his career.

"I tell Rick that all the time, and he just shakes his head," Jamison says with a laugh.

Early in the week of the 1988 Final Four, Jamison wagered a friend that Oklahoma would win the championship. Before the week was out, KU had started recruiting Jamison, and won the NCAA title a few days later.

"My life is full of things like that," he says with another laugh.

Notes on Alonzo Jamison

Years lettered: 1989-90 to 1991-92

Position: Forward

Height: 6-foot-6

Playing weight: 225 pounds

Hometown: Santa Ana, California

Current Residence: Shawnee, Kansas

Occupation: Product manager for Embarq Corp. and part-time assistant basketball coach for Mill Valley High School

Accomplishments: All-Big Eight Conference (second team), Big Eight All-Tournament Team, Big Eight player of the week (January 26, 1992), and Big Eight All-Defense team in 1992; two-time winner of the team's "Ted Owens Defensive Player" Award; named Most Outstanding Player in the NCAA Southeast Regional in 1991; honorable mention All-Big Eight (AP and UPI) in '92; All-Surprise Team and All-Defense Team for Big Eight (UPI) in '91.

Nickname: "Zo"

The Game: Kansas vs. Arkansas in Charlotte, North Carolina, March 23, 1991

College Life

Jamison visited Lawrence three weeks after the Jayhawks defeated Oklahoma to win the 1988 national championship.

"The city was still buzzing, and I knew that's where I wanted to be," he says. "Lawrence is like no other city. I have yet to see a town that I can put on the same map as Lawrence."

Kansas coach Larry Brown had declined an offer to return to UCLA as the Bruins head coach by the time Jamison committed to the Jayhawks.

"He told me he was not going to another college, period," Jamison says. "He was true to his word. He didn't."

But Brown's statement said nothing about the NBA. On June 13, Kansas' coach accepted the San Antonio Spurs head coaching job.

"I got a phone call from a reporter asking me how I felt [about Brown leaving Kansas]," Jamison explains. "I had just come in from playing ball, and nobody had told me what was going on. You can pretty much figure out how I reacted. I'll leave it at that."

Jamison cooled down and decided he would still come to Lawrence because of his fondness for the city and KU.

"You go to a university and you sign to play for a coach, but that's not all that goes into it," he says. "Fifty percent of it has to be the atmosphere, where you're playing, and the fans. Lawrence had it all, and that's why I ended up going there."

After Kansas hired Roy Williams as its seventh basketball coach, Jamison was quite impressed with his genuineness. Williams told Jamison that he liked the way he played and would honor his scholarship.

Jamison says Williams added, "If you decide to go back to junior college for a year, we will recruit you again [if needed]." Those words meant a lot to Jamison, who strongly reaffirmed his commitment to KU.

In reviewing Jamison's junior college transcript, Kansas officials discovered one of Jamison's classes would not transfer to the university, making him ineligible for the 1988-89 season. The determination came as news to Jamison, who says he would have taken care of the problem during the summer of 1988 had he known about it. Jamison also sat out the first semester of the 1989-90 season as he worked at becoming eligible to play.

"There are two sides of life as a student-athlete," he says. "Most know how to be athletes, it's the student part that they can have rough [times] with. I was a 20-year-old kid enjoying life, on my own pretty much. … It was one of those things that you have to learn how to grow up. Luckily, I did."

Kansas fans know the Jayhawk players regardless of how much they play. But Jamison made a name for himself at the first "Later with Roy Williams" event when he broke a backboard during a pre-scrimmage dunking session.

For the record, Jamison did not pull the rim off the glass, nor did he shatter the glass. Instead, he broke the backboard—with rim intact—clean away from its supports. The feat elevated Jamison into instant legend status

with the 10,000 cheering fans in attendance, even though it delayed the post-midnight scrimmage by 20 minutes.

"I remember doing the dunk and having the rim in my hands and noticing that I'm also on the ground. That's not supposed to happen," he says. "It shook me."

Jamison debuted with the Jayhawks on January 18, 1990, against Elizabeth City (N.J.) State at Allen Fieldhouse. In 21 minutes he scored nine points and had six rebounds in the 132-65 rout. In 17 games, Jamison averaged 4.9 points and two rebounds per game for the 30-5 Jayhawks.

The next season, Kansas welcomed a trio of determined freshmen— Patrick Richey, Richard Scott, and Steve Woodberry. Richey said he learned a lot about college basketball by battling Jamison daily in practice.

"It reminded me of when I was a freshman in high school and everyone was bigger, faster, and stronger," Richey says. "Alonzo used to steal the ball from me every day. He was so big and strong and his hands were so quick. He was one of the better defenders in college basketball, so going against him in practice every day helped me."

Jamison earned a starting role for the 1990-91 Jayhawks, averaging 10.4 points and 6.4 rebounds. By Kansas standards, the team started the season a little sluggishly with a 9-4 overall record and 0-2 conference mark after losing road games to Oklahoma and Oklahoma State in early January. Then the 'Hawks won 10 straight games before finishing with a 3-3 mark, including going 1-1 in the Big Eight tournament. Heading into the NCAA tournament, KU's record stood at 22-7. Whether the mid-winter team that went 10-0 or the "other" Jayhawks that went 12-7 at the beginning and end of the season would show up for the "Big Dance" remained a big question to Kansas fans everywhere.

The Setting

Kansas entered the 1991 NCAA tournament as a third seed in the Southeast Regional and a 30-1 long shot to win the championship. Those odds may have decreased after a shaky 55-49 decision versus New Orleans. KU shot a season-worst 41.4 percent from the field against the Privateers. Mike Maddox scored 12 and Mark Randall contributed 10 points to lead the

Jayhawks. The best part of Jamison's scoring line that afternoon in Louisville was his team-high five assists.

The 'Hawks rebounded in their second-round game against Pittsburgh by zooming to a 14-2 lead at the outset and cruising to a 77-66 triumph over the Panthers. Defense carried the day for KU as the Jayhawks limited Pitt to 38.2 percent shooting from the floor. Jamison and company held Brian Shorter, the Panthers' leading scorer, to only six points.

Next up for Kansas were the second-seeded and third-ranked Indiana Hoosiers, coached by the legendary Bob Knight. For the second straight game, the Jayhawks leapt to a decisive early lead, this time 24-6, en route to an 83-65 victory. Sharp-shooting guard Terry Brown led KU with 23 points. Sean Tunstall came off the bench to provide 15 points while Jamison scored 14 to go with a game-high 10 rebounds.

"We put Indiana out in the first 10 minutes," Jamison says. "I remember Coach Knight saying there was a loose board on the court and asking, 'Could we start the whole game over?'"

Arkansas hounded and pounded Alabama 93-70 in the other Sweet 16 matchup. KU's victory crimped the Razorbacks' plans to face Indiana. The 34-3 Hogs were looking to return to the Final Four, and Razorback coach Nolan Richardson admitted he was hoping to play the Hoosiers for the right to advance to Indianapolis.

"[Coach Knight] has a place in history," Richardson said. "I like to play against the great coaches of all time, and I've never played his team."

Richardson also gave Williams his proper due but not without a subtle warning.

"Roy is doing a great job," he said. "Roy is a newcomer, and Roy I like. But when we step on the floor, it's war. That's the way it is."

Arkansas' idea of "war" on the floor came from a constant pressure defense that forced more than 20 turnovers a game. The Razorbacks and their coach reveled in calling their style "40 minutes of hell." For most of the first half of the 1990s, Arkansas basketball was aptly described as such. But that wouldn't be the case on a late Saturday afternoon in the early spring of 1991 in Charlotte, North Carolina. For on that day, Kansas' last 20 minutes against Arkansas was about to turn the Razorbacks' idea of hell into nothing more than mild humidity.

The Game of My Life

BY ALONZO JAMISON
KANSAS VS. ARKANSAS, MARCH 23, 1991

We didn't play badly in the first half until the last three or four minutes. We actually took the lead midway through the half [29-26]. Then they went on a big run and it was a 12-point deficit at halftime.

It was one of those things where [Arkansas] had showed us no respect. I love playing the underdog role because you never know what the fight is inside "the dog." Arkansas had given us some bulletin-board material saying they wanted to play Indiana. We took that in stride and said, "Okay, we're here. You're going to have to deal with us. Please overlook us."

We showed a lot of perseverance, because when you're down 12 at halftime, most teams would think it's pretty much over when you're playing the second-ranked team in the country. But we had so much heart. We weren't going to go out that way.

I'll take the blame for Todd Day's 20 points in the first half. He was pretty much unconscious. I later saw that look from Anthony Peeler [who scored 43 points for Missouri in a 97-89 loss to Kansas in 1992 at Allen Fieldhouse]. They get that look in their eye when the basket looks like an ocean, and every time they throw something up it goes in. But luckily, I got in Day's head in the second half and got him away from that. I wish I knew how I did that; I would bottle it and sell it.

I wouldn't say Coach Williams was unhappy at halftime. He told us, "Guys, you are going away from what got you here. Keep doing what got you here—playing like a team, setting the right screens for the right people," things of that nature. But he did challenge our manhood when he told us, "Either you do the things that got you here, or you will be down by another 12 points at the end of the game."

It was a pretty good offensive explosion by us in the second half. It was one of those things where not only one person was hitting his shot, but everybody was. We pulled together more in that game than we did the whole year. We laid it out on the line and we came out on top of it.

We cut the lead down to four points in the first two minutes. That was a big pick-me-up. Terry [Brown] hit two layups, Mark hit a free throw, and I made a three. They might have gotten a couple of shots off, but obviously,

They ended up calling a timeout in the first two
ve knew the game was ours for the taking if we wanted

me was surreal, just like a dream, especially for me,
od game. People didn't think I was good enough to

when Coach got us up early to go to a 7:30 press
as asking questions and Coach Williams stopped
aid, "Somebody has to ask Alonzo a question. I'm
up and get them here and not have you guys ask
estion." There was dead silence for a minute or
ne one of the silliest questions—I forgot what it

is game, people swarmed me. It was like

-3); Assists:
, Tunstall);
stall, Scott,
dall, Jordan,

d Season Results

pretty good offensive explosion" for Kansas
8-34 second-half advantage for the 'Hawks,
ne deficit into a 12-point, 93-81 victory.
Arkansas lead in the second half. Jamison
way through to cut the Razorbacks' lead to
e the 'Hawks the lead for good at 63-62
three minutes, Jamison scored two other
three-point leads. When Mike Maddox
KU ahead 72-68 with 5:11 to go, the
e throws to pull away from Arkansas.
nd team-high) 26 points on 11-for-14
e three-pointer and 3-for-5 shooting
d a team-high nine rebounds and was
theast Regional.
ries and rewarded me. I was happy
t back from the Arkansas game and
nd talked to some friends at Wescoe

TP
26
11
16
7
3
14
2
0
2
81

0-1, Mayberry
Miller, Wallace);
ace 2, Mayberry,
, Morris, Murry).

,717.

BOX SCORE
KANSAS VS. ARKANSAS, MARCH 23, 1991

Kansas	35 58	– 93
Arkansas	47 34	– 81

Kansas (93)

	Min	FG	FT	Reb	PF	TP
Jamison	28	11-14	3-5	9	3	26
Maddox	22	3-4	2-2	4	2	8
Randall	27	4-5	2-4	2	4	10
Brown	26	5-12	0-0	3	4	11
Jordan	34	3-9	8-10	6	3	14
Richey	5	0-1	0-0	1	0	0
Woodberry	16	1-4	4-4	4	0	6
Tunstall	18	3-7	4-4	3	0	11
Wagner	5	1-1	2-2	0	0	4
Scott	16	1-5	1-2	3	2	3
Johanning	3	0-0	0-0	0	0	0
TOTALS	200	32-62	26-33	35	18	93

Three-point goals: 3-12 (Jamison 1-1, Tunstall 1-3, Brown 1-5, Jordan (
12 (Jordan 3, Randall 3, Jamison 2, Maddox, Brown, Woodberr
Turnovers: 14 (Randall 4, Jordan 4, Jamison, Maddox, Brown, Tur
team); Blocked shots 1 (Woodberry); Steals: 6 (Brown 2, Jamison, Rar
Woodberry).

Arkansas (81)

	Min	FG	FT	Reb	PF
Day	34	8-19	6-7	4	4
Morris	15	5-6	1-1	5	3
Miller	34	7-11	2-3	9	3
Mayberry	38	3-9	1-2	6	3
Bowers	20	1-4	0-0	0	3
Murry	25	6-13	0-1	4	5
Huery	18	1-7	0-0	1	2
Fletcher	5	0-1	0-0	0	0
Wallace	11	1-3	0-0	2	2
TOTALS	200	32-73	10-15	31	25

Three-point goals: 7-19 (Day 4-8, Murry 2-5, Bowers 1-1, Wallac
0-4); Assists: 16 (Mayberry 4, Huery 4, Bowers 3, Murry 2, Day,
Turnovers: 16 (Day 3, Miller 3, Morris 2, Bowers 2 Huery 2, Wall
Murry); Blocked shots: 6 (Day 3, Miller 2, Murry); Steals: 4 (Day

Officials: Mickey Crowley, Pete Pavia, Sam Croft. Attendance: 2

Beach and I heard people clapping. They were giving me applause for the game that I had."

The applause continued for Jamison and the Jayhawks. In the national semifinal game against North Carolina, Jamison keyed a second-half spurt to help lead KU to a 79-73 triumph. He scored nine points and snared 11 rebounds in the victory. But more importantly, Jamison and his teammates held Carolina star George Lynch to just 13 points and five rebounds.

"From UNO in the first round all the way up to the national championship game, I drew the other team's leading scorer," Jamison says. "But it wasn't just me on defense, it also was Steve Woodberry and Patrick Richey, and they were not slouches. As well as I did, they did just as well on those guys, too."

Two days later, the Duke Blue Devils controlled the championship game pretty much from the outset to defeat the Jayhawks, 72-65, for the national title. Despite coming up short for the championship, the return to the Final Four and the title game firmly re-established Kansas as a basketball program to be reckoned with.

What Became of Alonzo Jamison?

The 1991-92 Jayhawks outdid the previous KU team in the regular season by posting a 23-4 record and winning the Big Eight title outright. KU then decisively won the Big Eight tournament and headed into the NCAA tournament as the top seed in the Midwest Region.

Kansas ran through Howard 100-67 in the first round before the University of Texas-El Paso shocked the Jayhawks 66-60 in the second round. KU finished the season with a 27-5 record. Jamison started all 32 games as a senior, averaging 10 points and 4.6 rebounds. Playing in a bigger line-up with junior college transfer Eric Pauley and freshman reserves Greg Ostertag and Ben Davis, Jamison led the team in scoring three times, in rebounding seven times, and in assists 10 times during the season.

Later that year, Jamison went to camp with the Los Angeles Lakers as an undrafted free agent. Surgery kept him from making the team, so he headed to Sweden to play professionally in 1992-93. The next season Jamison played in France before rupturing his Achilles tendon, which ended his playing career.

"Everybody should go across the pond once in their lives to see how they view Americans," he says. "I was in eastern France, and there wasn't a lot of love there. It makes you appreciate home, I'll tell you that much."

Today, Jamison stays busy with three demanding jobs. His full-time duty is as a product manager for Embarq (formerly Sprint's local telephone service). He has three daughters, Michaela and twins Olivia and Elise, who keep him busy. During the basketball season, he also serves as a part-time assistant basketball coach for Mill Valley High School in Shawnee, Kansas.

"I would love to be a coach full time," Jamison says. "I think I have the personality to do it and the wherewithal. That'll be in the future, hopefully."

Should he become a head coach, Jamison definitely would share with his players just how special that time will be in their lives. From his own experiences, he deeply appreciates the opportunity to have been a recognized athlete while with the Jayhawks.

"Basketball is like a religion at Kansas," Jamison says. "You do well and you get rewarded for it. I loved being a part of that. The kids who are playing now, they probably won't know what they are going to be missing when they leave, but it will come sooner or later. It is a unique experience."

6

MARK RANDALL

The Life of Young Mark Randall

In the spring of 1983, 15-year-old Mark Randall faced a pivotal decision: keep playing baseball at the expense of his burgeoning basketball career, or give up the diamond and focus on hoops. He chose basketball, obviously, but it wasn't an easy decision. A day after hitting 4-for-5 for his sophomore baseball team at Cherry Creek High School in suburban Denver, freshman Randall told his coach he could no longer play baseball.

"I went in crying to the coach telling him that I needed to make a decision," Randall says. "I was playing basketball year-round by then, and baseball was going to cut out playing time for basketball. In hindsight, that's one of the biggest regrets I have. But there was a chance I could play basketball at the Division I level, and that had been a goal of mine."

Randall's decision turned out to be as correct as it was difficult. He grew six inches to 6-foot-8 the summer between his freshman and sophomore years. Usually in a growth spurt, a young athlete loses some coordination as his or her body tries to catch up. But in Randall's case, time spent playing soccer and street hockey helped him with his coordination.

Playing basketball—all the time—helped as well. In the driveway, Mark took on his younger brother, David; their friends; and their, dad, Thomas. Practice at school might happen during the lunch hour or even between classes.

Colleges began noticing Randall. Actually, his first recruiting letter arrived from the University of Colorado when he was in middle school.

Factor in his growth and improvement as a player, and the pace picked up to a "ridiculous" level by his senior year.

"I was getting six or seven calls a night from different colleges," Randall says. "I knew what the process was about but that didn't make it any easier in my life or my family's life." His brother and sister started screening the calls. "You couldn't live a normal life," he says. "It's something every high school boy dreams about, but it's just crazy."

Randall eventually narrowed his final three prospects to Arizona, Duke, and Kansas.

"I was on my plane ride home from Duke when I decided to go to Kansas," Randall explains. "I had a great time at Duke, would have loved to have gone to school there. [But] my family means a ton to me. We weren't in a financial position for them to be hopping on a plane to the ACC tournament every year.

"It was easier for them to get in a car and drive nine hours to get to Lawrence. (KU) came to Colorado every year to play the Buffs. That was the bottom line."

College Life

Randall acclimated to Lawrence and college life at KU fairly easily in late summer 1986, given that he had graduated from a 4,000-student high school in Denver. He came in with fellow freshmen Jeff Gueldner, Keith Harris, and Kevin Pritchard.

Formal basketball practice started off on a high note. Larry "Bud" Melman, a cult favorite from *Late Night with David Letterman*, attended "Late Night with Larry Brown," and the team sang "My Girl" during a skit.

"We actually sang it, which in hindsight might not have been the thing to do," Randall says. "But the crowd loved it."

When practice began, Randall admits to being overwhelmed at first. He learned, as 99 percent of freshmen do, that there's a big difference between high school and college players. Part of that discovery also had to do with playing the small forward position.

"I was more of a big man with foot speed, so it was tough for me to contain a lot of the 'threes' [small forwards] in college," Randall says. "Guys were bigger and stronger than I was used to."

Notes on Mark Randall

Years lettered:	1986-87; 1988-89 to 1990-91
Position:	Forward/center
Height:	6-foot-9
Playing weight:	235 pounds
Hometown:	Englewood, Colorado
Current residence:	Lonetree, Colorado
Occupation:	Community ambassador for the Denver Nuggets and Kroenke Sports Enterprises, Inc.
Accomplishments:	First-round draft pick of the Chicago Bulls; winner of the team's MVP award in 1991; first-team All-Big Eight (AP and UPI) and honorable mention All-America (AP and UPI) in '91; member of the bronze medal-winning 1990 U.S. basketball team at the World Championships in Argentina and the Goodwill Games in Seattle; third-team All-American, Naismith Award finalist, and second-team All-Big Eight (AP and UPI) in 1990; two-time Academic All-Big Eight Team; member of the gold medal-winning 1989 U.S. basketball team in the World University Games in West Germany; second-team All-Big Eight (UPI) and honorable mention All-Big Eight (AP) in '89; consensus All-America in high school.
The Game:	Kansas vs. Duke, NCAA championship game in Indianapolis, Indiana, April 1, 1991

Still, Randall averaged 10 minutes per game in the 31 games in which he played in 1986-87, averaging 4.5 points for the 25-11 Jayhawks. Randall then took what was called a "medical" redshirt in the championship season of 1987-88. He underwent surgery in early 1988 to correct breathing and jaw-alignment problems. His sinus cavities were drained and his jaw was broken in four places, resulting in him having it wired shut for eight weeks afterward. But playing time was the main reason for his decision.

"The reason I took the redshirt in the first place was that Danny [Manning] was a pre-season player of the year, and I was moving into the power forward position," Randall says. "We had size in Danny, Marvin Branch, and Mike Masucci. It was apparent that I wasn't going to get a lot of time that year. So, for my development, after talking with Coach Brown, I decided to take the redshirt that year. In hindsight, it turned out to be a great thing."

Great, but difficult: Randall practiced with the team but missed the 1998 championship. He keeps his championship ring in a safety deposit box ("never have worn it") and gets it out only to show friends and family who ask about it.

Randall was preparing for his sophomore year in June 1988 when Brown left to coach the San Antonio Spurs.

"We were shocked but not totally surprised that Coach Brown had taken off," Randall says.

Three and a half weeks later, Kansas hired Roy Williams as its new head coach.

"Coach Williams called a meeting when he first came to town, told us what he expected of us," Randall says. "We felt a little more at ease and excited about what the future was about."

The 1988-89 Jayhawks started 16-3 before hitting an eight-game losing streak. The team, unable to defend its national championship due to NCAA sanctions, finished the season 19-12. Randall showed no ill effects of taking a year off. He started every game for the Jayhawks and averaged 16 points, second best on the team behind Milt Newton's 17.7 average.

"Mark was unbelievably strong, did a great job of using his body, ran the floor well, and had a soft touch shooting the ball," says teammate Mike Maddox.

Though unranked to start the season, Kansas got off to an even better start in 1989-90, winning its first 19 games. The team was ranked first for four weeks during the season and second for 10 weeks. Overall, the Jayhawks went 30-5, getting upset in the second round of the NCAA tournament by UCLA. Randall again started all 35 games for the 'Hawks while averaging 13.3 points and 6.2 rebounds.

The 1990-91 team lost three senior starters from the previous season. Gone were Gueldner and Pritchard from Randall's recruiting class, along with transfer Rick Calloway. Randall, transfer Terry Brown, and Maddox comprised the heart of the '91 seniors. Their season started badly in a two-point loss to Arizona State in Tempe, and after 12 games Kansas' record was 8-4, including

0-2 in league play. The 'Hawks then rattled off 10 straight wins before going 2-2 in the last four games of the regular season. In the Big 8 tournament, Kansas defeated Colorado 82-76 before losing to Nebraska 87-83.

"Our season was so up and down that year," Randall says. "We had stretches where we played pretty well, then we got into the Big 8 Conference and played well against some teams, but other teams had our number. We had a high level of confidence that year. We believed in one another, and that is what made that year and the year before so special."

By mid-March, Kansas basketball resembled the proverbial half-full, half-empty glass of water. The team's record was 22-7, but only 3-3 in its last six games, including two losses to Nebraska. The team's highest poll ranking was eighth, but the Jayhawks drew a third seed in the NCAA tournament's Southeast Region.

Regardless how the outside world viewed the Jayhawks, the team had confidence in themselves.

"We knew our roles, we fit well together," Randall says. "The team took it personally when we got slighted."

But there was only one goal: win.

"When you're in college, your goal is to get to the NCAA tournament. When you play at Kansas, your expectations are higher," Randall emphasizes. "You want to get to the Final Four and ultimately to win it."

Heading into the tournament, college basketball "experts" didn't give KU much of a chance, which Randall says inspired the team. Then the games began. In Louisville, Kentucky, the Jayhawks edged New Orleans 54-49 in the first round. Kansas played solidly in defeating Pittsburgh 77-66 in the second round. Moving to Charlotte, North Carolina, the 'Hawks embarrassed Indiana 83-65 to set up an Elite Eight game versus Arkansas, which had reached the Final Four the previous season.

"Nolan Richardson was talking about his '40 minutes of hell,'" Randall recalls. "We said, 'Okay, we got our 40 minutes of hell on this side, too. Alonzo [Jamison] was huge, Terry was huge. Mike had a great regional. It wasn't one person stepping up. The team was the focal point."

The Kansas-Arkansas game turned into two 20-minute halves of hell. Arkansas took the first half 47-35. But then Kansas regrouped at halftime and controlled the thermostat in the second half, blistering the Razorbacks 58-34 and taking a 93-81 victory.

One impressive-yet-uncanny four-game winning streak in March propelled Kansas back to the Final Four for the first time in three years. The 'Hawks were bound for Indianapolis.

The Setting

"Can Kansas?" *Sports Illustrated* posed that question next to a picture of Randall on the cover of its magazine the weekend heading into the Final Four.

Well, Kansas certainly could. The Jayhawks had dismantled Indiana in the Regionals and then staged a mighty second-half comeback against Arkansas to reach the Final Four.

"We came back from the regional and were flying high with the two big wins," Randall says. "It goes back to what we felt in '88—you're just numb. You're going to class, you're studying, you're doing things, but you don't really understand what's going on in the world around you other than the NCAA tournament."

Randall and his teammates weren't the only people in Kansas who were managing distractions in the face of the Final Four. This story would not be complete without one an anecdote to show—once again—what place KU basketball has in the hearts and minds of many Jayhawk fans. For Lawrence resident Howard Wilburn, the end of the season meant he could cash in on a big prize. Wilburn, a KU basketball fan, won $2 million in a Lotto America (now Powerball) drawing just a couple of days before the Final Four. He didn't claim his winnings until mid-April. Part of the reason he waited to step forward, he said, was he didn't want to be distracted from watching the Jayhawks play in the NCAA semifinal game: Kansas versus North Carolina; Coach Williams versus his mentor, Dean Smith, a KU alumnus.

"Going in, we were hyped up but Coach Williams kept us under control," recalls Randall. "He kept our heads level. We went in looking to have fun. We had nothing to lose. In the first game against Carolina, obviously there were a lot of feelings there with Coach Williams and the connection between Carolina and Kansas with Dean Smith."

North Carolina took an early lead in the game, but Kansas answered with a 17-1 run and led 43-34 at halftime. The tables turned somewhat in the second half with the 'Hawks taking a 10-point lead in the first four and a half minutes before the Tar Heels outscored KU 14-5 to make it a one-point game at 58-57. Then Jamison sparked a 7-0 run to give the Jayhawks some much-needed breathing room. Kansas won 79-73. The team then waited to see who would win between Duke and top-ranked Nevada-Las Vegas.

"Can Kansas?" remained a viable question for one more game.

The Game of My Life

BY MARK RANDALL
KANSAS VS. DUKE, APRIL 1, 1991

We went in confident, knowing we could play with those guys, excited about the opportunity. But, as I said, we were just numb [to our] surroundings. It's just crazy. You first walk into the Dome in Indianapolis, it's just unbelievable to think there's going to be that many people there watching the game. Yet, it really doesn't faze you once it comes game time because you are so locked into the game.

I was excited to be playing Duke. I've always wanted to play against the best. I also got caught up in the irony of it, the fact that I'm playing my last college game against the team that was the last one I turned down coming out of high school. Coach Williams stated it best: There are not a lot of seniors in this country who know the last game they play in college is going to be the national championship game. That's pretty powerful.

I was guarding Christian Laettner. Our friendship started when we played on a summer team together. Coach K [Duke coach Mike Krzyzewski] coached a U.S.A. basketball team, and I played on it three out of five summers. We trained in Colorado Springs and played in the Goodwill Games in Seattle and then in the World Championships in Argentina. [Christian and I] both made the team and started hanging out during down time.

We never led in the first half. Duke takes pride in their defense. Coach K is a good defensive coach. That was the one thing going into that game—we were always good at executing our half court, running our plays, and taking what was given to us. If they tried to cut out one option, we went to another option. That's where our confidence came from. When we were playing "Kansas basketball," you couldn't stop us.

We were getting a lot of looks at the basket and were able to run a ton of our stuff. They were somewhat tired coming off their game versus UNLV. We were just not knocking down the shots we had been coming into that game. We were missing a lot of lay-ups, which was not characteristic of our team. If we make half of the lay-ups we normally make, we win going away.

With 3:26 left in the first half, I hit the only three-pointer I ever made in college to make the score 36-30 Duke. It came out of the flow of the game, and that's why it meant that much more. It just felt right.

We were behind 42-34 at halftime. We were disappointed. There were so many shots as a team we missed that were hard to take. Their defense was good that day, but we were still able to get the ball inside. But we could just not get the shots, the lay-ups to fall. The shots that had made us the team that we were ... those easy shots just would not fall.

Early in the second half, we cut Duke's lead to four points, but they pulled away. I don't recall when I picked up my third foul, but I know what my thought processes would have been from my whole career. Once you pick up three, you have to play more tentatively. You don't want to pick up the fourth and be sitting on the bench. The aggressiveness scales back a little bit. You play your best when you're not in foul trouble and you're able to take some chances here and there. In that game, I really didn't pull it all together.

Game and Season Results

Kansas played valiantly in the second half, but could never whittle Duke's margin away in losing 72-65. The Jayhawks finished 27-8 for the season. Randall scored 18 points and grabbed 10 rebounds, statistics he says he knows because Jayhawk fans have reminded him of his line from that game many, many times. Otherwise, Randall says he had never seen a boxscore from the game until preparing to be interviewed for this book.

"That's why that team was special, because we didn't care who scored the points," he says.

Tournament MVP Laettner complimented Randall, saying Randall wore him out during the game.

BOX SCORE
KANSAS VS. DUKE, APRIL 1, 1991

Kansas	34	31 –	65
Duke	42	30 –	72

Kansas (65)

	Min	FG	FT	Reb	PF	TP
Jamison	29	1-10	0-0	4	4	2
Maddox	19	2-4	0-0	3	3	4
Randall	33	7-9	3-6	10	4	18
Brown	31	6-15	0-0	4	1	16
Jordan	34	4-6	1-2	0	0	11
Richey	4	0-1	0-0	1	0	0
Woodberry	18	1-4	0-0	4	4	2
Tunstall	11	1-5	0-0	1	3	2
Wagner	3	1-1	0-0	1	0	2
Scott	15	3-9	0-0	2	1	6
Johanning	3	1-1	0-0	2	1	2
TOTALS	**200**	**27-65**	**4-8**	**32**	**21**	**65**

Three-point goals: 7-18 (Brown 4-11, Jordan 2-2, Randall 1-1, Jamison 0-2, Richey 0-1, Tunstall 0-1); Assists: 16 (Jamison 5, Maddox 4, Jordan 3, Randall 2, Brown, Johanning); Turnovers: 14 (Randall 3, Jordan 3, Maddox 2, Brown 2, Jamison, Woodberry, Tunstall, Scott); Blocked shots: 2 (Maddox, Scott); Steals: 10 (Jamison 4, Brown 3, Randall, Jordan, Woodberry).

Duke (72)

	Min	FG	FT	Reb	PF	TP
Koubek	17	2-4	0-0	4	1	5
G. Hill	28	4-6	2-8	8	1	10
Laettner	32	3-8	12-12	10	3	18
Hurley	40	3-5	4-4	1	1	12
T. Hill	23	1-5	0-0	4	2	3
McCaffrey	26	6-8	2-2	1	1	16
Lang	1	0-0	0-0	0	0	0
Davis	24	4-5	0-2	2	4	8
Palmer	9	0-0	0-0	0	0	0
(team)				1		
TOTALS	**200**	**23-41**	**20-28**	**31**	**13**	**72**

Three-point goals: 6-10 (Hurley 2-4, McCaffrey 2-3, Koubek 1-2, T. Hill 1-1); Assists: 14 (Hurley 9, G. Hill 3, T. Hill, Davis); Turnovers: 18 (Laettner 4, McCaffrey 4, Hurley 3, Koubek 2, G. Hill 2, T. Hill, Davis, Palmer); Blocked shots 2 (G. Hill 2); Steals: 6 (G. Hill 2, Hurley 2, Koubek, Laettner).

Officials: Mickey Crowley, Charles Range, James Burr. Attendance: 47,100.

"There were many times during this game when I was winded," Laettner said. "I think it was mainly because of Mark Randall. I chased him around all game. He's a very good runner."

Laettner matched Randall with 18 points. The Duke junior shot just 3-for-8 from the field, but was a perfect 12-for-12 from the line.

"It was a tough test," Laettner said. "We broke their continuity. I tell you, Kansas is a tough team to defend against."

When he looks back at the game now, Randall says, "It was the ultimate. To play Duke in the Finals, on national TV and all that good stuff, it couldn't be any better for me. In hindsight, getting a win would have meant that much more, but just to play in the game, to be able to say I'm a part of the team … I'm more proud of the ring we got out of that one than the one we got in '88 (when he redshirted)."

Randall averaged 15 points and 6.2 rebounds as a senior, and totaled 1,627 points in his career.

"He was so wise and knew what to do in certain situations," Jamison says of Randall. "He was deceptively athletic, and he's probably one of the best guys I've ever known."

What Became of Mark Randall?

In June 1991, the Chicago Bulls, led by Michael Jordan, won the first of what would become six NBA championships in the '90s. The Bulls drafted Randall in the first round with the 26th overall pick. The pairing was a terrible match.

"Going to the Bulls was perhaps the worst place I could have gone," Randall says. "I loved being around that team. I loved being around Phil Jackson. [But] the reality quickly hit me about what the NBA is about at that level. I got released just after Christmas. It was a tough thing for me."

Besides the Bulls, Randall played parts of four seasons with Minnesota, Detroit, and Denver. While in Detroit in 1992-93, Randall played with an aging "Bad Boys" team—Bill Laimbeer, Isiah Thomas, Dennis Rodman, Joe Dumars, and Mark Aguirre—that was three seasons removed from its last championship. Randall says he hadn't practiced with a teammate as strong as Richard Scott until he went up against Aguirre.

"That was fun but the team wasn't very good," he says of the 40-42 Pistons.

Randall's NBA career ended in 1995 with his hometown Nuggets. He averaged 2.6 points in 127 career NBA games.

Outside of the NBA, Randall tried out for a team in Milan, Italy, and played in the Continental Basketball Association with three different teams. He also tried returning to the NBA but missed the cut with the Miami Heat and Vancouver Grizzlies. Randall wouldn't make it back to the NBA for a few years.

He remained close to the players on the Denver Nuggets. During the strike-shortened season of 1998-99, his friend and former teammate, LaPhonso Ellis, noticed Randall was getting a little overweight.

"He said, 'You're not going out this way, buddy,'" Randall recalls.

So Randall worked his way into playing shape, made the team when training camp re-opened in early 1999, but then injured his shoulder before playing another game with the team.

"The Nuggets told me they were going to release me but asked if I was interested in staying with the organization. I said, 'You bet,'" he says.

Randall scouted college basketball for the Nuggets during the next two and a half years. His duties allowed him to "conveniently" return to Lawrence two or three times a year to check out Big 12 players. The job also took Randall back to Indianapolis for a Final Four, which gave him a different perspective on the event.

"I sat there and I watched all the blitz that was going on down on the court as the guys were going through their lay-up drills, and I thought, 'Wow, this is unbelievable, I would have never guessed that this stuff was going around me in '91,'" he says.

After scouting, Randall served as an assistant coach and worked in player development. For the last few years, he has worked as a community ambassador for the Nuggets and Kroenke Sports Enterprises, Inc.

"I'm at a point in my life where I'm doing what I'm supposed to be doing. I'm absolutely loving it," he says. "I talk to kids about education, staying away from drugs, and staying out of gangs. It's not about me; it's about these kids and what they are going to do with their future."

Other aspects of Randall's job include working with service groups and Fortune 500 companies. This interaction often means golf—lots of golf.

Randall considers the game a "passion" and has used his competitiveness and athleticism to fashion a one-handicap game.

"When I stand over a three-footer, it kind of gives me the same rush I had standing in front of 16,000 people in Allen Fieldhouse trying to make free throws," he says.

As with most of the former Jayhawk players, the talk about their lives often returns to the time they spent at Mt. Oread. Randall is no exception.

"My five years at Kansas were the greatest of my life," he says. "From the education I received, the people that I met, the faithfulness of the fans— to this day the bond that I feel with the university is as strong as it's ever been, even though I'm not able to get back and be a part of that community like a lot of my former teammates. You're a Jayhawk from the moment you step foot on the campus until the day you die."

7

REX WALTERS

The Life of Young Rex Walters

Rex Walters' father, Monte, didn't have many rules for his youngest son, but he made sure those rules were followed.

"Dad always said, 'You can't do anything until: number one, your homework is done; and number two, you shoot 100 free throws.' So, from eighth grade on, I shot 100 free throws every day, Monday through Sunday," Walters says.

And they weren't just any free throws.

"He'd put the rim up extra high and tilt the rim up, so I had to shoot with more arc—a higher, softer shot," Walters adds. "It had a lot to do with how I shot the ball the way I did."

Monte Walters was an ex-Air Force officer who later worked for Lockheed Missiles and Space. In short, he knew discipline, precision, and competition. He passed these attributes on to his two sons, Rex and Rick, Rex's older brother by 10 years. Walters says he enjoyed competing in many sports—none of which he liked as much as basketball, but he played other games just for the sake of competing and winning.

"There's nothing like the feeling of outworking somebody," he says.

Not that Rex always won. Rick "beat me down every day" when they competed in games.

"I just come from a very competitive family," Walters says. "Some kids, [getting beat] may turn them off. For me, it made me go harder for whatever reason."

Still, despite his free-throw shooting regimen and competitive streak, something went wrong during Walters' freshman year in high school. He averaged "only" seven points playing for the freshman-sophomore team.

"My dad and my brother were very disappointed," Walters says. "My brother re-focused me, and I worked real hard afterwards. I never wanted to disappoint my dad with what I did or said. His approval was big for me."

As a sophomore, Walters made the varsity team at Piedmont Hills in San Jose, California.

"That's when it really took off and I saw I could do some things on the basketball court," he says. "Another thing that drove me is we had a very talented high school team. I played year-round."

The dedication paid off. Walters had a great summer season before his senior year.

His AAU team won a national tournament in Los Angeles, and he was named most valuable player. Suddenly, Walters went from being an unknown player who had been told to consider junior college to a well-known recruit sought by Northwestern, Stanford, Santa Clara, and Pepperdine.

But no schools the caliber of Kansas were interested. North Carolina assistant coach Bill Guthridge traveled to San Jose to check on Walters, but the Tar Heels signed Hubert Davis instead.

"It was probably the two best weeks of my life thinking North Carolina was actually interested in me," Walters recalls with a laugh.

College Life

After a senior season in which Walters helped lead Piedmont Hills to a 24-4 record while averaging 17.7 points, 8.8 rebounds, and 6.1 assists per game, he signed with Northwestern. He loved the idea of playing in the Big 10 against all the powerhouse schools such as Indiana, Illinois, Michigan, and Michigan State.

"But we didn't have the success I thought we would," Walters says. "My sophomore year we were 7-3 in non-conference and won only two more games the rest of the season. We had good guys who had great character, but on the court there wasn't that love and passion that I thought I would get myself into. That's why I decided to leave."

Notes on Rex Walters

Years lettered:	1991-92 to 1992-93
Position:	Guard
Height:	6-foot-4
Playing weight:	190 pounds
Hometown:	San Jose, California
Current residence:	Boca Raton, Florida
Occupation:	Head coach, men's basketball, Florida Atlantic University
Accomplishments:	First-round draft pick of the New Jersey Nets in 1993; named team MVP in 1992 and '93; honorable mention All-America in '93; All-Big Eight first team (AP, coaches, and players) and two-time Big Eight Player of the Week in '93; Big Eight Newcomer of the Year and All-Big Eight first team (media and players) in '92.
Nickname:	"Sexy Rexy"
The Game:	Brigham Young vs. Kansas in Rosemont, Illinois, March 20, 1993

After he was given his release from Northwestern, Walters' AAU coach contacted Kansas assistant Kevin Stallings. By then, UCLA and a few other West Coast schools were interested in Walters. He chose Kansas because it struck him as "a fun place to play where they share the ball."

Walters had visited Lawrence in the spring of 1990 and returned to Mt. Oread in late summer to begin classes and the informal pick-up games the team plays before practice officially starts in October. The place was better than he remembered it.

"You walk into Allen Fieldhouse and you see the banners, the trophies," Walters says. "You see this old building just steeped in tradition. That was a basketball player's dream.

"I was a highly driven guy. I went to class, Robinson Gym, did my homework and went back to Robinson Gym and played some more. It was perfect for me."

So was "Late Night with Roy Williams"—or so he thought.

"I knew this was the only chance to show people what I could do on the basketball court, so I reverted back to what I did best—scoring," Walters says. "I played a good game, but it was a pick-up game, not Kansas basketball. The next day Coach Williams told me, 'You scored real well last night, but playing defense like that, you're never going to play here.' He said it real matter-of-fact. He wasn't mad, just firm.

"I'm the type of guy that if you tell me something, it's going to burn inside of me. I'm going to remember it for a long time. He's a really good psychologist for telling me that."

When practice started, Walters found adjusting to Kansas basketball to be difficult.

"We did things differently than I had done before," he says. "There were hard, long practices with a lot of running. On offense, it was about getting the best shot, not the shot you wanted. On defense, I had never played defense [man-to-man instead of zone] like that before. You had to see one or two plays ahead. You could never relax."

But Walters adjusted and appreciated being held accountable.

"You had to push yourself," he says. "You felt like you were prepared for every situation, and it got you closer to the other guys because you had to count on each other."

Counting on each other served as a good lesson for Walters and the Jayhawks. The team was 22-7 heading into the NCAA tournament, where it was seeded third in the Southeast Regional. Walters—who had to sit out the season in accordance with NCAA rules for transfers—watched the first four NCAA games on television, but was allowed to travel with the team to Indianapolis, where KU defeated North Carolina before losing to Duke in the championship game.

"After that season, I just wanted to get back there desperately," Walters says of the Final Four. "I saw that we had all the pieces. But I didn't know if I could be a guy like Mark [Randall] who could help lead us there, but I knew I could be a part of it."

That he was. Walters was in the best shape of his life and mentally prepared to play Kansas basketball. He started all 32 games in 1991-92 and led the team in scoring with a 16-point average. The team won the Big Eight regular-season and tournament titles, was ranked No. 1 during parts of the

season, and improved its record to 26-4 heading into the NCAA tournament.

Top-seeded Kansas slammed Howard in the first round of the Midwest Regional in Dayton, Ohio. In the second round, the 'Hawks faced the University of Texas-El Paso, led by veteran coach Don Haskins. In a major upset, KU fell to the Miners 66-60.

"UTEP really spread us out and drove it, just penetrate and kick, penetrate and kick," Walters says. "We played a pressure defense and tried to get in the lanes, but it was hard to pressure the lanes when guys would penetrate. They had good guards who could do that, and they had some big bodies down low that could finish.

"We didn't bring our 'A' game, to say the least. We weren't as focused as we should have been. We thought it was a game we should win and were going to win. We played a poor game and UTEP had a lot to do with it."

The loss deeply bothered Walters.

"It was like a wasted year," he says. "I thought we had the best team in college basketball. We had the best defensive power forward in Alonzo Jamison and one of the best point guards in Adonis [Jordan]. We had great post players in Richard Scott and Eric Pauley. And I thought Steve Woodberry was one of the best sixth men in college basketball."

On the bright side, KU lost only one starter (Jamison) after the 1992 season ended. Walters stayed in Lawrence and worked his way into even better shape. He and the team were motivated not to be ambushed again. But before the season, Walters endured a different kind of ambush when he severely sprained his ankle in a pick-up game. For most of the 1992-93 season he played without the ability to slide his feet or slash his way to the basket. Instead, Walters was relegated to being a jump shooter, and jumping proved problematic at times, too.

Still, Walters managed to average 15.3 points per game, and the Jayhawks again won the Big Eight regular-season title, going 11-3 in conference play and 24-5 during the regular season. In the last regular-season game, Walters felt the best he had all season. Playing in Stillwater, Walters torched Oklahoma State for 27 points in a 74-73 Jayhawk victory.

Things were looking up for KU and Walters heading into postseason play.

The Setting

Behind Walters' 22 points, Kansas rallied in the second half to dispatch Colorado 82-65 in the opening round of the Big Eight tournament. In the semifinals, KU went cold from the field (39 percent, including 25 percent behind the arc) and dropped a 74-67 decision to Kansas State.

On "Selection Sunday," the NCAA Tournament directors seeded the Jayhawks third in the Midwest Region and sent them to the Rosemont Horizon in suburban Chicago to take on Ball State. The assignment meant Walters would return to the city where he had played the first two years of his college career. In his first game back in Chicago, Walters staged a triumphant return by scoring 23 points in a 94-72 opening round win. He sank all six of his three-point attempts.

That victory set up the "second-round hurdle," which tripped up the 'Hawks the year before and caused them to crash land after a solid season. Walters and his teammates wanted to make sure history didn't repeat itself in 1993. They set their sights on defeating Brigham Young University.

"We took the Final Four for granted [the previous year]," says Walters. "We weren't going to let that happen again. There was an anger. As a team, it was an 'us against the world' kind of mentality."

Good thing for the world that KU "only" had to play BYU on March 20, 1993. Otherwise, a Jayhawk flag might be flying from every flagpole 'round the globe.

The Game of My Life

BY REX WALTERS
BRIGHAM YOUNG VS. KANSAS, MARCH 20, 1993

After we lost to Kansas State in the Big Eight tournament, one of the biggest things that coach said to us was, "Do what we ask you to do." I think that was on all of our minds. If we just do what Coach tells us to do, we're going to come out okay. The shots will take care of themselves, everything will take care of itself if we do it and do it hard. That was our mind-set.

I got lost in the system. I was in that zone. If you looked at me, I was probably looking right through you. I was focused on things like getting to the long-rebounding spot when the shot goes up, setting good screens, and finding the man on defense when I was setting the screen.

The shooting was easy. The shots just fell. There was no thought in it at all. The ball would touch my hand, it was fine, the follow-through was there—thank you, thank you. It was one of those games when you're just lost in the game. Everything was in slow motion and you see things clearly, two plays ahead.

[Kansas led 45-35 at halftime after outscoring the Cougars 17-6 in the last five minutes of the half. Walters had 12 points at intermission. In the second half, BYU rallied and led 68-67 with 4:38 to play. Then Walters made a play to key a big Jayhawk resurgence.]

They were playing a zone defense. I caught the ball on the wing, and the guy really closed out to me so hard that he went to my right inside shoulder, trying to make a play for the ball. I just spun off of it, put the ball on the floor to attack the gap and draw Adonis' man. I took two dribbles, kicked it to Adonis, and I knew the ball was going in.

[Jordan's three-pointer put KU ahead for good. Three minutes later, KU led 81-70 when Walters faced a breakaway opportunity.]

Greg Gurley was on my left. I should have given him the basketball. But I wanted to put an exclamation on this game, so I went up and flushed it. The Kansas band was right in front of us. I put my hands out to let them know, we're going to do this. Last year is over. All the ghosts of the past are gone. That was a good moment.

Game and Season Results

Walters' dunk was the last of his career-high 28 points that afternoon. Kansas finished off BYU 90-72 and moved on to the Sweet 16 round in St. Louis, Missouri.

"I learned that I was good enough to be a leader that could help lead a team beyond that point," he says.

Walters' discovery about his leadership represented something his teammates already knew about him.

"He was the most competitive guy I ever played against and with," says Steve Woodberry. "We would play against each other on the court and be ready to fight each other. We both wanted to win. And if we played five-on-five, it was like we were playing one-on-one. He would go into the gym and shoot after the game was over. I respected that about him."

Williams said of Walters, "He was fantastic. Like always, he was willing to step up and make the big, big play."

Kansas faced the University of California next. The Golden Bears, led by future NBA all-star Jason Kidd, had knocked off two-time defending national champion Duke in the second round. Besides the Final Four goal, Walters further motivated himself by remembering how Cal had snubbed him as a recruit and how Kidd had considered coming to KU out of high school, a decision that may have bumped Walters from the Jayhawk lineup.

"I just wanted everyone to know that on that night, he wasn't going to be as good as me," Walters says.

He wasn't. Walters scored 24 points to Kidd's 13, and most importantly, KU scored 93 points to Cal's 76. Now, to reach the Final Four, Kansas would have to get past Indiana. The Jayhawks had decimated the Hoosiers in the 1991 NCAA tournament and had defeated IU 74-69 in Indianapolis in the second game of the 1992-93 season. For Walters, the game presented another opportunity for him to pay back a team that had "whipped up" on Northwestern when he played in the Big 10.

"This was going to be a toughness game, to see who was going to be mentally tough enough to keep running their stuff," he says. "It came down to who was going to be tougher. And we were."

Final score: KU 83, Indiana 77. Next stop, the Final Four at the Louisiana Superdome in New Orleans. In their last college games, Walters and Jordan each scored 19 points for the Jayhawks. Their effort, and that of the team, wasn't enough this time. North Carolina defeated Kansas 78-68. The Tar Heels would defeat Michigan two nights later to win the 1993 national championship.

"It was just disappointing," Walters says. "Their physical-ness really bothered us that night."

He acknowledges the team felt good about its tournament performance, but still …

"Playing for Coach Williams, we felt that every year we had a chance to play for the national championship," Walters says. "It was disappointing we didn't get that done for Coach, because the man puts you in position to be successful."

BOX SCORE
BRIGHAM YOUNG VS. KANSAS, MARCH 20 1993

Brigham Young	35	41	– 76
Kansas	45	45	– 90

Brigham Young (76)

	Min	FG	FT	Reb	PF	TP
Larson	25	3-8	4-5	5	3	10
Durrant	14	2-3	0-0	2	3	4
Trost	36	4-9	4-4	6	4	12
Sanderson	37	7-18	4-4	1	2	24
Reid	32	1-3	6-6	3	5	8
Christensen	8	0-0	0-0	0	0	0
Lindquist	1	1-1	0-0	0	0	2
Cuff	2	0-0	0-0	0	1	0
Nixon	16	1-2	0-0	5	2	3
Astle	1	0-0	0-0	0	0	0
Knight	1	0-0	0-0	1	0	0
Miller	28	5-9	3-6	10	5	13
(team)				3		
TOTALS	**200**	**24-53**	**21-25**	**36**	**25**	**76**

Three-point goals: 7-19 (Sanderson 6-15, Nixon 1-2, Trost 0-1, Reid 0-1); Assists: 21 (Trost 8, Reid 4, Durrant 2, Sanderson 2, Nixon 2, Larson, Cuff , Knight); Turnovers: 21 (Reid 7, Durrant 3, Trost 2, Sanderson 2, Christensen 2, Nixon 2, Miller 2, Larson); Blocked shots: 2 (Larson, Miller); Steals: 5 (Larson 2, Miller 2, Durrant).

Kansas (90)

	Min	FG	FT	Reb	PF	TP
Hancock	12	2-8	0-0	3	3	4
Scott	17	1-2	3-4	1	4	5
Pauley	28	5-7	2-3	7	1	12
Walters	30	9-15	8-8	6	2	28
Jordan	35	4-8	1-3	0	4	13
Ostertag	12	0-1	0-0	2	1	0
Rayford	5	0-0	0-0	0	1	0
Whatley	1	0-1	1-2	0	0	1
Richey	22	3-5	7-8	4	1	13
Woodberry	28	4-6	5-6	2	2	14
Pearson	4	0-0	0-0	0	1	0
Weichbrodt	1	0-0	0-0	1	1	0
Gurley	5	0-2	0-0	0	0	0
(team)				1		
TOTALS	**200**	**28-55**	**27-34**	**27**	**21**	**90**

Three-point goals: 7-17 (Jordan 4-8, Walters 2-6, Woodberry 1-2; Gurley 0-1); Assists: 20 (Walters 6, Jordan 5, Ostertag 2, Richey 2, Woodberry 2, Pauley, Rayford, Pearson); Turnovers: 10 (Scott 2, Jordan 2, Ostertag 2, Hancock, Pauley, Walters, Richey); Blocked shots 3 (Scott, Pauley, Ostertag); Steals: 14 (Pauley 4, Jordan 3, Hancock, Scott, Rayford, Richey, Woodberry, Pearson, Gurley).

Officials: Frank Bosone, Tim Higgins, Leonard Wirtz. Attendance: 17,463.

What Became of Rex Walters?

After graduating from Kansas, Walters played seven years in the NBA with the New Jersey Nets, Philadelphia 76ers, and Miami Heat. He scored 1,547 points in the league and played for three of its most successful coaches: Chuck Daly in New Jersey, Larry Brown in Philadelphia, and Pat Riley in Miami.

"I learned a tremendous amount from Pat Riley," Walters says. "There are two guys who inspired me to be a coach—Roy Williams and Pat Riley."

Walters explains that Riley is "unbelievable" at organization and motivation. "He puts on a persona that it's 'show time,' but he really cares about his players," Walters says.

Toward the end of his professional career, Walters also played for the Kansas City Knights of the ABA (coached by former Jayhawk Kevin Pritchard) and in Spain, where he injured himself in two separate stints. He then entered college coaching as an assistant for Valparaiso University in 2003. He spent two years with coach Homer Drew before departing for Florida Atlantic University as an assistant to former Jayhawk assistant Matt Doherty. After a successful season with the Owls, Doherty left FAU to coach Southern Methodist University in Dallas. In the spring of 2006, FAU promoted Walters to head coach.

In time, coach Rex Walters may encounter a recruit similar in temperament and ability to a player named Rex Walters from the early 1990s. Could the two co-exist?

"There's no question," the new coach says. "You have to have unbelievable confidence. When you're 6-foot-3 and slow all your life until you get to college—because I made myself an athlete—you have to have great confidence in yourself."

8

PATRICK RICHEY

The Life of Young Patrick Richey

Patrick Richey grew up in the pastoral Lakewood neighborhood in Lee's Summit, Missouri, where the people were always friendly. With plenty of kids living in the area and three older brothers living in his house, some sort of game was always going on somewhere for Richey. Up until his freshman year in high school, those games included baseball, football, soccer, and lots and lots of hoops.

"My parents got me into leagues," Richey says. "My brothers [Brian, Mark, and Todd] were always playing. So I got to play with the older kids in the neighborhood. When you're playing with older kids, day in and day out, and getting beat up on, that helps improve your game."

When he wasn't in league play, the basketball games usually took place on a full-length court at a park a mile from Richey's house.

"I spent hours and hours and hours there," he says. "I dribbled the ball a mile there, played, and then would stay up there and shoot around after the games. And I dribbled the ball back home."

All of that play—leagues, between brothers, and at the neighborhood court—began paying off for Richey. He played AAU basketball in the Kansas City metro area in grades six through eight and hit the national AAU circuit as a freshman.

"It was great," Richey says. "You played against the best of the best. You saw where you stacked up. It helped me grow as a player."

Richey grew with his game, hitting 6-foot-5 as a freshman (point guard, no less). That's when he started hearing from college recruiters, beginning with Arizona. Once the letters started coming in, Richey gave up all other sports to commit everything to basketball.

Another key development for Richey during his freshman season was the implementation of the three-point line in high school play. His coach at Lee's Summit High School, Glen McDonald, started the team on Steve Alford shooting and workout drills to take advantage of the new rule.

"Those Alford drills really developed my skill as a player," Richey says. "A lot of high school coaches look at summer as their break. But Coach opened the gym for us every day, provided us an opportunity to improve ourselves, to work out, which is all you can ask for

"I took it to the next level my freshman year in high school. There are a lot of guys who have the talent and skills but not the heart or desire to take it to the next level, all those intangibles it takes to become a successful college player. You could almost go to any park and pick out guys who [are talented enough to play] college ball, but the attitude may not be there, the desire, will, commitment, academics aren't.

"The games with my brothers were real competitive. Afterwards, one of us was crying, usually me, because I didn't like losing. When I started getting better, I'd sneak up and beat my brother Todd every now and then."

As a sophomore, Richey's team took second place in the Missouri state tournament. In his junior season, he earned second-team all-state honors and would come home to 10 to 15 recruiting letters daily.

"It was ridiculous ... you can't read them all," Richey said of the college mail. "I made a decision early in my senior year that I wanted to get it over early, because it had become so hectic—calls every night, constant mail."

So Richey narrowed his choices to Kansas, Kentucky and Missouri. He visited all three schools and then eliminated Kentucky because of his desire to play closer to home. Patrick knew more about KU because his brother Brian had graduated from there.

"The thing that made me consider Missouri was when KU went on probation after the '88 season, when they won it all," Richey recalls. "I thought, 'Maybe I should go somewhere else.' So I got serious about Missouri.

"Roy Williams convinced me the only probation that was going to affect me was the word 'probation.' There weren't postseason sanctions [after

Notes on Patrick Richey

Years lettered:	1990-91 to 1993-94
Position:	Guard/forward
Height:	6-foot-8
Playing weight:	200 pounds
Hometown:	Lee's Summit, Missouri
Current Residence:	Olathe, Kansas
Occupation:	Communications products salesman
Accomplishments:	Career 40-percent three-point shooter; Big Eight All-Bench Team in 1993; Big Eight All-Freshman and All-Newcomer Team in 1991.
The Game:	Indiana vs. Kansas in Lawrence, Kansas, December 22, 1993

1989] or anything. He did a great job selling KU. Coming off probation is always a hard time for recruiting. I'm sure Coach Williams feels a sense of loyalty to Steve [Woodberry], Richard [Scott], Adonis [Jordan], and me for that reason, because we stuck with him and the University of Kansas when times were tough."

Richey also appreciated that KU and Williams stuck with fellow recruit Chris Lindley, who had a foot amputated after a serious accident involving a train in early 1990. The university and coach awarded an institutional scholarship to the 6-foot-9 Lindley from Raytown (Missouri) South High School after the accident ended his basketball dreams.

After committing to Kansas the last day of the early signing period, Richey enjoyed an all-state senior season, averaging 18 points, seven rebounds, and five assists per game. He played all five positions for his team that season.

"KU didn't need me as much as I needed them, that's for doggone sure," Richey says. "But I feel like I have a place in the history of the program."

It was a history that began with a somewhat unlikely trip to the Final Four in 1991.

College Life

As he entered college in the late summer of 1990, Richey brought his determination and a set of realistic expectations with him. He knew he would not start, but he also knew he would play.

"When you come to KU under Coach Williams, you know 10 guys are going to play," Richey says. "We played defense at a high level. We denied every pass. We were in passing lanes all game long. We made it difficult for a team once they got across half court.

"As a player, you cannot play 40 minutes like that. So I knew right away I was going to get 10-15 minutes a game. Then you've got games where you shoot the ball well and get a few extra minutes here and there. So pretty soon I was getting 20-25 minutes per game. There was a lot of playing time to be had. You had to earn it all in practice. You had to be there daily. You had to play defense if you were going to see the court."

Richey played in 32 of the Jayhawks' 35 games as a freshman, averaging 4.2 points and 1.9 rebounds per game. One of Richey's fondest memories from the regular season occurred in a road game against Missouri.

"We were just stinking up the joint," he says. "Coach Williams got so upset that he put Richard, Steve, and me in the game about five minutes before halftime. Coach was notorious for yanking all five guys and putting five new guys in when they weren't performing.

"We were too naïve to understand the circumstances. We turned the game around. Going into halftime we had some momentum. We ended up winning that game [by four points]. We were down 12-14 points but turned it around."

After that game, Kansas went 3-2 the rest of the regular season and was defeated by Nebraska in the Big Eight tournament. Despite a 22-7 record, Jayhawk fans were concerned their favorite team lacked momentum going into the NCAA tournament. Richey credits the senior leadership of Mark Randall and Mike Maddox for helping the Jayhawks to right their course.

"When we lost the Big Eight tournament, we came together as a team and said, 'Let's put this behind us and focus on what we need to do as a team,'" Richey says. "The seniors did a great job of bringing us together, and we had a great run.

"You think of the teams we beat during that run: Pittsburgh was solid back then, Indiana and Arkansas. Indiana was one of those games where everything goes right for you. It doesn't happen that often, but we had a couple of them in the tournament. Arkansas clearly had better players, but we had the better *team*. That's the key word."

In the national semifinals against North Carolina, Richey was the first substitute off the bench to get into the game. In all, six Jayhawk subs played in the game for a total of 54 minutes—including some big minutes at the end of the first half—and scored 25 points, the bulk of which came from Scott's 14 points. The Jayhawks won 79-73.

"We had some experience early in the year, so that when we got to the Final Four, we weren't overwhelmed," Richey says. "We felt like we belonged there.

"You can look up at the bright lights and be in awe, or you can tune everything out and get lost in the game. That's when you're successful. You forget everything that goes on during the game, but at the end, late that day, all these images of the game pop up, and then you remember all the things that happened. That's when I played my best games, when I got lost in the game."

Kansas lost the championship to Duke 72-65 but had re-established itself as a team to be reckoned with in NCAA tournament play.

"Starting that season I wanted to come here and help the team be successful and play for a championship at some point," Richey summarizes. "Little did I know that I'd be playing in the championship game my freshman year."

A degenerative injury to his back during his sophomore season limited Richey to just 24 games. His statistics dipped slightly to 3.9 points and 1.8 rebounds per contest.

"Anyone who's ever had back pain knows that controls every movement you make," Richey explains. "With my back problems, I wasn't as quick, and I couldn't jump as high. I was able to do some physical therapy and get back to about 85 or 90 percent. It set me back. That's something I had to deal with the next three years at KU."

Richey's situation and the Jayhawks' season illustrate the vagaries of sport. His injury limited his playing time, yet the team responded with a better season than the year before, going 27-5 overall and winning the Big

Eight regular-season and tournament titles. But then the stronger of the two Kansas teams did not fare as well in postseason play.

"It's kind of ironic," Richey says. "My freshman year we were not even ranked in the Top 20 to start the season and we ended the year playing in the championship. Sophomore year, we're No. 1 going into the NCAA tournament, and we lose the second game to UTEP."

More determined than ever, Richey and the Jayhawks rebounded in 1992-93, certain they would not be denied in March. The Jayhawks won the Big Eight regular-season title with an 11-3 mark and went 29-7 for the season. Richey played in 34 games and improved his averages to 6.7 points and 3.4 rebounds.

"We felt we were as good as anyone," Richey says. "It was Rex's [Walters] final year. He brought a lot to the team. It was a great ride."

Walters shared his admiration for his teammate.

"Richey was just a great team guy," Walters said. "He made a lot of sacrifices for our team with his back and playing positions that he wasn't accustomed to playing, such as the power forward. He did it willingly and never thought twice about it."

Kansas advanced to the Final Four and again faced North Carolina. This time the Tar Heels enacted revenge on the Jayhawks by defeating KU 78-68 in New Orleans.

"Adonis and Rex played really good in that game," Richey says of the duo's 19-point performances. "But Donald Williams [game-high 25 points] played tremendous. Unfortunately for us, had he not been on fire we would have won that game. He was the difference-maker."

The Setting

The 1993-94 season represented the time for Richey, Woodberry, and Scott to exert their senior leadership. Gone were the days when the team could look to the guidance of the ever-steady Jordan and the ultracompetitive Walters. The team would break in a freshman point guard named Jacque Vaughn this season and rely more heavily on junior Greg Ostertag inside.

The transition to the "new" Jayhawks worked well from the outset. Kansas won its first four games that season, including the preseason NIT in New York against Minnesota and Massachusetts. A tough Temple team surprised the Jayhawks at home 73-59, but KU recovered to win its next six games, including road contests against DePaul and North Carolina State and a neutral-site game versus Georgia in Atlanta.

Finals had ended by December 22, but Kansas' student section was not missing a soul that Wednesday night as coach Bob Knight brought his vaunted Indiana Hoosiers to Lawrence for the first time in almost 20 years. Coach Williams said ticket manager Bernie Kish told him that he could have sold "40,000 to 50,000 tickets" for the game.

The Jayhawks stood 10-1 and were ranked sixth nationally. Indiana's record was 5-1, good for a 12th-place ranking. In recent history, Kansas had won three straight games against Indiana, including a Sweet 16 triumph in 1991 and an Elite Eight victory that sent KU back to the Final Four in 1993.

The contest marked the 501st game at Allen Fieldhouse. KU had won 408 games there since it opened in March 1955. It's a good thing the venerable fieldhouse was built sturdily. Any other material but native limestone may not have been able to withstand the cumulative decibel level of the previous 39 seasons, or the one-night, two-and-a-half hour blast that was about to occur that crisp early winter evening.

The Game of My Life

BY PATRICK RICHEY
INDIANA VS. KANSAS, DECEMBER 22, 1993

Playing home games is indescribable. It was everything I thought it would be while I was being recruited, if not better. It's hard to explain to someone what you feel when you run out of that tunnel at the fieldhouse and you have 16,000 people yelling your name.

The anticipation of that game was like no other. There was an electricity, a little extra enthusiasm that I can't remember at Allen Fieldhouse. Perhaps it was the "Bobby Knight Factor." We were both highly ranked. Their seniors had never beaten us. We had knocked them out of the tournament two times. They're coming into Allen Fieldhouse mad. We recognized that we were going to have to bring our best to beat these guys.

When you play Indiana, you have to have your head on a swivel, because they are screening you all game long. If you're not paying attention, they are going to come up and screen you in the back and give you whiplash. You have to be arms out, knees bent, ready to go, or else they are going to knock you around. And that goes on all game long. It feels like you played a football game, you're so sore.

I was guarding Brian Evans. I played a little power forward in that game as well, so I also guarded Alan Henderson. And at some points, I was guarding Damon Bailey as well. It was Indiana, so you could be guarding anybody. They screen so much and switch.

I had a pretty good first half. I scored some points [10] and had three baskets in a row early on. But I also picked up my third foul just before halftime. I had to be a little smarter after that. In the first half I could drive in and shoot lay-ups [even if] my body was out of control; or potentially [I could have taken] some charges. I wasn't as aggressive in the second half as I was in the first half for that reason. They were getting back on defense better, so I didn't have the opportunity for fast breaks. They played a better second half.

[KU led by nine points early in the second half and was up 50-43 with 11:57 to go in the game when Indiana mounted its comeback. The Hoosiers tied the game at 65 and then took a 68-65 lead on two three-point shots by senior Pat Graham with 3:08 to play. The two teams then traded free throws and a basket for a 70-all score at the end of regulation.]

A lot of teams might have panicked if they had an eight-to-10-point lead and a team comes back at home in front of a big crowd. Some teams might have folded. But we had the maturity to overcome. We were an experienced enough senior class. We'd been to two Final Fours, we'd played at difficult places, we'd played at Kentucky, we'd been in difficult situations, so we weren't going to panic.

We knew what we had to do. It was what we'd always done: execute, turn up the defensive pressure, just what Coach Williams had always asked us to do. It had always been successful.

When I fouled out in the first minute of overtime, I felt helpless. However, I was a senior and I needed to be a vocal leader for my team. Once you're out of the game, it doesn't mean your responsibilities are over. You have to cheer your teammates on. When they come over for timeouts, give them support. If their legs are getting tired, tell them, "Hey, you can rest over the holiday break."

BOX SCORE
INDIANA VS. KANSAS, DECEMBER 22, 1993

Indiana	30	40	13	– 83
Kansas	33	37	16	– 86

Indiana (83)

	Min	FG	FT	Reb	PF	TP
Evans	25	0-6	1-2	2	2	1
Henderson	32	6-13	4-6	11	5	16
Lindeman	27	2-5	0-2	7	5	4
Wilkerson	8	0-0	0-0	1	1	0
Bailey	43	9-20	15-17	5	4	36
Graham	34	6-8	7-8	1	3	22
Knight	5	0-0	0-0	1	0	0
Leary	24	0-1	0-2	1	2	0
Hart	14	1-4	0-0	3	1	2
Mandeville	13	1-2	0-0	4	2	2
(team)				3		
TOTALS	**225**	**25-59**	**27-37**	**39**	**25**	**83**

Three-point goals: 6-15 (Bailey 3-9, Graham 3-4, Evans 0-1, Leary 0-1); Assists: 12 (Leary 7, Bailey 4, Graham); Turnovers: 14 (Evans 4, Graham 4, Bailey 3, Henderson, Lindeman, Wilkerson); Blocked shots: 7 (Henderson 2, Lindeman 2, Evans, Graham, Hart); Steals: 5 (Henderson 3, Evans, Bailey).

Kansas (86)

	Min	FG	FT	Reb	PF	TP
Richey	31	5-10	2-3	6	5	12
Scott	34	8-13	7-10	10	1	23
Ostertag	14	1-6	4-6	9	4	6
Vaughn	33	3-8	5-5	1	3	13
Woodberry	29	4-11	3-4	1	4	13
Pollard	30	3-4	4-6	5	2	10
Williams	8	0-3	0-0	1	1	0
Gurley	15	0-4	0-0	4	1	0
Rayford	12	1-1	0-0	2	1	2
Pearson	19	3-7	0-1	1	3	7
(team)				2		
TOTALS	**225**	**28-67**	**25-35**	**42**	**25**	**86**

Three-point goals: 5-15 (Vaughn 2-4, Woodberry 2-4, Pearson 1-2, Richey 0-2, Gurley 0-2, Ostertag 0-1); Assists: 14 (Vaughn 5, Pearson 3, Woodberry 2, Rayford 2, Richey, Pollard); Turnovers: 16 (Scott 4, Ostertag 3, Woodberry 3, Richey 2, Vaughn, Pollard, Gurley, Rayford); Blocked shots 5 (Pollard 3, Richey, Williams); Steals: 5 (Vaughn 2, Richey, Woodberry, Pollard).

Officials: Ed Hightower, Verl Sell Tom Clark. Attendance: 15,800.

Game and Season Results

When Richey fouled out, Bailey hit both free throws to open the scoring in overtime. From that point until Sean Pearson's three-pointer with 1:21 to go to put KU ahead 81-80, the two teams alternated scoring in overtime. Woodberry's jumper broke that pattern and made it 83-80 Kansas with 30 seconds to go. But Bailey hit a trey, the last of his 36 points, with 18 seconds left to tie the game.

When Kansas got the ball back for the final shot, Vaughn was not the team's first option. Woodberry was who they wanted to take the shot, but he was too well covered. Todd Leary had Vaughn defended pretty well, but the freshman pump-faked and shot from beyond the arc as time wound down.

"Over the years it's become slow motion for me," Richey says. "I can see Jacque hitting that shot. I can see the fans, as soon as the ball goes through that basket, throwing their arms up and going crazy. I'll be envisioning that in my head forever.

"I have a bunch of game tapes and occasionally take them out. Every time I bring that Indiana game out it gives me chills. It was probably the most rewarding game in terms of giving everything I've got and being spent when it was over. Not having anything left.

"We ran around on the court a little bit. We all hugged Jacque and jumped up and down. By the time we got to the locker room, we were too exhausted to celebrate anymore. There were big smiles on everyone's faces, including the coaches. We had a sense of relief that we were able to hold them off."

Following the 86-83 victory, the Jayhawks won their remaining four non-conference games and started 6-2 in league play (including another overtime buzzer-beater versus Oklahoma State) before losing three straight Big Eight games, the team's longest losing streak in five seasons. The Jayhawks finished third in the Big Eight with a 9-5 record.

In the NCAA tournament, KU impressively defeated the University of Tennessee-Chattanooga and Wake Forest before running into a human buzz saw named Glenn Robinson. Purdue's "Big Dog" scored 44 points in leading the Boilermakers to an 83-78 victory.

"That's the thing about why it's so hard to win it all: You have to put together six perfect games in a row," says Richey, who averaged a career-best 6.8 points and 4.4 rebounds that season. "You never know when a guy on the other team is going to come out and score 40 points on you. He has one of those games that no matter what you do, everything he shoots goes in.

"You've got to be good, but you've got to have some luck and catch some breaks."

What Became of Patrick Richey?

The Purdue loss ended Richey's competitive basketball career.

"I had a couple of offers overseas, Spain and the Netherlands," he says. "But my back was so bad, I knew I couldn't keep it up. I had spinal fusion surgery after college. That ended my playing career."

Richey hasn't played basketball for nine years.

"I can shoot around, and I work out quite a bit. But I can't run," he says. "Since the surgery, I have better days, and I have worse days. It's limited me in that I can't get up and down the court anymore."

Richey is living proof that it's good for college players to have their education to fall back on. He's also living proof to keep your options open and even have a "Plan C" if necessary. In Richey's case, he planned to use his degree in broadcast journalism, broadcast sales, and promotions to get into radio broadcasting. But during a sales class, he realized he could make more money faster in sales than in on-air broadcasting. So, for his first four years he worked in liquor sales in Lawrence. Then a friend hooked him up with another sales job in the electrical industry, which he did for six years before moving over to another electrical firm, Panduit, in 2005.

Richey and his wife, Mary Ann, live in Olathe, Kansas, with their young daughter, Lauren. When he can, Richey enjoys working out, watching sports on TV, and attending games, particularly ones in Lawrence. It's a place he can return to and recall the many victories and good times he enjoyed from 1990 to 1994.

"The experiences I had during those four years are still with me today and will be with me forever," Richey says.

9

STEVE WOODBERRY

The Life of Young Steve Woodberry

Steve Woodberry grew up with basketball. He had no other choice, really.

Woodberry was the youngest of nine children. His five brothers and three sisters almost always had a game going, often at a playground that was a two-minute walk from their Wichita home.

"We were all playing basketball," Woodberry says. "We never got into trouble."

As a youngster, the only trouble Woodberry experienced was getting into their games.

"When you're young, the older guys don't want to let the little guys on the court," Woodberry recalls.

So, Woodberry took his game to "Biddy Basketball" at age eight. He played for a traveling team that played in Pennsylvania, Texas, and Louisiana. As his skills improved, Woodberry earned more playing time with his family. These experiences paid off well for him.

"When you get older and better, they pick you up all of a sudden and then you start beating them," he says. "My brothers didn't take it easy—that was part of it. I always looked to them. When you play against older guys it helps you become more competitive, helps you get your toughness with all the bumps and bruises."

The "older players as mentors" role continued for Woodberry when he arrived at Wichita South High School to play for coach Steve Eck. Most of the team's players went on to play junior college or major college basketball. The talent helped the Titans win state championships Woodberry's sophomore and junior years. As a senior, Woodberry's team lost in the championship game to Shawnee Mission South on a last-second shot by his future Jayhawk teammate Greg Gurley.

As one of the better players on a top high school team, Woodberry barely did what most players in his situation would do: play AAU summer basketball. He only played the summer going into his senior year, and he didn't particularly like the experience.

"It wasn't as huge as it is now," Woodberry says. "I was more into winning state championships for my school than trying to get notoriety for myself. I feel that if you win and your team is good, someone will notice."

When it was pointed out that his outlook then would differ compared with 99 out of 100 of today's high school stars, Woodberry says firmly, "We're getting away from the team game. If you look at who wins NBA championships or college championships, the team that plays like a team always wins. The San Antonio Spurs and Detroit Pistons are great examples of that. So was North Carolina."

As a result of little AAU exposure, Woodberry wasn't highly recruited.

"I didn't go to all the Nike camps," he says. "I went to local camps with all the high school teams. Like I said, I wanted to win state championships."

Wichita State was Woodberry's first choice for college. But coach Eddie Fogler left the Shockers for Vanderbilt, so Kansas became his top school. Coach Roy Williams started recruiting Woodberry during his junior year, he recalls.

"Coach Williams came to watch Val Barnes play and practice one day— he was a senior, I was a junior—and that day in practice I don't think I missed a shot. He started recruiting me then," Woodberry says.

He also considered Kansas State, but coach Lon Kruger's team was too deep at guard to suit Woodberry's taste. So he took an unofficial visit to Lawrence and later an official one. Woodberry came away impressed with what Williams told him.

"When I met with Coach Williams, I never spoke much at all, I just listened. I like to sit back and observe," Woodberry says. "To me, he was straightforward and honest. I asked about playing time. [He said] 'That depends, you work your butt off, you've got a chance to play a lot. If you don't, you're not going to play.'

Notes on Steve Woodberry

Years lettered:	1990-91 to 1993-94
Position:	Guard
Height:	6-foot-4
Playing weight:	190 pounds
Hometown:	Wichita, Kansas
Current residence:	Springfield, Missouri
Occupation:	Assistant basketball coach, Missouri State University
Accomplishments:	Winner of the team's "Dr. Forrest C. 'Phog' Allen MVP Award" and the "Ted Owens Defensive Player Award" in 1994; first team All-Big Eight (players) and second-team All-Big Eight (AP and coaches) in '94; Big Eight All-Defensive Team in '94.
Nickname:	"Woody"
The Game:	Oklahoma State vs. Kansas in Lawrence, Kansas January 26, 1994

"Everything he said to me was the truth. I respected him for that. He did everything the right way. Richard Scott committed without even coming to visit. We had a real good recruiting class with Patrick Richey, too."

College Life

Adjusting to Lawrence and college life came easy for Woodberry. At times he found it to be almost too quiet.

"I roomed with Patrick Richey the first year," Woodberry says. "He probably said about 10 words the first couple of months. I didn't know the guys, but they talked to you and made you feel at home. I was observing everyone."

He also observed "Late Night," the first practice of the season held at midnight in mid-October before a capacity crowd at Allen Fieldhouse. Woodberry tore the meniscus in a knee and sat out for the first month, thus missing the "Late Night" scrimmage.

"That was my first injury, so I took it easy," he says. "It's tough coming off a knee injury—you're a lot slower and the game is a lot faster than high school. I was learning to play point guard, which is the toughest position on the court. It was an eye-opener, the speed of the game. I'm not a fast person anyway.

"I practiced against Adonis [Jordan], which was good for me because he was a lot quicker, and I learned the position behind him. And Sean Tunstall was really tough defensively."

The 1990-91 Jayhawks relied on seniors Terry Brown, Mike Maddox, and Mark Randall to lead them to a 22-7 record entering NCAA tournament play. Kansas defeated New Orleans, Pittsburgh, Indiana, and Arkansas to reach the Final Four. In a national semi-final game, the Jayhawks outfought North Carolina for a tough 79-73 win before 47,100 fans at the Hoosier Dome in Indianapolis. The victory set up a championship game against Duke.

"It was great," Woodberry says of the experience. "You seem like a rock star. We had police escorts down the middle of the street. You'll never experience anything like the Final Four. You can watch all the championship games you want to, but you have to be there to experience it."

Duke defeated Kansas 72-65 for the championship. Woodberry played 18 minutes off the bench, scored two points, and grabbed four rebounds. For the season he averaged three points.

Woodberry's sophomore season saw the Jayhawks win the Big Eight regular season and tournament titles. The team soared to No. 2 in the AP poll but was upset by the University of Texas-El Paso in the second round of the NCAA tournament. KU finished with a 27-5 record. Woodberry's playing time increased off the bench, and his scoring average improved to 7.2 points.

The Jayhawks won their first 17 games in the 1992-93 season and returned to the Final Four, losing to North Carolina in the semifinals. KU won 30 games and lost only six. Woodberry continued his steady play and averaged 10.1 points and 4.2 rebounds.

"You appreciate your second Final Four a lot more," Woodberry says. "I think my sophomore team was our best team, but it doesn't matter, because we picked the wrong year to have a terrible game."

Heading into his senior year, Woodberry had started only six of the 103 games the Jayhawks had played. But he had played almost 30 minutes per game as a sophomore and junior.

"Sometimes it's not who starts but who finishes," Woodberry says. "I was in there when it counted. When you play for a team, you need to sacrifice something.

"When I came off the bench, I had a better feel for the game. You get the scouting report and read about a guy's tendencies. But on the bench you see it right in front of you. You can watch and focus, and that prepares you a little more."

With a positive attitude and an unselfish, team-first approach, Steve Woodberry and the Jayhawks were poised for another successful season in 1993-94.

The Setting

The thing you have to understand about KU basketball fans is the white-hot intensity of their passion for the Jayhawks. In KU fans' eyes, *all* games are big games. Some games are bigger than others, of course, but all games are big.

The Oklahoma State game in 1994 was a really, really big game. Oklahoma State was 13-5 and featured a dominant center, 7-foot, 290-pound junior Bryant Reeves, the Big Eight's player of the year in 1992-93; the conference's top three-point shooter, senior guard Brooks Thompson; and the league's best three-point marksman the season before, junior guard Randy Rutherford.

Kansas entered the game with a 17-2 record and was ranked third nationally. The Jayhawks' two losses had uncharacteristically occurred at home, the first to Temple in the season's fifth game and the second nine days earlier to Kansas State, which cost KU its No. 1 ranking in the media polls. Plus, the Jayhawks were hurting. Richard Scott was recovering from a concussion suffered in the Kansas State loss and then his left shoulder was pulled out of place during practice two days before the game. He would start for Kansas but not be close to 100 percent.

So a matchup of this stature with an intriguing sub-plot meant students would be camping out for tickets a few days ahead of tip-off, instead of the day of a game, a tactic used only for run-of-the-mill "big" games. Students camped out from 6 a.m. to 10 p.m. in the north end of the fieldhouse. The students, who took shifts in line, would sign a sheet of paper that listed their place in the queue. If a student missed roll call the next morning, his or her group lost their place in line.

Some students found the area's relative quiet to be quite conducive for studying. But most listened to music, played cards, or just napped until it was time to get their tickets a couple of hours before the game.

"You know you're in a special place when fans camp out in cold weather just to get a seat to watch you play," Woodberry says. "The fans are out there waiting for a chance to watch you play for two hours, and they've been there about a week."

Oklahoma State coach Eddie Sutton said Allen Fieldhouse was the toughest place to play in the conference, thanks in part to KU's passionate fans.

"I don't think there's a place where fans understand better what a home crowd can do to help their team," he said.

The fans understood perfectly. What they didn't know as the game started, however, was just how happy the campers would be afterward.

The Game of My Life

BY STEVE WOODBERRY
OKLAHOMA STATE VS. KANSAS, JANUARY 26, 1994

To me, Oklahoma State was always one of our toughest teams to play. They were well coached by Eddie Sutton, and defensively they're tough. They were talented every year. It was never a blowout. It was a battle the whole game. So we had to be prepared to play the whole 40 minutes.

Oklahoma State led 24-22 at halftime, which shows you how defense dominated the game. I had six points at halftime from two three-point shots. I was focused on guarding Randy Rutherford and Brooks Thompson, and they were tough to go against, too.

We led most of the second half, but Oklahoma State outscored us 10-3 in the final 3:06 to take the game in overtime tied at 54. I missed a shot with two seconds left in regulation that would have won the game. But it didn't bother me.

I've always been a player who wants to take the last shot of the game. In my mind, if you miss it, so what? Some people can't take the last shot, because they don't handle pressure well. I've always handled pressure well. You have to have a tough mental capacity. After I missed it, I didn't think anything of it. We were going into overtime. We had another five minutes to win the game.

What gave us a lift in the second half was Sean Pearson hitting four-for-four threes. That really helped us. In the past we'd had people like Adonis [Jordan], Rex [Walters], and other guys who could shoot the ball, too. We struggled my senior year because I was the only consistent shooter. With Sean, he could shoot but sometimes he put up shots he shouldn't have. But when he was making shots that really opened up things for me—they had to find him and me.

In overtime, Thompson made a three, and then Sean hit his fifth three-pointer to tie the game. Jacque Vaughn hit a jumper with 2:18 left to give us a two-point lead. Rutherford shot a three with 1:24 remaining to put OSU ahead 60-59.

With 18 seconds to go we fouled Fred Burley. He made the first free throw but missed the second. Greg Ostertag missed the box out and should have had the rebound. But he got the ball away from an OSU player and threw it to Jacque. I was on the right wing, and Jacque kicked it up to me. It was one of those moments where I was locked in. I checked the clock, dribbled between my legs, kind of fell back, and shot. It felt good when it left my hand.

Game and Season Results

Woodberry's shot over Randy Rutherford gracefully arced through the rim with eight seconds left. Oklahoma State tried a desperation shot that failed, and KU had won its 18th game of the season and Roy Williams won his 150th game at Kansas. Woodberry led the Jayhawks with 17 points, and Pearson scored 15.

Ostertag grabbed 11 rebounds and blocked eight shots, which tied a team record for most blocks in a game. The 7-foot-2 center outdueled Reeves, who made only six of 18 shots. Ostertag made a near-game-costing turnover with 23 seconds when he inadvertently threw a pass to an Oklahoma State player after rebounding a missed free throw. Fortunately for the Jayhawks, his last rebound set up Woodberry's game-winning shot.

"I started to cry, but it was a happy cry," Ostertag said of Woodberry's final shot. "He's a great shooter, and I'll take him on my team for a last-second shot any day."

Williams said he "sort of had a feeling" Woodberry would make the shot.

"I have a lot of confidence in this team, and it starts with Woodberry," he said. "It was appropriate that he got that shot because he has played his tail off for four years. He has always acted as a student-athlete and represented this university well."

The Jayhawks won three of their next four games after the Oklahoma State game and improved its national ranking to second by mid-February. But the cumulative effect of injuries to Scott, Richey, Gurley, and Nick Proud began to slow the team's momentum.

On February 16, Oklahoma State exacted revenge on Kansas by defeating the Jayhawks 63-59 in an overtime game in Stillwater. KU lost two more games before winning its final three regular-season league contests to finish 9-5 in the Big Eight, which Missouri won with a perfect 14-0 record.

Kansas rolled over Kansas State in the first round of the Big Eight tournament, setting up a third game of the season with the Cowboys. Again the two teams were evenly matched, and Oklahoma State won the "rubber game" 69-68 behind Bryant Reeves' 27 points. Woodberry scored a team-high 20 points for Kansas. Six points separated the two teams in the three games played between them in 1994.

The Jayhawks won their first two games in the NCAA tournament, a 102-73 blowout over UT-Chattanooga and then a 69-58 decision against Wake Forest, which featured Tim Duncan. Woodberry had team highs with 18 points and seven assists, earning CBS "Player of the Game" honors. Purdue ended the Jayhawks season on March 24 with an 83-78 victory. National player of the year Glenn "Big Dog" Robinson scored 44 points for the Boilermakers.

What Became of Steve Woodberry?

After a year of "retirement" from playing basketball overseas, Steve Woodberry added the title of coach to his resume. First, Woodberry served as head coach of the Kansas City "Pump N Run" AAU team. He guided the team to three titles in 16-17 age group tournaments in the summer of 2005. In May 2006, Missouri State University hired Woodberry as an assistant men's basketball coach. He joined head coach Barry Hinson's staff, which includes former KU assistant coach Ben Miller. Hinson targeted Woodberry for his overseas connections and involvement in AAU coaching.

OKLAHOMA STATE VS. KANSAS, JANUARY 26, 1994

Oklahoma State	24 30 7	–	61
Kansas	22 32 8	–	62

Oklahoma State (61)

	Min	FG	FT	Reb	PF	TP
Burley	25	1-5	1-2	5	2	3
Collins	17	0-3	0-0	4	1	0
Reeves	40	6-18	1-4	9	2	13
Rutherford	36	5-12	0-0	11	2	15
Thompson	40	7-15	3-5	2	0	23
Sutton	15	0-2	0-0	0	1	0
Pierce	21	0-2	1-2	5	4	1
Roberts	17	2-6	0-0	3	2	4
Manzer	9	0-1	2-2	1	0	2
Phillip	5	0-0	0-0	0	1	0
(team)				5		
TOTALS	**225**	**21-64**	**8-15**	**45**	**15**	**61**

Three-point goals: 11-23 (Thompson 6-9, Rutherford 5-8, Roberts 0-2, Sutton 0-2, Burley 0-2); Assists: 16 (Thompson 4, Collins 3, Rutherford 3, Roberts 2, Burley, Reeves, Sutton, Pierce); Turnovers: 13 (Burley 3, Collins 2, Rutherford 2, Thompson 2, Reeves, Pierce, Roberts, team); Blocked shots: 5 (Reeves 4, Pierce); Steals: 9 (Thompson 3, Collins 2, Reeves 2, Roberts 2).

Kansas (62)

	Min	FG	FT	Reb	PF	TP
Richey	35	1-4	4-4	7	3	6
Scott	21	0-4	1-4	3	0	1
Ostertag	31	2-5	5-6	11	1	9
Vaughn	31	2-9	0-0	2	1	4
Woodberry	38	6-12	0-1	2	0	17
Pollard	14	3-7	0-0	3	3	6
Williams	13	2-3	0-0	0	0	4
Gurley	8	0-1	0-0	1	0	0
Pearson	20	5-6	0-0	2	1	15
Rayford	14	0-1	0-0	1	3	0
(team)				3		
TOTALS	**225**	**21-52**	**10-15**	**35**	**12**	**62**

Three-point goals: 10-16 (Woodberry 5-7, Pearson 5-5, Vaughn 0-2, Richey 0-2); Assists: 17 (Vaughn 6, Woodberry 4, Rayford 3, Richey 2, Scott, Gurley); Turnovers: 16 (Vaughn 4, Pearson 4, Scott 3, Woodberry 2, Ostertag, Gurley, Rayford); Blocked shots: 12 (Ostertag 8, Woodberry 2, Pollard, Williams); Steals: 5 (Ostertag 2, Scott, Woodberry, Gurley).

Officials: Stanley Reynolds, David Hall, Scott Thornley. Attendance: 15,500.

Woodberry established himself as a stellar player on two continents—Australia and Europe—after leaving KU in 1994 with an economics degree. He averaged 24.5 points, 7.6 rebounds, and 7.4 assists in 16 games for the Gold Coast Rollers in his first season in the National Basketball League of Australia in 1995. But a severe knee injury ended his rookie season, and he returned to Kansas to rehabilitate.

"I took one year off because I had knee surgery—actually, four knee surgeries in eight months," Woodberry says. "I kept coming back too early."

Woodberry returned to the NBL in 1996 with the Brisbane Bullets. He was selected to the all-NBL second team in that season and the all-NBL third team in 1997. His best season was 1999, when he earned the league's MVP award, also with the Bullets. In all, Woodberry played six seasons in Australia and met his wife there. The couple has one son, Shaylan, who is five years old.

"Australia was nice. It is a lot like America—a lot of land but with a lot less people," he says.

Woodberry's professional career then took him to Europe after six years in Australia. He played three years in Lithuania and also played for teams in Greece, Finland, and Sweden before retiring in 2005. Lithuania has emerged as a national power in men's basketball since the break up of the Soviet Union in 1991. The U.S. team split with the Lithuanian national team in the 2004 Summer Olympics in Athens, losing in the preliminary round before prevailing in the Bronze Medal game.

"They do a great job of moving the ball," Woodberry says of Lithuanian players. "It's easy for them because they have a lot of shooters, four or five per team. But they can't guard anybody.

"The people love basketball there. When you played a top team and the game was a sellout, you couldn't hear the officials blow their whistles because of all of the air horns going off."

Woodberry played in 80 to 90 games his first season in Lithuania. Road trips took his team all over Europe, from Russia to Italy.

"I liked Italy. And playing in Northern Europe, I visited Amsterdam and Denmark," Woodberry recalls. "Those were good places to get out and see what they had when I went shopping."

Until taking the Missouri State job, Woodberry had made his off-season home in Lawrence. The city, like Woodberry, is laid back.

"It seems like a family atmosphere around here," he says. "A lot of former players settle here. Plus, I liked watching practice and practicing with the Jayhawks when I could, just to see how Coach Williams ran a program and the team."

Before he makes a new set of memories in the college coaching ranks, Woodberry says he would always remember his two Final Four appearances as a Jayhawk and hanging out with people from different schools and various cultures.

"I tell people it was the best four years of my life," he says. "It was a great experience. You get to go to all the big places, eat at nice restaurants, meet some 'important people' that you see on TV. Other people didn't have those opportunities. Basketball has created a lot of opportunities for me on and off the court."

10

JEROD HAASE

The Life of Young Jerod Haase

If South Lake Tahoe, California, sounds idyllic, it's only because it is.

The sun shines on the city's 20,000-plus residents 300 days a year. Situated at 6,220 feet above sea level just across the Nevada state line, the city features Lake Tahoe and its famous clear blue water; the El Dorado National Forest to the north and west, which offers extensive hiking trails and several skiing resorts in the Sierra Nevada mountains; and Yosemite National Park is located an hour-plus drive south.

The climate also produces snow—lots of snow. When Jerod Haase was growing up in South Lake Tahoe, the two to three feet of snow he shoveled off of his backyard basketball court sometimes took the edge off paradise but not for long. Once Haase started shooting hoops, he was transported back into his element, even when he missed and the ball bounced into a drift.

"If it snowed five or six feet, I'd shovel below the basket to the free-throw line," Haase says. "Once in a while it would freeze over or be covered from sleet, so I'd take an axe to the free-throw line to chip away to the pavement. To this day, there are still axe marks out on the court."

Haase is the youngest of five children of Carol and Gary Haase. Sisters Mara and Karin are the oldest, followed by David, Steven, and Jerod. Basketball entered Haase's life when he was a second grader tagging along to Steven's fifth-grade team's practice.

"Seeing my brother play basketball was big for me because he was one of my role models," Haase says. "By third grade I was playing up a level at my elementary school. It was easy for me to pick up, and I had success right away with it. It fit my personality because it is non-stop and up-and-down."

In high school, Haase played for a school located in California that played in a Nevada league. The area's terrain made it so: Nevada high schools were easy 30- to 60-minute drives from South Lake Tahoe; similar-sized California schools were two hours to three hours away, some of which were inaccessible because of snow-covered passes in the winter.

Coach Tom Orlich had developed South Tahoe into a dynasty in Nevada. Haase played during a span when the Vikings were winning 10 league titles in 12 seasons. South Tahoe won the Nevada state championship in 1987 and Haase's senior season in 1992, the only two championships won by a northern Nevada school in 30 years.

"Besides Coach Williams, I learned the most from Coach Orlich," Haase says. "He's as good a coach that there is. He taught us a ton through his work ethic and passion for the game."

College recruiters began contacting Haase after his junior year, a process the family was familiar with. Both of Haase's sisters attended college on cross-country skiing scholarships. Both of his brothers earned appointments to the U.S. Air Force Academy in Colorado Springs, Colorado, and both currently serve in the Air Force. Steven, an F-16 pilot who has seen duty in the Iraq War, played basketball for the Falcons. David completed a tour of Afghanistan in 2006.

Haase's college choices came down to California, Santa Clara, Santa Barbara, and Loyola Marymount. He chose Cal, his parents' school, because it was close to home. Two events—one life altering, one career altering—occurred during Haase's freshman year at Berkeley that would change his world. His father died two days before the Golden Bears played UCLA in Los Angeles. Haase played in honor of his father's memory and scored 16 points as Cal won 104-82, the Bruins' worst loss ever at Pauley Pavilion.

A couple of week's later, Cal fired coach Lou Campanelli during the season and replaced him with assistant Todd Bozeman. The Bears reached the NCAA tournament and dethroned two-time defending national champion Duke in the second round. Ninth-ranked Kansas then defeated Cal in the Sweet 16 round in St. Louis.

Notes on Jerod Haase

Years lettered:	1994-95 to 1996-97
Position:	Guard
Height:	6-foot-3
Playing weight:	190 pounds
Hometown:	South Lake Tahoe, California
Current residence:	Durham, North Carolina
Occupation:	Director of basketball operations for the University of North Carolina
Accomplishments:	First team Academic All-America and Big 12 All-Academic team in 1997; awarded "James Naismith Captain's Award" with fellow seniors Jacque Vaughn, Scot Pollard, and B.J. Williams in '97; All-Big 12 Conference third team (AP) and All-Big 12 Conference honorable mention (coaches) in '97; Naismith Award and Wooden Award candidate in '96; All-Big Eight honorable mention (players) and Big Eight All-Defense team in 1996; member of the 1995 gold medal-winning U.S. World University Games basketball team in Japan; Big Eight Newcomer of the Year in '95; All-Big Eight second team (AP, coaches, players) in '95.
The Game:	Kansas vs. UCLA in Los Angeles, California, December 7, 1996

After the coaching change, Haase says he did not fit in as well as he would have liked.

"I felt more comfortable moving on," he says. "I did not see my role there being what I wanted it to be."

Haase did not consider many colleges when transferring.

"I wanted to get to the biggest, best basketball program I possibly could," he says. "Kansas was first on my list. I knew the situation—Rex Walters was leaving and Steve Woodberry was going to be a senior, so they would need a two-guard at some point. It was the first place I contacted, and it worked out from there."

College Life

With a year of college experience, Haase easily transitioned from the one and only Berkeley to the "cornfield Berkeley," a nickname given to KU and Lawrence in past editions of the *Fiske Guide to Colleges* guidebook.

"Lawrence is a great place, and people welcomed me with open arms," he says. "It was great joining the team. Coach [Roy Williams] preaches the family atmosphere, and I fit right in and knew I made a good choice."

In practice, Haase faced off against guards Calvin Rayford and Jacque Vaughn.

"They whipped me every day," Haase recalls. "Coach had me at point guard that year, and I was going against the two quickest guys in college basketball every day.

"Red-shirting was tough for me, but I enjoyed getting better and getting experience. In that point in my life, it wasn't a bad thing to sit out for a year."

After that season ended, the 1994-95 Jayhawks found themselves in transition after losing seniors Patrick Richey, Richard Scott, and Woodberry. Haase says Vaughn assumed most of the leadership roles for the team, which won the Big Eight regular season title with an 11-3 record and finished 25-6 overall, losing to Virginia in a 67-58 upset in a Sweet 16 NCAA tournament game at Kemper Arena in Kansas City, Missouri.

Haase averaged a career-best 15 points that season and earned second-team all-conference honors.

"It was a fun year for me," he says.

As a junior, Haase and the Jayhawks won the last regular-season Big Eight title with a 12-2 mark and finished 29-5, losing to Syracuse in an Elite Eight game in Denver. Though pleased with the team's success, Haase was not happy with his play in 1995-96.

"I was awful in terms of shooting the basketball," he says of his 35.6 percentage from the field including 29.8 percent from three-point range. His scoring average dipped to 10.8 points.

"It was a real low point for me because I had worked my tail off, and played for a U.S. team overseas," Haase says. "In some ways, I probably spent too much time playing team-organized basketball; it was the only summer I had done something like that instead of just working on my own game."

Heading into his senior year of 1996-97, Williams asked Haase to seek higher quality shots to increase his shooting percentage.

"I had no problem doing that," Haase says. "We knew we were good, and we were good. The whole goal was to keep it going as long as we can. The only goal any of us on the team had was to just win ballgames."

The Jayhawks won their first six games of the season but at a price. In the season opener versus Santa Clara, Haase broke his wrist but does not remember the play in which he was injured. His wrist was sore, but X-rays didn't indicate any broken bones. KU won the opener 76-64, in what was Haase's homecoming game before many South Tahoe fans that traveled to San Jose, California, for the contest.

From there, Kansas flew to Hawaii, where the Jayhawks won the Maui Invitational by handily defeating LSU, Cal, and Virginia. KU returned to Lawrence to beat San Diego and then traveled to Chicago as the nation's new No. 1 team to face fourth-ranked Cincinnati in a "Great Eight" game before 21,062 fans at the United Center. Cincinnati intimidated Kansas into a 35-23 halftime lead over the Jayhawks. KU outscored the Bearcats 49-30 in the second half after a blistering speech from Williams to capture a 72-65 victory.

"Coach never berates us or curses at us," senior Scot Pollard said at the time. "Now, his tone of voice may go up some, but we needed a good chewing out."

Now the Jayhawks would return to California to play UCLA in Pauley Pavilion, a storied arena where KU had never won before.

The Setting

Williams scheduled the Kansas-UCLA game as a homecoming for Jacque Vaughn, but the senior point guard had missed the entire season up to that point with a right wrist injury. Haase and Vaughn (Pasadena) represented two of six Californians on the Kansas roster in 1996-97. The others were fellow seniors Pollard (San Diego) and junior college walk-ons Joel Branstrom (Half Moon Bay) and Steve Ransom (Mission Viejo), and junior Paul Pierce (Los Angeles).

Kansas was favored to win the national championship in 1997. UCLA won the title in 1995 but replaced its coach, Jim Harrick, with 32-year-old assistant Steve Lavin a month before facing the Jayhawks. By losing to Tulsa in the first round of the preseason NIT, the Bruins had only played two games compared with six for KU.

The two teams knew each other well. A year earlier, UCLA led Kansas 41-26 at halftime in Lawrence before the Jayhawks staged a massive second-half rally to win 85-70. The defending Pacific 10 Conference champions returned all five starters from that game, and Kansas would have, too, had Vaughn not been injured.

"I think this game will be very emotional," Williams said of the match-up and how the game played out the previous season.

True enough, but what he or no one else could foresee would be just how dominant KU would be for another half of college basketball played at its best.

The Game of My Life
BY JEROD HAASE
KANSAS VS. UCLA, DECEMBER 7, 1996

This game had me reliving a lot of memories since the last time I had played there as a freshman for Cal. It was kind of a milestone for me to see where my life had gone since that point. Obviously, things had gone pretty well for me.

I think in this game we had UCLA down by as much [28 points in the first half] as they had ever trailed playing in Pauley Pavilion. The two times I had been to Pauley, home to one of the most storied programs in college basketball, my team beat the heck out of them both times, and both times were very emotional for me.

We were ready. We saw what happened when you came out flat, as we did against Cincinnati. That was fresh in our minds. And playing UCLA gets your attention. We did not come into that game with doubt in our minds. We were not passive or worried about playing UCLA at their home. We were determined.

I'm not one to remember a lot of details about a game. I do know it was a heckuva game and every one of us was involved. Going into halftime, they had a little run, so instead of being up by 28 points we were ahead by 21. Basically, we played a fantastic half of basketball.

Before they made their run, the fans were booing and were pretty tough on their team. They knew we had basically dominated them. We did not think the game was over, but it was pretty darn close. If they didn't make that run, it definitely would have been over.

The game was not as close as the final 13-point margin indicates. It was never in jeopardy or in doubt. Everyone got minutes and contributed. It was awesome to get everybody on our team into the game. That's a huge goal. It really was a group effort.

The start of the season—with the travel we did and the school that we missed—was unbelievable. It was a testament to this team to be able to play that well.

Game and Season Results

Kansas defeated UCLA handily, 96-83. Raef LaFrentz led the Jayhawks with 31 points, and Haase scored 22 points on 7-for-12 from the field and 7-for-7 from the line.

"One nice thing or interesting thing or emotional thing was getting to the game and sitting at the same locker as I had when I was a freshman at Cal," Haase says. "I spent some time there after the game kind of reflecting and being very appreciative for every thing that had happened in my life."

The 1996-97 Jayhawks became one of the best teams in university history. Kansas won its first 22 games that season before losing to Missouri 96-94 in double-overtime at Columbia. The 'Hawks proceeded to win the first Big 12 Conference regular-season title with a 15-1 record. KU breezed through the conference tournament and then defeated Jackson State 78-64 and Purdue 75-61 in the NCAA Tournament in Memphis, Tennessee, before venturing to Birmingham, Alabama, to take on the Arizona Wildcats. In one of the most disappointing endings to a great Kansas season, Arizona—the eventual national champions—upset the Jayhawks 85-82. KU's dream season ended with a 34-2 record.

Haase's wrist continued bothering him during the season. X-rays taken during conference play showed his wrist was broken and had been broken for a while—probably in the season opener versus Santa Clara. Even with a broken wrist, Haase averaged 12 points per game.

BOX SCORE
KANSAS VS. UCLA, DECEMBER 7, 1996

Kansas	54 42	– 96
UCLA	33 50	– 83

Kansas (96)

	Min	FG	FT	Reb	PF	Pts
Pierce	30	3-10	5-6	5	3	12
LaFrentz	30	13-21	5-7	11	3	31
Pollard	20	3-7	4-6	7	5	10
Haase	30	7-12	7-7	6	3	22
Robertson	38	0-4	0-0	2	1	0
Williams	22	0-2	1-2	2	1	1
Thomas	15	7-10	0-0	1	1	18
Pugh	6	0-1	0-0	0	2	0
McGrath	2	0-0	2-2	1	0	2
Bradford	4	0-1	0-0	1	2	0
Ransom	1	0-0	0-0	0	0	0
Nooner	1	0-0	0-0	0	0	0
Branstrom	1	0-0	0-0	0	0	0
(team)				3		
TOTALS	**200**	**33-68**	**24-30**	**39**	**21**	**96**

Three-point goals: 6-11 (Thomas 4-6, Pierce 1-2, Haase 1-2, Robertson 0-1); Assists: 20 (Robertson 11, LaFrentz 3, Pierce 2, Haase 2, Thomas, McGrath); Turnovers: 19 (Pierce 6, Haase 6, Robertson 2, Thomas 2, Pugh 2, Pollard); Blocked shots: 3 (Pierce, LaFrentz, Pollard); Steals: 12 (Pollard 3, Haase 3, Pierce 2, LaFrentz 2, Williams 2).

UCLA (83)

	Min	FG	FT	Reb	PF	TP
O'Bannon	35	6-10	7-10	6	3	20
Henderson	24	4-6	3-5	7	4	11
McCoy	28	7-8	1-2	5	4	15
Bailey	32	5-10	2-4	4	3	14
Dollar	30	3-8	2-2	0	4	8
Johnson	28	3-9	2-4	3	4	9
Loyd	16	2-3	0-0	1	1	6
Myers	7	0-0	0-0	0	0	0
(team)				2		
TOTALS	**200**	**30-54**	**17-27**	**28**	**23**	**83**

Three-point goals: 6-12 (Bailey 2-3, Loyd 2-3, O'Bannon 1-2, Johnson 1-4); Assists: 13 (Dollar 5, O'Bannon 3, Bailey 2, Henderson, McCoy, Loyd); Turnovers: 26 (McCoy 8, Johnson 7, O'Bannon 4, Bailey 3, Dollar 3, Henderson); Blocked shots 5 (McCoy 3, O'Bannon, Bailey); Steals: 9 (Dollar 5, O'Bannon 2, Henderson 2).

Officials: Ed Hightower, Paul Kaster, Scott Thornly. Attendance: 12,060.

"I look at that season as absolutely what's right about college basketball," Haase says. "We were a team that was a model of how to do things right. The majority of the players made really good grades. We worked extremely hard. We cared about how the team did. We represented the university, each other, the coaches and the fans in the right way.

"It also showed that life is not fair. We lost to a team that I think we were better than. My wrist ended up giving out at the end of that season. But for every time you say, 'Life isn't fair,' if you keep battling and making yourself better, there's some pretty good things in there, too."

What Became of Jerod Haase?

For a year after his final college basketball game, Haase stayed in the limelight in Kansas by co-writing a book, *Floor Burns,* with Mark Horvath. The book detailed Haase's senior season and was a bestseller in the Sunflower State.

"It was a fun project and great learning experience," Haase says.

At first the two authors could not find a publisher for the book. Then Haase went to Macedonia for a brief attempt at playing professionally. By the time he returned to Kansas, they decided to self-publish the book, which meant they also handled its distribution and marketing by picking up copies in Newton and then driving around the state for various signings. As the book sales were winding down, Haase spent 1998-99 revisiting towns throughout Kansas by conducting 100 basketball camps at 30 to 40 venues. He also took graduate classes at KU, eventually earning a masters of science degree in human resource management.

When Jayhawk assistant coach Matt Doherty accepted the Notre Dame head coaching job in 1999, Haase and his former roommate, C.B. McGrath, joined the KU staff.

"I never knew what I wanted to do," Haase explains. "I really enjoyed being an entrepreneur, and to this day I think it would be fun starting something from scratch and seeing if I could make it work. While I was in Europe, I knew I didn't want to play basketball, and my gut was telling me I wanted to be a coach."

Haase worked at KU for four years doing behind-the-scenes work such as selling calendars, dealing with team travel, and coordinating special events. When Williams took the North Carolina job, Haase and McGrath were among the coaches who joined him in Chapel Hill.

Today, Haase and McGrath alternate years on the bench and working behind the scenes. Haase was scheduled to be behind the scenes in 2006-07, which is probably a good thing, because he and his wife, Mindy, became first-time parents in September 2006.

In time, Haase intends to be a head coach. In the meantime, he says the way the 1997 season ended will stick with him for years to come.

"To this day I still feel that I owe Kansas even something more, something better," Haase says. "Not just Kansas and Kansas fans, but Coach Williams, too. When Coach Williams won the national championship here at North Carolina, some of that burden was lifted knowing he had won one. But at the same time, I'm still pulling like heck for Kansas to get another national championship."

11

SCOT POLLARD

The Life of Young Scot Pollard

Like several of his Jayhawk teammates, Scot Pollard grew up in a basketball family and never lacked for a game.

Unlike his teammates, he didn't relish the experience.

Pollard is the youngest of six children in the Pearl and Marilyn Pollard family. Three of his brothers—Carl (7-foot-3), Mark (7 foot), and Neal (7 foot) are taller than he is, and Pollard is only an inch taller than his brother Alan (6-foot-10). Plus, Pollard is at least five years younger than his brothers.

"By the time I could even try to compete with them, they were in high school and were 7 feet tall," Pollard says. "I could try to compete with them, but it wasn't even close. It got to the point that I did not play with them a lot."

Still, basketball was always there. His father, Pearl, had excelled in the sport in high school and at the University of Utah. Pearl built the family— which also included sister Susan—a cusom-made home that featured an outdoor basketball court. Pearl and Scot's brothers worked with Scot on the game, and Scot attended many of his brothers' games when he wasn't playing them at home.

In sixth grade, Pollard's family moved to San Diego, and Pollard's interests changed with the territory.

"I was a wannabe surfer dude, always in the ocean or on the beach," he says. "I also played a lot of volleyball."

Out of the shadow of his brothers—all of who played basketball in college—Pollard stuck with the sport and starred at Torrey Pines High School. When he was 16, his larger-than-life father died. Pollard and his mother moved to Kennewick, Washington, for his senior year of high school to live with his oldest brother, Alan, who was playing for the Tri-City team in the Continental Basketball Association.

Despite the tragic turn of events, Pollard led Kamiakin High School to a 27-2 record and was named Washington Gatorade Player of the Year and a third-team *Parade* All-American after averaging 18.5 points, 10.4 rebounds, and 3.2 blocked shots. Before he completed his senior year, Pollard moved back to San Diego on his own to graduate with his friends at Torrey Pines.

The family considered Scot to be the most driven of his brothers. Before his dad died, Pollard bought fully into the laid-back Southern California lifestyle. When his dad died in October of his junior year, Pollard took a couple of weeks off and thought about his future. He considered quitting basketball, but then he decided to dedicate himself to being the best player he could be to honor Pearl's memory.

"From that point on, I haven't had a single problem getting motivated to play basketball," Pollard says.

For the record, Pearl Pollard was inducted into the inaugural class of the Utah Hall of Fame in 1999 along with Utah Jazz owner Larry Miller and former Brigham Young and NBA star Danny Ainge, among others. Despite Pollard's lengthy NBA career and notoriety with his different hairstyles and unique look, people still stop him when he visits Utah and ask, "Are you Pearl Pollard's son?"

When choosing a college, Pollard was determined to find a place with a strong coach and an established program. He considered San Diego State—two of his brothers had played there—but the Aztecs were not a national powerhouse. UCLA interested him, but Pollard was concerned that coach Jim Harrick would not be there for all four of Pollard's seasons. He visited BYU for his mother's sake, but he was not interested in the Cougars. Then, Pollard thought Arizona, given its similarity to San Diego, was a perfect fit for him—until he visited Kansas.

"I thought Roy Williams would be a better father figure for me, which I definitely needed at that time," Pollard says.

Pollard committed to KU after visiting "Late Night," which would not be the only time he made headlines during those festivities.

Notes on Scot Pollard

Years lettered:	1993-94 to 1996-97
Position:	Center
Height:	6-foot-11
Playing weight:	265 pounds
Hometown:	San Diego, California
Current residence:	Cleveland, Ohio
Occupation:	NBA player for the Cleveland Cavaliers
Accomplishments:	Named co-recipient of the "James Naismith Captain's Award" in 1997; honorable mention All-America (AP) and All-Big 12 honorable mention (coaches) in '97; All-Big Eight Conference second team (AP and players) and All-Big Eight Conference honorable mention (coaches) in 1996; All-Big Eight honorable mention, Big Eight All-Underrated and All-Bench teams in 1995; Big Eight All-Freshman team in 1994.
The Game:	Kansas State vs. Kansas in Lawrence, Kansas, February 22, 1997

College Life

Pollard arrived in Lawrence knowing he wasn't going to start for the Jayhawks, and so he worked to earn his minutes. Ahead of him at center was 7-foot-2 junior Greg Ostertag. Starting at power forward was 6-foot-6 senior Richard Scott, who Pollard calls "a dominant, great low-post offensive player who used every inch of his body and played as if he were 7-foot-6."

At times frustrated with his playing time, Pollard worked through his issues with Coach Williams and averaged 7.5 points and 4.9 rebounds in 17 minutes, all off the bench. The Jayhawks finished 27-8 and won two games in the NCAA tournament before bowing to Purdue 83-78.

As a sophomore, Pollard still played behind Ostertag, but Pollard's minutes increased to 20 per game. His scoring and rebounding averages improved to 10.2 and 6.2, respectively. The 1994-95 Jayhawks won the Big Eight regular-season championship and again advanced to the Sweet 16 before losing to Virginia 67-58 at Kemper Arena in Kansas City, Missouri, ending KU's season with a 25-6 record.

Pollard underwent surgery to repair his right shoulder after the season.

"I had always been a bit ambidextrous ... in high school I used to shoot with both hands until my coach told me to pick a hand," he explains. "After the surgery, I decided to switch back to my left hand because I wasn't allowed to use my right for a while. To this day when I'm in the post, going to my left is a lot more comfortable, so I think it helped further develop my game."

The surgery, rehabilitation, and Pollard's inventiveness as a part-time southpaw worked out well for him during his junior year in 1995-96. Pollard started all but "Senior Night" and averaged 10.1 points and 7.4 rebounds for the 29-5 'Hawks, which won the final regular-season Big Eight championship.

As a freshman, Pollard lived across the hall from an attractive student named Mindy. Coach Williams would visit his players from time to time, and during one visit to Pollard and Jacque Vaughn's apartment, the coach noticed Mindy and asked Pollard if he had met her.

"She's gorgeous," Williams told Pollard.

"Yeah, Coach, I know," Pollard replied, adding, "It was a mutual feeling—Mindy thought Roy was gorgeous, too."

In time, Pollard and Mindy dated while they both attended KU. But Mindy graduated first and the couple broke up, which Pollard blames on himself. Mindy moved to Phoenix "and acted like she didn't miss me," Pollard says of their summer apart. But he visited her and they eventually reconciled, which brings us to "Late Night" in October 1996.

Pollard decided to propose to Mindy at "Late Night." He ran his idea past Williams and Vaughn, both of whom approved of his decision. A plot was hatched that Williams would walk Mindy to half court, where Pollard was waiting to propose to her in front of 16,300 of their closest friends. She accepted, and the couple added to "Late Night's" lore.

The Setting

The 1996-97 Jayhawks became one of the top teams in Kansas history. The team won its first 22 games, captured the Big 12 regular-season title with a 15-1 mark in conference play and then swept the Big 12 tournament by an average of 22 points.

Although the 'Hawks were dominant, the season was far from easy. Vaughn missed the first 10 games due to injury. Jerod Haase broke his wrist in the season's first game but the extent of the injury wasn't discovered for a couple of months. And Pollard severely sprained his ankle on January 11, 1997, against Baylor, which sidelined him for eight games.

"I decided rather than wait and let it heal—we were undefeated at that point—so I decided to wrap it up real tight and keep playing," he explains. "I just wrapped it up like a boot and we fit everything we could into my shoe around my ankle. I ran like I had a boot on and there was no range of motion. It turned out not to be that smart of a deal, but it was me, it wasn't the training staff."

After Pollard played two games in his "boot," he was walking home from class when the middle bone in his left foot snapped. He limped to the team's training table, and the trainers also discovered Pollard had a stress facture in the bone next to the broken bone.

Looking back, missing eight games does not seem like that big of a deal in a season of 36 games. But the time missed seems like an eternity when the player is a senior, like Pollard was, and the season and his career were winding down.

Therefore, the February 22 game against Kansas State loomed large for Pollard. The date not only meant his return but also his farewell—the game was "Senior Night," and it marked the last Allen Fieldhouse appearance for Pollard, Haase, Vaughn, B.J. Williams, and walk-ons Joel Branstrom and Steve Ransom.

Although Kansas State didn't represent the toughest of opponents, Senior Night was an event not to be missed—especially if Pollard was involved in it.

The Game of My Life
BY SCOT POLLARD
KANSAS STATE VS. KANSAS, FEBRUARY 22, 1997

It was my first game back, and I was so excited to get back on this team that was having a magical season. I didn't want to miss one more second of action.

The training staff said I could play but I shouldn't play a full game because I wasn't ready and they didn't want me to break the foot again. Coach said, "All right, we'll start you and let you play a few minutes."

Coach couldn't decide who to start, so we "started" Raef LaFrentz and six seniors. [Before the tip-off, Branstrom and Ransom returned to the bench and later got into the game.]

I had never shot a three-pointer until that game. I had always joked with Coach that I'm a better shooter than he thought I was, but I always gave that responsibility to the guys who were the best shooters—Jerod, Paul [Pierce], Billy [Thomas]—anybody but me.

But I always bragged that I was a better shooter and could shoot threes. I promised Coach that one of these days I was going to shoot a three, like on Senior Night. He said, "If you do, I'm going to take your ass right out of the game," jokingly, I think.

The game was getting out of hand a little bit toward the end, and I knew I was coming out anyway, when I got the ball at the top of the key. They didn't guard me 'cause they had no reason to guard me at the three-point line. I shot it up there and it went in.

To me, that was just my dad grabbing it and stuffing it in for me, 'cause there was really no reason for that ball to go in.

Then I got taken out. I went over to Coach and said, "I told ya!"

Game and Season Results

Despite trailing by one at halftime, Kansas soundly defeated the Wildcats 78-58. Pollard played 13 minutes in his triumphant return and scored eight points.

"This was as emotional a day as there's been since I've been here, and it got so emotional that it became a distraction," Williams said afterward.

Pollard says he doesn't remember anything from his postgame senior speech except for feeling joyful but also a sense of loss.

"We knew that the next time we walked through that tunnel, the cheering and all that noise would not be for us," he says. "I've made it back since then ... but it's a sad feeling, because there's nothing like running through that tunnel, hearing the noise, the band strikes up, the girls dancing and the crowd going nuts. There's not a whole lot of arenas in the country like that, and none are as special as this place."

No. 1 Kansas played "only" eight more games that season. Most Jayhawk fans anticipated that number to be 11, but eventual national champion Arizona stunned KU 85-82 in a Southeast Regional Sweet 16 game. Kansas finished the season at 34-2.

What Became of Scot Pollard?

If you ask Scot Pollard a question, you're liable to get an explanation as well as an answer. Not that there's anything wrong with that—it's not like he's some publicity hound baring his soul on a TV talk show. Instead, the added details lend more credence to his answer. In other words, you know Pollard is telling you the truth.

Question: Scot, what do you enjoy most about the NBA?

Answer: "That's easy, the money," he says with a telling laugh. "You can call me a sap or whatever, but there's absolutely nothing like playing college basketball. I think it's the purest form of basketball. I think it's the best mixture of talent, pureness of heart, desire, and effort.

"I think high school kids give that effort but they don't have the talent, and I think in the pros they have that talent, obviously, but not always the effort because believe it or not, with 100 games, it's hard to show your best effort every single night. For a guy who has been injured as much as I have been lately, I think that the fact that I've given my effort so much, I think that's maybe why I'm injured so much now because my body is starting to break down from all those charges, diving on the floor and doing those things that I love doing.

"I really do think that college was a lot more fun, but to be fair, there's only 35 games. There's only one game a week and sometimes two. In the NBA, we play two or three and they're back-to-back or in different cities. You give your best effort every night—I'm not saying you're not giving 100 percent every night by any means. You give your best effort every night, but you don't always have the energy to give your best effort every single night, because you may have played the last four nights or four of the last five."

See?

The short answer to what happened to Pollard since he played at Kansas is that he has enjoyed a nine-year NBA career with Detroit, Atlanta, Sacramento, Indiana, and now Cleveland, where he plays alongside former Jayhawk Drew Gooden. Despite such attention-getting behavior as painting his fingernails and sporting an array of hairstyles and colors during his time

BOX SCORE
KANSAS STATE VS. KANSAS, FEBRUARY 22, 1997

Kansas State   31 27 – 58
Kansas   30 48 – 78

Kansas State (58)

	Min	FG	FT	Reb	PF	TP
Dies	24	1-4	0-1	3	1	2
Young	25	5-10	0-0	8	1	12
Rhodes	32	0-4	2-2	5	2	2
May	36	4-11	2-4	4	2	11
Swartzendruber	31	1-3	4-4	4	3	7
Griffin	13	1-3	0-0	1	1	2
Reid	1	1-1	0-0	0	0	2
Marsh	1	0-0	0-0	0	0	0
Jones	1	0-0	0-0	2	1	0
Eaker	22	6-11	0-2	9	4	12
McCollough	14	4-6	0-0	4	1	8
(team)				2		
TOTALS	**200**	**23-53**	**8-13**	**42**	**16**	**58**

Three-point goals: 4-8 (Young 2-2, May 1-1, Swartzendruber 1-3, Rhodes 0-1, Griffin 0-1); Assists: 13 (Griffin 7, May 2, Young, Rhodes, Eaker, McCollough); Turnovers: 25 (Young 5, Swartzendruber 5, Rhodes 3, Griffin 3, McCollough 3, May 2, Dies, Marsh, Eaker, team); Blocked shots: 2 (Dies, Griffin); Steals: 7 (Swartzendruber 2, McCollough 2, Dies, May, Griffin).

Kansas (78)

	Min	FG	FT	Reb	PF	Pts
Williams	25	1-2	0-0	5	2	2
LaFrentz	28	9-15	3-4	11	3	21
Pollard	13	2-2	3-5	1	1	8
Vaughn	35	2-9	2-2	3	3	6
Haase	29	6-13	3-7	6	1	16
Robertson	7	1-4	0-0	3	2	2
Nooner	1	0-1	0-0	0	0	0
Thomas	14	1-6	0-0	1	1	3
Branstrom	1	1-1	0-0	2	0	2
Bradford	9	1-4	0-0	0	1	2
McGrath	1	0-1	0-0	0	0	0
Pugh	12	0-0	0-0	0	1	0
Pierce	24	5-12	3-4	5	0	14
Ransom	1	1-2	0-0	0	0	2
(team)				3		
TOTALS	**200**	**30-72**	**14-22**	**40**	**15**	**78**

Three-point goals: 4-23 (Thomas 1-6, Haase 1-4, Pierce 1-2, Pollard 1-1, Robertson 0-3, Bradford 0-3, Vaughn 0-2, Nooner 0-1, McGrath 0-1); Assists: 11 (Vaughn 6, Williams, Haase, Bradford, McGrath, Pierce); Turnovers: 11 (Haase 4, Pierce 3, LaFrentz 2, Vaughn 2); Blocked shots: 3 (Williams 2, Thomas); Steals: 15 (Williams 4, Vaughn 4, LaFrentz, Pollard, Haase, Robertson, Thomas, McGrath, Pierce).

Officials: Tom Harrington, Stanley Reynolds, David Maracich. Attendance: 16,300.

at KU and after, former Jayhawk teammates deeply appreciate what Pollard brought to the team.

Billy Thomas called him "a great, great teammate. He was a guy you want in your corner, the protector for our team. He would set the hard screen. He enforced the 'no layup rule.' He was so selfless in his play. He didn't score a lot of points or do the glamorous things, but we couldn't have won without him."

Fellow Californian Haase says, "I don't think Pollard is as weird as he likes to make himself out to be. He's a good guy and a fun guy to be around. He's extremely smart and worked hard to get where he is."

For Pollard, the emphasis of his life has been family—his first one as a son and brother, and his current one as husband to Mindy and father of two young daughters, Lolly and Tallulah. Then there's his extended family of fellow Jayhawks. Pollard says Mindy and he have run into people wearing Jayhawk T-shirts in Thailand and been reminded of his marriage proposal at "Late Night" by KU fans in Bermuda.

"You don't see that from other colleges," he says. "There's a strong sense of family with the Jayhawks, and it's a great thing that my wife and I have enjoyed."

1 2

BILLY THOMAS

The Life of Young Billy Thomas

The neighborhood where Billy Thomas lived the first 18 years of his life is called "The Bottoms," and it is aptly named.

"It's pretty hard, like a lot of areas for a young black kid growing up," Thomas says. "It's tumultuous. You've got drugs, gangs, violence, and everything that comes along with it."

But Thomas would be spared the undertow of such a place. He came from a strong family led by his mother, Eddie Mae, and two supportive sisters. And his athletic skills in football and especially basketball earned him such a high degree of respect in the neighborhood that he was left out of any potential trouble, either as a participant or a potential victim.

"It was sort of like I had a halo over me the whole time, which never allowed me to get into any of the bad things that I could have easily gotten in to," Thomas says. "The guys in the neighborhood looked out for me to make sure I didn't do any of that."

Thomas improved his basketball game by constant play at the neighborhood courts.

"I'd go all day, in the sun, never getting tired. Then I'd eat a little something and go to sleep. I wasn't fortunate to have any individual instruction, so I learned mostly from watching the older guys play. And then play, play, play."

By the time he was a high school freshman, Thomas was playing with the older guys in his neighborhood on a regular basis. He often went up against his cousin, Michael, a former high school star, and his two uncles, Jimmy and Eddie.

"My confidence grew," Thomas says of those early playground games. "Those guys saw that I could compete with them. That's when they—and I—saw I might be able to get away from that neighborhood by playing basketball."

That realization helped Thomas become more interested to leave the neighborhood. He gave up football after his junior season to avoid injury, even though colleges had started recruiting him in that sport. He focused on basketball and continued to stay trouble-free.

"I got my determination from growing up in that neighborhood, growing up watching guys come before me who were talented but not get a break here or there, not to make excuses for them, or they made terrible decisions on their own," Thomas says. "I saw how talented they were and the mistakes they made. I thought if I'm as talented as they are but don't make the same mistakes, then I'm blessed. A lot of the attributes I have now come from growing up in that neighborhood."

Thomas recalls his college recruiting as "crazy." Thomas met Valparaiso assistant Scott Drew at LSU's summer camp, where Drew was working. Valpo sent Thomas his first letter, but Thomas favored the in-state Tigers. In time, Georgetown, Wake Forest, and Clemson, among others, came calling. Thomas listened but waited to decide on his college choice.

"I realized this was a pretty big deal for a small-town kid like me," he says. "Those are great schools. But I had the inclination to just hold off."

Kansas recruited Thomas later. Coach Roy Williams first saw Thomas on tape while evaluating another player. Williams was impressed with Thomas, who averaged 28 points, 12 rebounds, five assists, and two blocks as a senior for Loyola Prep High School in Shreveport.

Thomas visited Lawrence for the Missouri game in February 1994. Even though the Jayhawks lost, Thomas was extremely impressed.

"It was the loudest thing I ever heard. I couldn't even hear myself think," Thomas says. "Afterward, Coach Williams takes you into the locker room and you see your jersey hanging in the locker and the story of how you helped lead KU to the Final Four and the National Championship. It blew me away. I was sold at that point. Then, Wanda, Coach's wife, cooked biscuits and gravy for me the next morning. Man, I was sold."

Notes on Billy Thomas

Years lettered:	1994-95 to 1997-98
Position:	Guard
Height:	6-foot-4
Playing weight:	208 pounds
Hometown:	Shreveport, Louisiana
Current Residence:	Olathe, Kansas
Occupation:	Professional basketball player Serbia
Accomplishments:	"Clyde Lovellette Most Improved Player Award" in 1995 and 1998; Big 12 All-Improved team and All-Big 12 honorable mention in '98; Big Eight All-Bench team in 1996; Big Eight All-Freshman team in 1995.
Nicknames:	"B.T." and "Thrill"
The Game:	Kansas vs. Texas in Austin, Texas, January 10, 1998

Thomas wasn't the only person in Shreveport sold on the Jayhawks. After Thomas signed with KU, Williams spoke at his high school athletic banquet that spring and made a huge impression on the crowd.

"From that point on, everybody at school, parents of people I didn't know were Kansas fans from that day forward," Thomas says.

College Life

When Thomas arrived in Lawrence for the 1994 fall semester, he missed his family but not his neighborhood. Not in the least.

"It was totally different and a welcome change," Thomas says. "I had come from such a fast and furious, crime-ridden place. This was different from anything I'd ever known. It was laid back. It wasn't nearly as poverty stricken, there weren't any guys walking up and down the streets with guns.

"I took big sighs of relief when I got here and started to move around a little bit. It took me a while before I could let my guard down, relax, and be comfortable here. I used to have to be on the lookout for things in the neighborhood where I came from. I took a few nice, deep breaths and said, 'Man, I can start to live the second part of my life.'"

That next phase of his life started a little on the rocky side for Thomas. In pick-up games, he felt unsure of how he was doing. Coach Williams reassured him that the other players thought Thomas could play with them just fine.

"After hearing that those guys thought I was holding my own and thought I had a good knowledge of the game, that instilled more confidence in me," he says. "Every day from that point on I felt like I belonged."

Thomas roomed with fellow freshman Raef LaFrentz (as he would for the next two years) and spent a lot of time with him and also Jacque Vaughn. In practice he went up against Sean Pearson and worked on his ball-handling and defense, which Williams stressed with all the players.

Thomas says he was eager to improve.

"I used every day as a learning tool to get the tricks of the trade from some of the older guys—that you can get away with a shirt pull or blocking an arm, little-bitty things, but as a younger player you don't know that until you experience it," he says.

As a freshman, Thomas improved his defense, which led to more playing time and two starts. He averaged 7.3 points per game and was named to the Big Eight's all-freshman team.

Nagging injuries and a virus late in the season limited Thomas' playing time his sophomore season. He averaged 4.7 points per game but continued excelling from beyond the arc for Kansas, which reached the Elite Eight.

Thomas returned to form as a junior, averaging 7.7 points per game for the 34-2 Jayhawks, which were ranked No. 1 for most of the 1996-97 season before being upset by eventual national champion Arizona in the NCAA tournament. By this season, Thomas also had established himself as one of the more entertaining players on the team, says former teammate Scot Pollard.

"He was one of the funniest guys I have ever been around," Pollard says. "We loved it when he'd go home for the summer, because he would come back with a whole new set of slang. He'd come back and start saying something, and we'd start laughing before we even knew what he meant. We'd have him repeat it a few times so we could try and copy it."

Some of Thomas' expressions made lasting impressions on the Jayhawks years after he was finished with school. In 2001, when KU ended a three-year skid of second-round losses in the NCAA tournament, the team

presented Williams with a stuffed monkey to represent getting the monkey off his back. The monkey's name? "Stank 'em," which came from one of Thomas' expressions after draining a series of threes.

All joking aside, Thomas had earned and accepted a role as co-captain and team leader his senior season.

"It was a natural progression," he says "As a senior, you look upon it as your duty to guide the younger guys through, because the guys before you did the same thing. So it was natural helping guys like Kenny Gregory, going through the things I went through, the intensity change between high school and college and what Coach Williams expects, especially defensively."

Thomas became a full-time starter and KU enjoyed another fast start early in his senior year. Thomas scored a career-high 27 points against Ohio State in the Rainbow Classic in Hawaii and became a dominant outside force. "Stank 'em," indeed!

The Setting

Kansas entered its 21st game of the 1997-98 season with an 18-2 record, including a 2-0 record in Big 12 Conference play and a number-four national ranking. Judging by those numbers, KU's centennial season of basketball appeared to be on cruise control.

Still, the Jayhawks faced uncertainty. All-American Raef LaFrentz had been injured in late December in Hawaii and would miss his sixth of nine games. Paul Pierce, in the midst of his All-America season (and last at KU) had incurred a mild knee sprain in the previous game against Colorado. Junior forward T.J. Pugh was recovering from a stress fracture in his right foot. Plus, KU had played only two "true" road games and had gone 1-1 in those contests.

Coach Williams went beyond the typical coach-speak in describing his feelings about the Jayhawks playing their first conference road game of the season in Austin.

"We have to prove we can play on the road," he said. "We've had teams in the past who have done a great job of that. So far this team has not shown what they'll do."

In Texas, though, the Jayhawks were facing a young team off to a slow start. The Longhorns were 6-7 overall, 0-2 in league play (including a home loss to Baylor) and were only 5-2 at home. Texas started all underclassmen, including freshman guard Luke Axtell, who would transfer to KU after the season in a series of events that would cost 10-year head coach Tom Penders his job. The 'Horns also were minus their leading scorer, Kris Clack, who was out with a knee injury.

Billy Thomas was the only senior to start for either team that day. He may have had the largest individual cheering section in the stands, too. Twelve family members and friends—his mother, both sisters, two uncles, two nephews, a cousin Michael, his godmother, his "godsister," and two friends—had traveled 275 miles from Shreveport for the 11 a.m. game.

"It was one of the last times they saw me play," Thomas recalls.

That morning and afternoon the Jayhawks and Thomas would silence most of the other 16,163 fans at the Erwin Center while giving a dozen people plenty to talk about on the trip back to northwestern Louisiana.

The Game of My Life
BY BILLY THOMAS
KANSAS VS. TEXAS, JANUARY 10, 1998

We didn't prepare differently for this game, but as a team we had to take our game to another level when we went on the road. Every team gave us their best shot. We had to ratchet up our intensity. What helped us do that was that we were so closely knit as a team.

The first half was tight for a while. We started pulling away in the last 10 minutes of the half. I made a lay-up with 5:14 left in the half to put us back up by 10 points. Later I made a three-pointer to give us a 15-point lead with 1:48 to go. We led Texas 39-25 at halftime.

Things opened up in the second half. Their defense was trapping the whole game because they wanted to speed the game up. We were the kind of team that loved to play fast as well—but under control. We didn't have a problem breaking their press, because we worked on it so hard in practice. When we broke that press I was wide open.

Our "press-breaker" depended on the way we called it. You'd either be in the far corner or the guard at half court. I was always the one in the far corner. Once I started to make baskets, my teammates did a great job of looking for me. The rim looked huge. Every time I let it go it felt like it was going in. I made five three-pointers in the first seven and a half minutes of the second half and another to put us ahead by 30 points with 4:41 remaining before coming out.

I've always been blessed being able to shoot the ball. That was the first thing I noticed when I started playing: I was shooting the ball out farther than the other kids. That day, I was smiling and laughing every time I caught the basketball. That's what our team was about. We had so much fun that game. Everybody was making plays. There was no selfishness involved in this game at all.

This game summed up my experience as a basketball player at Kansas. You look at the newspaper photos and you see people laughing, cheering, jumping up and down. Raef was injured, but he was on the bench cheering us on. They tried to put me back in the game so I could score 30 points. I said, "That's not important to me." At the end, Terry Nooner got in and made a three-point shot. It was so much fun.

The game also was a real tribute to Coach Williams for not letting us get ahead of ourselves. He challenged us before the game because we hadn't played well on the road. At halftime he wanted us to continue to play hard. He knew what the score was, but we were playing to get better. And my family was there, so I knew I had to play hard.

Game and Season Results

The Jayhawks routed the Longhorns 102-72 deep in the heart of Texas. Thomas matched his career high in points with 27 on nine-for-13 shooting from the field (including eight-for-11 three-pointers) and a free throw. He earned CBS "Player of the Game" honors for his shooting prowess. Pierce's knee held up just fine and he led KU with 31 points. Lester Earl also scored in double figures with 15 points.

Thomas says having his family and friends at the game meant a lot to him that day.

"I wanted to play well because they made that trip all the way up there," he says. "But when you play for Kansas, you can play well and have 15 points. I think I made the trip worthwhile for them. They were ecstatic after the game. You hate to see them turn around and drive home, but they had seen a really good basketball game. They went back smiling."

BOX SCORE
KANSAS VS. TEXAS, JANUARY 10, 1998

Kansas	39 63	– 102
Texas	25 47	– 72

Kansas (102)

	Min	FG	FT	Reb	PF	TP
Pierce	27	11-20	9-13	10	2	31
Earl	30	5-15	5-6	8	0	15
Chenowith	26	2-7	0-1	8	5	4
Robertson	28	1-4	4-4	2	2	6
Thomas	30	9-13	1-2	4	1	27
Gregory	18	3-7	1-4	2	0	7
Bradford	19	2-3	0-0	4	4	4
McGrath	13	0-0	1-2	5	2	1
Janisse	3	1-1	0-0	2	0	2
Nooner	3	1-1	0-0	1	0	3
Martin	3	1-4	0-0	0	1	2
(team)				5		
TOTALS	**200**	**36-75**	**21-32**	**51**	**17**	**102**

Three-point goals: 9-17 (Thomas 8-11, Nooner 1-1, Pierce 0-2, Robertson 0-2, Gregory 0-1); Assists: 22 (Robertson 6, Earl 5, McGrath 4, Chenowith 3, Bradford 3, Gregory); Turnovers: 15 (Chenowith 4, Robertson 3, Bradford 3, Pierce 2, Earl 2, Nooner); Blocked shots: 5 (Chenowith 4, Pierce); Steals: 6 (Pierce, Earl, Chenowith, Robertson, McGrath, Janisse).

Texas (72)

	Min	FG	FT	Reb	PF	TP
Muoneke	18	5-10	2-2	7	4	12
Vazquez	22	1-3	4-4	6	4	6
Mihm	31	3-13	1-6	13	4	7
Wagner	27	4-11	2-4	5	3	10
Axtell	32	5-18	6-7	3	0	18
Perryman	18	1-6	0-0	1	3	3
Goode	1	0-0	0-0	1	0	0
Smith	20	4-7	0-0	2	0	10
Carter	1	1-1	0-0	0	0	2
Clark	18	2-5	0-0	2	2	4
Drakes	12	0-0	0-0	3	2	0
(team)				5		
TOTALS	**200**	**26-74**	**15-23**	**48**	**22**	**72**

Three-point goals: 5-20 (Axtell 2-7, Smith 2-3, Perryman 1-6, Wagner 0-3, Vazquez 0-1); Assists: 14 (Wagner 4, Axtell 3, Smith 3, Vazquez, Perryman, Goode, Clark); Turnovers: 17 (Wagner 4, Vazquez 3, Axtell 3, Muoneke 2, Perryman 2, Smith 2, Mihm); Blocked shots: 6 (Mihm 4, Vazquez, Drakes); Steals: 7 (Muoneke, Vazquez, Wagner, Axtell, Perryman, Clark, Drakes).

Officials: Larry Lembo, Wally Tanner, Charles Range. Attendance: 16,175.

Kansas gave its fans plenty to smile about in 1998. The Jayhawks won their fourth consecutive regular season conference crown going 15-1 in league play. The only loss was a one-point defeat versus Missouri in Columbia. The Jayhawks avenged that loss in Lawrence before more than 300 former KU players and coaches who reunited in Lawrence to celebrate the university's 100th year of basketball.

Thomas suffered a hamstring injury late in the season and missed the conference tournament. But Kansas still won its second straight Big 12 title, defeating Oklahoma in the championship game.

In NCAA tournament play, KU routed Prairie View in the opening game but fell to red-hot Rhode Island in a second-round upset. For the season, Kansas went 35-4, a record that matched the 1985-86 Jayhawk team for most wins in school history. KU also extended its school-record home-court winning streak to 60 games. In fact, the senior class of Thomas, LaFrentz, and C.B. McGrath won more career games (123) than any other class in KU history, and they never lost at Allen Fieldhouse.

Thomas averaged a career-best 13.6 points per game in 1997-98, third best on the team behind All-Americans Pierce and LaFrentz. Thomas' 269 three-point baskets also broke the school record for treys.

As teammate Ryan Robertson noted, "Billy was so energetic and was probably the best shooter I ever played with."

What Became of Billy Thomas?

One of the television sponsors for the NCAA basketball tournament the past couple of years is a motel chain that uses the Johnny Cash song "I've Been Everywhere" to tout its many locations.

No doubt Thomas could relate with the legendary "Man in Black" during these spots and add another verse of his own to the tune.

Since leaving Lawrence, Thomas has played minor league basketball in Salina, Kansas (twice); Cincinnati; Greenville, South Carolina; Bismarck, North Dakota ("the coldest I've ever been in my life"); and on three other continents.

Concerning his overseas experiences, he rated two out of three sites highly: Argentina ("It wasn't that bad, but not that great"); The Philippines ("They are rabid basketball fans. They have good tradition and they play good basketball."); and Italy ("It was cool to get a chance to see the culture, dealing with the language barrier. Basketball is so universal, you can communicate through it.")

Another universal in basketball is players' desires to play at the highest level, which means the NBA. In the fall of 2004, Thomas was the last player cut from the Washington Wizards. Being that close to making the NBA left him with a big decision: return overseas for a lucrative paycheck or stay stateside in the minors and hope for "the call" from the NBA. He chose the latter.

"You have major opportunities to play in Italy or Greece for 25 times what you'll be making here," Thomas said. "But you have to make those decisions. When you're told you're close, you have to give yourself a chance."

In January 2005, Thomas got "the call." The New Jersey Nets signed him to a 10-day contract from the Continental Basketball Association's Dakota Wind. Thomas had lit up the CBA with a league-leading 70 three-pointers that season and then held his own in the NBA, earning a second 10-day contract and then being signed for the rest of the season. He averaged 3.7 points off the bench for the Nets in 25 games.

"It was a wonderful experience," Thomas says. "The first two weeks of being there, I was floating on Clouds 9, 10, and 11. Once that wears off, it's just basketball."

While on the Nets, Thomas was reunited with former KU teammate Jacque Vaughn, who he says helped him with his transition. Thomas says he learned about being a professional and staying ready to play.

"You could go 10 straight games without playing and be called upon on the 11th game and they expect you to be able to play," he says. "That's what being a professional is all about. I think of myself as a fierce competitor; so that's what I did every day. When shots aren't falling and nothing's going well, that's one thing that's constant: I am going to compete. It makes me better and makes the team better."

In the fall of 2005, the Washington Wizards cut Thomas before the season, so he returned to the CBA's Dakota Wizards. In February 2006, Washington signed him to a 10-day contract, then another, and then kept him for the rest of the season. Thomas averaged 2.2 points for the NBA's Wizards in 17 games.

Thomas is playing for Crvena Zvezda ("Red Star") in Belgrade, Serbia, in 2006-07.

Although Thomas has bounced around in his professional career, he has found a home in Olathe, Kansas.

"I like the area. It's quiet," he says of suburban Kansas City. "You can live comfortably. I've stayed in this area because of where I went to school and the way people continue to receive me to this day."

No matter where Thomas plays in the future, his story of perseverance and determination can be summarized as one from "The Bottoms" to the top.

13

RYAN ROBERTSON

The Life of Young Ryan Robertson

Before she knew she was raising two college basketball players, Angie Robertson taught one—Stacey King—at Lawton High School in Oklahoma. King later starred for the University of Oklahoma and started for the Sooners at center in the 1988 championship game against Kansas. Mrs. Robertson also taught future OU quarterback Charles Thompson.

But her main job, along with that of her husband, Johnny, was bringing up their two sons, Ryan and Troy. For Ryan, that meant learning to dribble a basketball when he was three or four years old in the family garage.

"I can remember my dad taking me to the high school gym and we'd practice shooting," Robertson says. "I also remember playing first-grade basketball and being competitive but not necessarily good at it. By the end of the season, I was the best player on the team.

"It's like a lot of things when you first start, if people tell you you're good at it you end up liking it a lot more. I enjoyed it, from there it just took off."

Johnny Robertson had played football at Kansas State and briefly for the New York Giants. He worked as a homebuilder and built many apartment complexes in Lawton, in large part because the Fort Sill Army base expanded in the 1980s. By the end of the decade, though, the market cooled off and the family moved to St. Charles, Missouri, in suburban St. Louis.

Robertson worked on his game in the family's driveway in his new hometown. One of his favorite things to do was watching basketball on

TV—Magic Johnson was his favorite player—and see a certain play such as a no-look pass, reverse lay-up, or a behind-the-back pass in the game, practice it in the driveway and try it out in his next game.

In seventh grade in St. Charles, Robertson attended a local high school basketball camp and impressed the coach enough to be asked to try out for a select eighth-grade team.

"I made the team and ended up being one of the better players on the team as a seventh grader," Robertson says.

The next year, Robertson played for a small Lutheran school that made it to the national finals of the Lutheran tournament in Valparaiso, Indiana.

"We got beat in the semifinals by Clearwater, Florida, at the buzzer," he recalls. "Those were six- or seven-minute quarters and I had 34 points. There were games like that."

Robertson had many more "games like that" in store for him at St. Charles West High School the next four years. Terry Hollander, the man who asked him to try out for the select eighth-grade team, coached Robertson at West.

"He's the patron saint of St. Charles basketball," Robertson says of Hollander. "He's been there for 30 years and has coached generations of kids in this county. He's done a phenomenal job of shaping young men on and off the court."

Hollander and Robertson led the Warriors to the 1995 Missouri state championship. Robertson averaged 24 points, 10 assists, five rebounds, and two steals per game as a senior. His career total points (2,751) and assists (1,166) broke Jason Kidd's high school career record of most combined points and assists.

Such accomplishments brought a raft of coaches to Robertson's games, an experience he appreciated and disdained.

"It was a little uncomfortable for me," he says. "I loved that Coach Williams, Lon Kruger, Charlie Spoonhour, and Norm Stewart would come to my games. That made me feel special. But I also think it's asinine to have someone like Roy Williams feel compelled to stay in constant contact with me. I was happy when it was over."

Kansas recruited Robertson first after he attended Williams' summer camp in Lawrence as a freshman. KU sent him letters starting two months after the camp and then many schools began contacting him a month later. Kansas was Robertson's leading school, but then Missouri's recruiting efforts took off.

Notes on Ryan Robertson

Years lettered:	1995-96 to 1998-99
Position:	Guard
Height:	6-foot-5
Playing weight:	190 pounds
Hometown:	St. Charles, Missouri
Current residence:	St. Charles, Missouri
Occupation:	Regional marketing director for Hartford Mutual Funds
Accomplishments:	Third-team All-Big 12 in 1999; first-team GTE Academic All-American and PaineWebber Scholar-Athlete of the Year in '99; Academic All-Big 12 in 1997, 1998, and '99; "Dr. Forrest C. 'Phog' Allen MVP Award" winner in '99; "Dutch Longborg Free-Throw Percentage Award" in 1996, '97, and '99; honorable mention All-Big 12 in '97 and '98; Big 12 All-Underrated team in '98 and Big 12 All-Bench team in '97.
The Game:	Kansas vs. Kentucky in New Orleans, Louisiana, March 14, 1999

"The longer we went, the more difficult it got," Robertson says. "Missouri really put on a full-court press, especially during the last three months. They did a lot of things that made me and my parents consider them a lot more. It got to the point where it was a very difficult decision."

On his 18th birthday, October 2, 1994, Robertson ended his recruiting by calling the coaches still seeking his services to tell them he had chosen Kansas.

"I remember crying a little, not because I was happy but because of the stress and the relief that it was over," Robertson says. "I felt a loyalty to Coach Williams. I didn't think I could live with myself, after all he had done for me during recruiting, that I could spurn him and go somewhere else."

College Life

As with all Kansas players before and after him, Robertson acquainted himself to his new teammates during informal workouts and on the basketball court in pick-up games before practice started in October.

"You have a relationship with the guys once you get there," he says. "But you really get to know them and have them become your allies when you start to practice, going 'to work' with them every day and running through the same things they are. That's how you gain respect. They know how difficult practice is and they see you right there next to them doing the same stuff and busting your butt just as hard as they are."

The official start of practice meant "Late Night with Roy Williams," an evening of tradition featuring skits, warm-ups, and an intra-squad game.

"The thing I remember most was that Digger Phelps was interviewing the entire team on the court before we started," Robertson says. "It was so loud. I remember looking up into the stands, and it kind of took the wind out of me because it was an ocean of people. I wasn't used to that. But I had a great time."

Robertson faced a dilemma concerning playing time soon after practice began. Jacque Vaughn was the starting point guard backed up by Calvin Rayford. Jerod Haase was the starting shooting guard backed up by Billy Thomas. Robertson served as the backup's backup for both positions.

So Williams reluctantly suggested that Robertson redshirt. He and his parents discussed it briefly but decided against it. But as the 1995-96 season started, Robertson understood Williams' concern.

"The first half of the year was a struggle for me," he says. "I played in every game, but sparingly, five to 10 minutes a game."

Rather than hit the "freshman wall," Robertson's performance began improving.

"Right around Christmas, I got some confidence and had a couple of good games," he says. "From there, in the second half of the season, my five to eight minutes a game turned into 15 minutes a game. For a freshman, that wasn't too bad."

Robertson averaged 4.3 points per game for the 29-5 Jayhawks, which lost to Syracuse in an Elite Eight game in March.

The 1996-97 Kansas team featured seniors Scot Pollard, Vaughn, and Haase. The team went 34-2 in one of its most successful seasons in school history but lost to eventual champion Arizona in a Sweet 16 game. Robertson's playing time doubled that season, and he started 11 games in place of an injured Vaughn during the middle of the year. Robertson averaged 4.5 points that season.

Robertson took over as starting point guard as a junior and dished out 248 assists while committing only 93 turnovers, one of the best ratios in

Jayhawk history. He also improved his scoring average to 8.3 points per game and helped lead KU to a stellar 35-4 record in 1997-98, along with a second straight Big 12 regular-season and tournament championship. But KU again endured March disappointment, losing to a sharp-shooting Rhode Island team in the tournament's second round.

In Robertson's sophomore and junior seasons, Kansas won 69 games and lost only six, the best two-year stretch in school history. The team sported four NBA first-round draft picks—Pollard and Vaughn in 1997 and Raef LaFrentz and Paul Pierce in 1998. Billy Thomas, then the school's all-time three-point shooter, also graduated.

Robertson and his younger teammates would endure difficulty trying to replicate the previous two years' success in 1998-99. They were braced for a bumpy ride.

The Setting

"Fits and starts" most aptly describes the Jayhawks' 1998-99 season. The oft-injured team went 8-4 in its non-conference games with victories including Gonzaga and DePaul at home, Illinois at Kemper Arena in Kansas City, Missouri, and Pennsylvania in Philadelphia's storied Palestra.

Human nature being what it is, some fans were discouraged by the losses that included defeats to Kentucky in the Great Eight in Chicago (KU shot only 29.4 percent from the floor), Iowa at home (ending the Jayhawks' record 62-game winning streak at Allen Fieldhouse) and Saint Louis on the road (to a team that included Robertson's younger brother, Troy).

The conference season went better—mainly. Kansas won its first five games but then dropped an eight-point decision to Missouri in Lawrence and a 15-point defeat to Nebraska in Lincoln. KU won its next three, lost two more, won another three—including a Senior Night triumph over Oklahoma State in which Robertson hit the winning free throw with no time on the clock in overtime—before losing the season finale to Iowa State in Ames.

But the Jayhawks finally clicked in postseason play. Kansas won its third straight Big 12 tournament, defeating Nebraska by 24, Kansas State by 11 and then grinding out a gritty 53-37 victory against Oklahoma State.

Kansas drew a six seed in the NCAA tournament and defeated Evansville 95-74 in the first round in New Orleans. Five Jayhawks scored in double figures, led by Jeff Boschee's 17 points.

The second-round game pitted Kansas against eighth-ranked Kentucky, the same team that embarrassed the Jayhawks 63-45 on December 1. The game also offered a match-up between two of college basketball's top schools in history. Heading into the contest, Kentucky ranked first with 1,746 victories, ahead of North Carolina's 1,733 and Kansas' 1,688.

In NCAA tournament play, Kentucky had played the most games (116) and had the most wins (82) to Kansas' 85 games and 58 wins. The Wildcats had reached 13 Final Fours to Kansas' 10 and had won seven championships to the Jayhawks' two.

"This is a game you'd expect to see in the Final Four or a regional final," Robertson said at the time.

Kentucky also led the series between the two schools by a whopping 18-3. But statistics are more relevant for the media and fans than the players and coaches. Kansas improved vastly since its first meeting with Kentucky.

"I think they'll be respectful of Kentucky but not scared," Williams said. "I think we are more efficient. We are healthier."

Teams earn respect on the court. That Sunday afternoon in the Superdome, Kentucky was about to pay its respects in full to the Jayhawks.

The Game of My Life
BY RYAN ROBERTSON
KANSAS VS. KENTUCKY, MARCH 14, 1999

The Superdome was the first dome I had played in during college. Somebody mentioned offhand that it was very difficult to shoot in a dome. So I thought, "It is?" Then I started to think about it. We had our day of practice and I swear I didn't make a shot. And even before we played Evansville, I thought this was going to be an absolute disaster because I can't make a shot in a dome. I don't know what changed, but I got it figured out and things started to happen.

On my first basket [against Kentucky] I got a breakaway lay-up. T.J. Pugh knocked the ball away at the top of the key and I happened to be there. I picked it up and laid it in uncontested. When you get your first or second basket real easy, it gives your confidence a boost. Then our defense stepped it up. Because of that, I got a few easy shots and that added to my confidence.

We were down by four points [40-36] at the half and I had scored eight points. In the McDonald's All-American game when I was in high school, I played against Wayne Turner who was Kentucky's point guard. I remember guarding him during parts of that game. I also guarded Desmond Allison, Saul Smith, and Ryan Hogan. They were younger kids. Maybe that was a reason I could have an explosive game. I could focus on my game and not what they were doing.

[Robertson scored 19 points in the second half. He shot 7-for-8 from the line and was twice fouled while attempting three-pointers. He converted all three of the free throws both times.]

That was the weird thing about that game. Everything that I had done in the past came to fruition in that one game. There were only about five to 10 games of the 140 or so that I played in college that I got in a zone. That was one of them. Everything quiets. You concentrate. And the 40,000 people or so in the dome and millions watching on TV all of a sudden aren't there, and it's like you're on the driveway shooting with your dad. It was fun.

I remember taking two three-pointers at the end of the game that I normally never would have taken. But I had such good game up to that point that my confidence was high and we needed them. [In overtime, Kentucky never trailed and defeated Kansas 92-88.]

I've never seen a replay of the Kentucky game and I never will—or the [1997] Arizona game. To this day the losses are still painful, some more than others. People will say, "It's just a basketball game." I realize that. I take it with perspective. But it's hard to talk about. I still have a pit in my stomach when I think about those two games.

Game and Season Results

Robertson scored a career-high 31 points that day on seven-for-10 shooting from the field (4-for-6 on three-point attempts) and an extraordinary 13-for-14 from the line.

Still, he had to defend himself for a shot he didn't take. Robertson had a chance to take the final shot in regulation but two defenders collapsed on him as time wound down. So he passed to teammate Kenny Gregory, who missed a 10-foot baseline jumper, and the game went into overtime.

The media and the fans discussed the play in the days to come, but Williams ended the talk when he later said: "Ryan thought he had to make the play and that's the way it has to be done in basketball. Ryan played his tail off. To make a big to-do about that [decision to pass] is not fair."

Regardless, Robertson's collegiate career ended when the horn sounded at the end of overtime. He says the disappointment hit him while he was walking off the court.

"I was sitting in the locker room and Coach Williams opened the room up to reporters," Robertson recalls. "My freshman year began with the wind being taken out of me as a young kid from St. Charles looking up into the fans at Allen Fieldhouse. The same feeling happened to me as a senior, sitting down at my locker in the Super Dome.

"I never had more reporters packed around me. They were piled on top of each other. Someone I knew from the *Kansas City Star* asked a question, and as I started to answer I had to ask him to hold on a minute because I needed to choke back some emotions. I had to compose myself."

What Became of Ryan Robertson?

Robertson enjoyed a short but happy professional basketball career. The Sacramento Kings drafted him No. 45 overall in 1999 and he spent almost the entire season on injured reserve. The one game he played came against the Utah Jazz, and Robertson guarded future Hall of Famer John Stockton during the contest.

The next season brought Robertson back to the area with the Kansas City Knights of the ABA coached by former Jayhawk Kevin Pritchard. Then Europe beckoned: three years in Holland, a year in Greece and a year in France.

"The years in Holland were great," Robertson says. "My wife, Andrea, and I would take a weekend off and hop in the car and drive to France or take a flight to Italy. She traveled around while I was playing, and I was playing at a high level, making a decent living. We really have fond memories of Europe."

Robertson retired in May 2005. His agent enticed him with an offer to play in Italy, a favorite country of the Robertsons. But the couple had had a

BOX SCORE
KANSAS VS. KENTUCKY, MARCH 14, 1999

Kansas	36	43	9	– 88
Kentucky	40	39	13	– 92

Kansas (88)

	Min	FG	FT	Reb	PF	TP
Bradford	22	3-6	2-2	3	5	8
Pugh	24	1-1	0-0	4	5	2
Chenowith	41	4-9	3-4	10	4	11
Robertson	42	7-10	13-14	5	0	31
Boschee	34	6-21	0-0	1	2	18
Earl	10	0-2	0-0	2	2	0
Nooner	1	0-0	0-0	0	0	0
Gregory	28	4-8	2-4	3	3	11
Carey	2	0-0	0-0	1	1	0
Janisse	1	0-0	0-0	0	0	0
London	20	2-6	2-2	1	1	7
(team)				4		
TOTALS	**225**	**27-63**	**22-26**	**34**	**23**	**88**

Three-point goals: 12-31 (Boschee 6-18, Robertson 4-6, Gregory 1-1, London 1-4, Chenowith 0-2); Assists: 17 (Pugh 4, Boschee 4, Robertson 3, Bradford 2, Chenowith 2, Gregory, London); Turnovers: 14 (Bradford 3, Boschee 3, Pugh 2, London 2, Chenowith, Robertson, Earl, team); Blocked shots: 2 (Chenowith 2); Steals: 5 (Pugh 2, Chenowith 2, Robertson).

Kentucky (92)

	Min	FG	FT	Reb	PF	TP
Evans	28	7-11	0-0	2	4	14
Padgett	37	6-14	13-17	10	3	29
Bradley	13	0-1	2-4	2	2	2
Turner	39	6-11	5-6	6	0	19
Allison	22	2-2	0-0	0	4	5
Smith	11	2-3	0-0	0	1	6
Prince	27	1-5	0-0	3	0	3
Hogan	8	1-3	0-0	0	0	3
Camara	8	1-3	0-0	4	0	2
Magloire	32	4-7	1-2	7	3	9
(team)				5		
TOTALS	**225**	**30-60**	**21-29**	**39**	**17**	**92**

Three-point goals: 11-24 (Padgett 4-8, Turner 2-4, Smith 2-3, Allison 1-1, Prince 1-3, Hogan 1-3, Evans 0-2); Assists: 17 (Turner 7, Smith 3, Evans 2, Allison 2, Padgett, Hogan, Camara); Turnovers: 13 (Turner 3, Bradley 2, Allison 2, Prince 2, Magloire 2, Hogan, Camara); Blocked shots: 7 (Magloire 3, Padgett, Bradley, Prince, Camara); Steals: 7 (Padgett 2, Turner 2, Evans, Bradley, Allison).

Officials: Joseph Silveste, Rick Hartzell, Reggie Greenwood. Attendance: 15,804

baby daughter, Kylie, and they decided to stay stateside for the sake of the family. He also has a new younger brother, Dima, who his parents adopted from Russia.

Today Robertson works as a regional marketing director for the Hartford Mutual Funds, a mutual fund wholesaler.

"I call on stockbrokers and financial advisors," Robertson says. "There is a bit of travel, but at my discretion."

Former teammate Billy Thomas recalls Robertson as "a fun guy" who steadily improved his game while in college.

"He wasn't a typical KU point guard for his time; they were all shorter than him, faster," Thomas says. "But the one thing he did better than them was shoot. He had an unbelievable stroke, and he was a great passer, too. He had quiet confidence. We were backcourt mates starting my senior year. At the end of the game, we both felt like we could take big shots and both felt like we could make big shots."

14

NICK BRADFORD

The Life of Young Nick Bradford

Nick Bradford enjoyed an all-American life growing up in Fayetteville, Arkansas. He lived across the street from his elementary school. Besides convenience, the school's playground provided the perfect place to play all sorts of sports. When he wasn't playing basketball, he and his family followed the University of Arkansas Razorbacks led by Lee Mayberry and Todd Day. The Bradfords attended many games and traveled to Dallas every March for the Southwest Conference tournament.

Bradford picked basketball as his sport because, "I did really well in it. It was fun and other people were showing interest in me, so I decided to stick with it."

By fifth or sixth grade, Bradford played summer AAU basketball against the best players in the state and eventually traveled around the country as he got older. He played AAU ball through his junior year in high school.

"It got my confidence and everything else going," Bradford says.

Between his freshman and sophomore years of high school, college coaches started noticing Bradford as he faced the best competition in the nation.

"My brother, Ramon, pushed me and worked with me every day across the street and in the driveway," Bradford recalls.

As a senior, Bradford averaged 21 points, seven rebounds, and four assists for the 24-6 Fayetteville Bulldogs. Gatorade and *Scholastic Sports Magazine* both named him Arkansas Player of the Year.

Recruiting often is a double-edged sword for many high school players, and Bradford was no exception. He called the experience both "cool" and "tiring," while admitting he enjoyed the attention that went with the territory.

Bradford narrowed his college choices to Kansas, Oklahoma State, Arkansas, and Connecticut. Kansas won out, he says, because "I liked that it was close but still far enough way that I could do my own thing. And they had a great coach."

College Life

Bradford realized he might be in for a tough transition to college, but he didn't think the adjustment would include a broken nose during an abbreviated stay in Lawrence over the summer.

"I realized that basketball was kind of like a job, you have to do it every day and take a lot of time to work out," he says. "But everybody took me in. I was the only newcomer on the team; everyone else was back."

When practice started in the fall of 1996, Bradford backed up his roommate, Paul Pierce, at small forward and also filled in at point guard with Ryan Robertson for the injured All-American Jacque Vaughn. Bradford broke his nose a second time, and the injury kept him out of his first "Late Night with Roy Williams" scrimmage. "It was exciting and I was ready to get going," he says. "Seeing the fan base and everything, it was good."

Once Bradford was cleared to play, Williams had him working on his shooting and guarding the basketball. As Pierce's back-up, practice meant that Bradford faced the future All-American on a daily basis.

"I think playing against Paul helped me get better," Bradford says. "It helped my confidence. After guarding him every day, I knew I could guard anybody."

As a freshman, Bradford played in 34 of Kansas' 36 games. He averaged 2.3 points and scored 11 points versus North Carolina-Asheville. In 1997-98, Bradford doubled his minutes and averaged 4.2 points.

"We were still a really, really good team," he says of the Jayhawk squad that went 35-4 that season. "I think I improved and was heading in the right direction."

All of Bradford's hard work paid off as a junior. He earned a starting role and he essentially doubled his statistics from the previous season. In

Notes on Nick Bradford

Years lettered:	1996-97 to 1999-2000
Position:	Forward
Height:	6-foot-7
Playing weight:	205 pounds
Hometown:	Fayetteville, Arkansas
Current residence:	Fayetteville, Arkansas
Occupation:	Professional basketball player in France
Accomplishments:	Earned the team's "Forrest C. 'Phog' Allen MVP award" in 2000; All-Big 12 Conference honorable mention (coaches) in 2000; earned the team's "Clyde Lovellette Most Improved Player" and "Dick Harp Field Goal Percentage" awards in 1999; named Arkansas Player of the Year and fourth-team *Parade* All-American in 1996.
Nickname:	"Slick"
The Game:	Missouri vs. Kansas in Lawrence, Knasas, March 5, 2000

1998-99, Bradford averaged 9.1 points, 6.1 rebounds, and almost three assists per game. His top point performance came against Colorado when he scored 23 points. Bradford also led the team in rebounding and assists in six games.

"I became more of a leader," he says. "It was my best year scoring-wise, and Ryan and I took the responsibility of being leaders by making sure everybody was ready to play at practice."

Bradford was excited for his senior year in 1999-2000, not just for the prestige of his final season but also because the team had recruited three stellar freshmen in Nick Collison, Drew Gooden, and Kirk Hinrich.

"We had a great group of young guys coming in," Bradford says. "We wanted to make sure they came in, worked hard, and continued what we'd been doing the last couple of years."

The Setting

That season the Jayhawks raced to a 15-2 start through mid-January before losing handily to Missouri 81-59 in Columbia. After rebounding with a home victory against Colorado, the 'Hawks lost two road games, first to Iowa State and then to Iowa in a non-conference contest. Kansas went 5-3 in its next eight games to stand at 21-8 overall and 10-5 in Big 12 play before hosting Missouri on Senior Day at Allen Fieldhouse.

Missouri came to Lawrence with a 17-10 season record and an identical 10-5 conference mark. Emotionally, the stakes were always sky-high for Kansas and Missouri. But this time, the best the winner could do was finish fifth in the conference while the loser would settle for sixth. In other words, neither team was playing for a first-round bye in the conference tournament.

"I don't think there's a question that there's disappointment," Williams said. "Our goal at the start of the season was to win the conference championship, and we're not going to do that."

Bradford assessed Missouri and concluded that KU needed to take advantage of its size.

"We are going to need to pound it inside and hit the boards hard," he said before the game. "Defensively, we need to stop their penetration."

Bradford also understood the importance for the Jayhawks of keeping their emotions in check in the last home game of his career (and that of fellow seniors Lester Earl, Ashante Johnson, and Terry Nooner).

"I've seen three senior days that have been great," Bradford said. "They've been great because we've fought hard and won."

When it came to a Kansas-Missouri game, both teams knew all about fighting hard. The 2000 Senior Day match-up between the Jayhawks and Tigers would be no exception.

The Game of My Life

BY NICK BRADFORD
MISSOURI VS. KANSAS, MARCH 5, 2000

No matter what they did during the year, Missouri was always going to be a tough game. We always had to be ready to play Missouri. We wanted to come out really strong and play our last game to the fullest.

I drew Kareem Rush to defend but also would be switching to guard Clarence Gilbert and Jeff Hafer. These players were tough assignments.

We did not start out great, but then we calmed down a little bit and just started playing basketball. We got off the hype a bit and just played to get to the second half.

[Kansas led 45-42 at halftime. In the second half, KU led 65-61 when Bradford scored seven straight points to increase the Jayhawks advantage.]

I had missed a couple of free throws that I was pretty upset about. I got some open looks and wanted to be aggressive. I wanted to take the shot that came to me. I also stole a pass and made a dunk. Coach told us to dig in a little deeper at the end. I was usually pretty good at jumping in the passing lanes, so I wanted to see if I could do that. That's always big for momentum for the team and the fans. It was super loud.

Near the end of the game, we called a play and ran it to perfection, which gave Drew a good look. Hafer pulled Drew down for an intentional foul. I knew Drew would hit at least one free throw for us.

Game and Season Results

With 12.9 seconds left in regulation play, Gooden hit both free throws to put KU ahead 81-80. Hinrich added another pair a few seconds later and the Jayhawks held on to win 83-82. Bradford finished with 15 points and eight boards, second only to Gooden's 20 and 13.

In his senior speech, Bradford credited his brothers Eric and Ramon for inspiring him. Ramon, who had worked with Bradford for countless hours on his game, was killed in an auto accident when Bradford was in junior high. Bradford wore number 21 in his honor and won an award in high school named for his brother.

"He taught me how to play the game—ball handling, shooting, to keep getting better and good things will happen," Bradford told the appreciative crowd. "He helped me get a scholarship to this great university."

In the Big 12 tournament, Kansas defeated Kansas State before falling to Oklahoma State. The Jayhawks made the NCAA tournament as an eight seed in the East Regional. KU edged DePaul 81-77 in overtime in the first round and then dropped a 69-64 decision to top-seeded Duke. Kansas finished the season at 24-10.

BOX SCORE
MISSOURI VS. KANSAS, MARCH 5, 2000

Missouri	42	40	– 82
Kansas	45	38	– 83

Missouri (82)

	Min	FG	FT	Reb	PF	TP
Rush	31	8-14	1-3	2	4	20
Soyoye	24	1-6	3-4	9	3	5
Gilbert	35	7-17	0-1	5	2	18
Dooling	27	5-13	2-2	4	2	13
Hafer	28	5-10	0-0	2	5	14
Grawer	22	0-3	0-0	0	1	0
Kroenke	9	1-1	0-0	0	2	3
Parker	19	2-4	2-3	4	3	7
Gage	3	0-0	0-0	2	0	0
Schumacher	2	1-1	0-0	0	3	2
(team)				1		
TOTALS	200	30-69	8-13	29	25	82

Three-point goals: 14-33 (Hafer 4-7, Gilbert 4-10, Rush 3-5, Parker 1-1, Kroenke 1-1, Dooling 1-6, Grawer 0-3); Assists: 15 (Rush 4, Dooling 4, Gilbert 2, Hafer 2, Parker 2, Grawer); Turnovers: 13 (Hafer 2, Kroenke 2, team 2, Rush, Soyoye, Gilbert, Dooling, Grawer, Parker, Schumacher); Blocked shots: 4 (Soyoye 2, Hafer, Parker); Steals: 11 (Soyoye 4, Gilbert Hafer 2, Rush, Gilbert, Dooling, Grawer).

Kansas (83)

	Min	FG	FT	Reb	PF	TP
Earl	10	2-2	1-1	3	1	5
Bradford	28	6-8	3-7	8	4	15
Johnson	5	0-1	2-2	3	0	2
Nooner	2	0-0	0-0	0	0	0
Hinrich	35	3-10	4-4	3	1	11
Boschee	17	2-6	0-0	2	4	6
Gooden	27	8-13	4-4	13	1	20
Collison	26	6-12	2-2	6	2	14
Gregory	22	2-5	0-2	2	1	4
London	16	0-1	2-2	1	1	2
Chenowith	12	2-6	0-0	1	3	4
(team)				5		
TOTALS	200	31-64	18-24	47	18	83

Three-point goals: 3-9 (Boschee 2-5, Hinrich 1-3, Collison 0-1); Assists: 18 (Hinrich 6, Gooden 4, Bradford 2, London 2, Earl, Boschee, Gregory, Chenowith); Turnovers: 19 (Hinrich 4, Collison 3, Bradford 3, Gregory 2, Johnson 2, Earl, Gooden, Boschee, London, team); Blocked shots: 4 (Chenowith 2, Hinrich, Collison); Steals: 6 (Bradford 3, Boschee 2, Chenowith).

Officials: Scott Thornley, Bill Kennedy, Bob Sitov. Attendance: 16,300.

Bradford closed out his career averaging 7.6 points and 4.8 rebounds. He was named to the All-Big 12 Conference honorable mention team by the league's coaches and earned the team's "Phog Allen Award" as Jayhawk most valuable player for the season.

Williams said of Bradford, "Nick Bradford comes in with the high knee socks ... the whole thing last year where he gives up 30 to 40 pounds a game to play the four spot because of injuries. To give up his starting spot the last couple of weeks ... he's all about what is best for the team."

What Became of Nick Bradford?

After leaving KU, Bradford continued playing basketball. He first played for the Kansas City Knights of the ABA and then headed to Europe, first to Iceland and then to France, where he plays for Dijon in the country's top league.

Bradford remains very popular with his former Jayhawk teammates. Ryan Robertson considers him, C.B. McGrath, and T.J. Whatley as his "brothers." Jeff Boschee remains indebted to Bradford for helping him land a spot on a rival team in Iceland.

"Nick became a good friend of mine," Boschee says of their days together on Mount Oread. "He's the one I keep in touch with the most."

Jerod Haase appreciated Bradford coming to North Carolina's basketball camp to help out during the summer of 2006.

"He's as flamboyant and as good of a personality that there is," Haase says. "He's never met anyone he doesn't like, and I don't think that anyone who has met him doesn't like him. He's always upbeat and fun to be around."

15

DREW GOODEN

The Life of Young Drew Gooden

Most kids in the United States would consider a trip to Europe as a once-in-a-lifetime event. Not Drew Gooden. He traveled to Europe—Finland, to be exact—every other summer from the time he was six years old through his sophomore year in college. That's because Gooden's mother, Ulla, is a native Finn. The trips allowed Ulla and Drew to visit her family, spend time fishing and relax in the sauna after a dip in the lake.

Ulla met Gooden's father, Andrew Gooden, when he played professional basketball in Finland during the mid-1970s. They married, and later Drew was born in Oakland, California; a 9-pound, 2-ounce, 21-inch-long baby that the doctors proclaimed would grow to be 7 feet tall. Once Andrew Gooden heard that statement, he placed a basketball in Drew's crib. Gooden doesn't remember that gift, of course, but one of his earliest memories deals with shooting a Nerf ball through a little hoop that his dad hung on a wall at the family's home.

"I was around basketball since the day I was born," Gooden says.

Gooden stood almost 6 feet tall by the time he entered junior high school in Richmond, California, a suburb of Oakland. It was there he played his first organized game of basketball.

"I scored four points. I think we only had 16 or so, but I had four points," Gooden says. "I was like, 'Wow, so that's what a real basketball game feels like.' I'll always remember that."

From seventh grade through his junior year, Gooden grew to 6-foot-4 and practiced basketball as often as he could. He usually played against area high school players and neighborhood kids at the East Shore Community Center in Richmond, where his father had a job when he wasn't working construction.

By then, Gooden's parents had divorced, and Gooden and his father faced some tough times financially. While growing up, Gooden attended only two Golden State Warriors NBA games and one University of California basketball game at Berkeley despite the proximity to their home.

"Sometimes it was rough growing up, but getting past that made me a better person," Gooden says.

The events of the summer of 1998 helped make Gooden a much better player. In the midst of a four-inch growth spurt before his senior year, he wowed his fellow players and big-name college basketball coaches at the ABCD basketball camp in New Jersey.

"I wasn't ranked in the top 200 kids in high school that year," Gooden recalls. "I went to the camp and came out as the No. 1-ranked player. That's when I knew I could play. I went from local and D-2 schools offering me scholarships to Duke, Kansas, North Carolina, Kentucky, and other programs of a high caliber recruiting me.

"It was overwhelming. I had maybe 10-15 letters before I went to ABCD camp, then I got 500 letters from USC in one day alone. I went from off the radar to one of the hottest high-school prospects in the country. I enjoyed every moment of it. It was a great experience, and I'm glad I went through it."

Gooden's recruitment ended soon after it began. He and his father made a two-day trip to Lawrence in September 1998. Both were impressed with the University of Kansas' basketball tradition, and Gooden canceled his other trips and committed to the Jayhawks.

"On my official visit I met Paul Pierce and Nick Bradford, who was my host," Gooden says. "A lot of people who go there feel comfortable because Coach Williams recruits a lot of good guys. Considering the family atmosphere, I thought that would be the best decision for me."

Completing his recruiting brought Gooden peace of mind. He knew where he was going, and his parents wouldn't have to pay for his education. So Gooden focused on his senior season at El Cerrito High School in

Notes on Drew Gooden

Years lettered:	1999-2000 to 2001-02
Position:	Forward
Height:	6-foot-10
Playing weight:	230 pounds
Hometown:	Richmond, California
Current Residence:	Cleveland, Ohio
Occupation:	NBA player with the Cleveland Cavaliers
Accomplishments:	First-round draft pick of the Memphis Grizzlies in the 2002 NBA draft; named *Basketball America's* Player of the Year and the National Association of Basketball Coaches' co-Player of the Year in '02; named first-team All-America in 2002 and earned the team's "Dr. Forrest C. 'Phog' Allen Most Valuable Player" and the "Bill Bridges Rebounding" awards; named "Power Forward of the Year" (*ESPN The Magazine*) and "Big Man of the Year" (Pete Newell) in '02; selected as '02 Big 12 Player of the Year and All-Big 12 first team (AP and Coaches); All-Big 12 first team (AP and *The Sporting News*) and All-Big 12 second team (Coaches) in 2001; honorable mention All-Big 12 (AP), first-team Freshman All-America (*CBS Sportsline*), and Big 12 All-Freshman and All-Bench teams in 2000.
Nickname:	"The Truth"
The Game:	Missouri vs. Kansas in Lawrence, Kansas, January 28, 2002

Richmond. He led the Gauchos to a second-place finish in the state tournament (after winning the Division III Northern California title) while averaging 18.5 points, 13 rebounds, and three blocked shots per game.

In August 1999, Gooden packed up and headed east to Lawrence. He would become the 14th player (out of 15) from California to play for Williams at KU as either a recruit or walk-on.

College Life

On the basketball court, Gooden and his fellow freshmen recruits Nick Collison and Kirk Hinrich were seldom, if ever, lost. The same could not be said about the trio navigating KU's campus soon after arriving in Lawrence.

The three attended Traditions Night with a couple thousand other freshmen at Memorial Stadium the Monday night before classes started in August 1999. Traditions Night is an annual event in which school officials and student leaders instruct incoming freshmen on KU's many traditions, from the "Rock Chalk" chant to the significance of walking down Campanile Hill.

Finding Memorial Stadium in the fading sunlight was easy for Gooden and the two Iowa stars. Returning home to Jayhawk Towers in the dark proved more challenging.

"It was the first day we were really together," Gooden recalls with a telling laugh. "We were walking back to the dorms after it was over, and somehow, some way, we ended up on Iowa and 9th streets. We ended up walking all the way back down Iowa street to campus."

As Collison explains, "If you go from the football field west to the Towers, you can get into a neighborhood of curved streets, and that's where we got lost. We knew the direction we needed to go but we couldn't get there. We finally made it to Iowa Street and got home from there.

"Once you've lived in town for a while, you know how to get around, but at that point we really didn't have a clue. It probably took us two hours to get home."

Despite taking the long way home, Gooden says he adjusted easily to college life in a Midwest college town.

"You're there to go to school and play basketball," he says. "What else is there to do?"

Great question. In Gooden's case, it was learning to conform his free-flowing, run-and-gun game to coach Roy Williams' style of team play. At times, Gooden found the answer to that question hard to pin down.

As Collison recalls, "Coach Williams gets young guys and breaks them down a little bit, and then gets them to play hard and play unselfish, play the way he wants them to play no matter how long it takes. Drew was a perfect example of that. When Drew got there, he was all over the board. He would

not throw a basic chest pass; it would be a behind-the-back pass or no-look, or something.

"Drew was a little wild when we first got to school. His concentration wasn't very good. But everyone could see his talent. Some coaches would let him get away with things because they knew he was talented, but Coach made him play a certain way. I think if you ask Drew he'll say that Coach Williams did a great job with him and made him so much tougher and a better player."

Despite a quick hook from Williams whenever he free-lanced on offense or missed a defensive assignment, Gooden still played considerable minutes as a freshman in 1999-2000. He averaged 10.6 points and 7.5 rebounds for the 24-10 Jayhawks.

As a sophomore in 2000-01, Gooden led the team with averages of 15.8 points and 8.4 rebounds. The team improved to a second-place finish in the Big 12 regular season (12-4) and went 26-7 for the season. The Jayhawks also ended three years' frustration in the NCAA tournament by winning their second-round game for the first time since 1997 and advancing to the Sweet 16. With Gooden, Collison, and Hinrich returning for their junior year, along with sharp-shooting senior guard Jeff Boschee, the 2001-02 season outlook shined exceptionally bright in Lawrence.

The Setting

Ball State initially dimmed that optimism by upsetting No. 4 Kansas 93-91 in the Jayhawks season opener, a first-round game on November 19, 2001, in the EA Sports Maui Invitational in Hawaii. Gooden led Kansas with 31 points and 10 rebounds.

The team quickly shook off the loss.

"Coach Williams said the first team he took to the Final Four lost their first game," Gooden says, adding that the loss was a good wake-up call. "That's when we started winning games, the unity was there. Everyone was playing well. We were leading the nation in scoring, field-goal percentage, just about everything. We knew that we were better than our opponent every night."

Kansas won its next 13 games, and Gooden produced 11 double-doubles in the season's first 14 games. His top games in that span included a 23-point, 15-rebound performance versus Arizona in Tucson (KU won

105-97); 25 points and 21 rebounds in a 106-73 victory against South Carolina State in Lawrence; a 30-point, 18-rebound game on January 2, 2002, against Valparaiso (an 81-73 KU victory) in Lawrence; and a 27-point, 14-rebound effort three days later in a hard-fought 97-85 defeat of Colorado in Boulder.

UCLA broke the 'Hawks winning streak 87-77 on January 12, 2002, in Los Angeles. The loss cost the Jayhawks their No. 1 ranking in the polls, but KU returned to Big 12 play to defeat Oklahoma State, Oklahoma, Iowa State, and Texas A&M (all but the OU game was on the road).

Through its first 19 games, Kansas stood 17-2 overall and 6-0 in league play. The Jayhawks were ranked second in the nation. And Gooden, who led the Big 12 conference in scoring and rebounding, was gaining more national attention for possible player-of-the-year honors along with Duke guard Jason Williams.

Sports Illustrated followed the Jayhawks during the team's three games against UCLA, Oklahoma State, and Oklahoma in eight days for a story headlined "Hell Week."

The story included a segment about Gooden's appearance on Fox Sports' *Best Damn Sports Show Period,* in which he held his own with co-hosts Tom Arnold and John Salley and even played a Boyz II Men song on a synthesizer.

The Jayhawks story in *Sports Illustrated* ran in the issue dated January 28, 2002. That date coincided with Kansas' highly anticipated "Big Monday" showdown versus 18th-ranked Missouri at Allen Fieldhouse. The Tigers (15-5 and 5-2), like the Jayhawks, sported four starters that averaged in double-figures in scoring: senior Clarence Gilbert, junior Kareem Rush, and sophomores Arthur Johnson and Rickey Paulding.

The Kansas-Missouri rivalry needs stoking no more than a nuclear reactor needs a meltdown. But on January 28, 2002, both the *Lawrence Journal-World* and *Kansas City Star* ran stories depicting colorful incidents from past Jayhawk-Tiger contests. The *Journal-World's* story was headlined "Hatred has deep roots in rivalry," which featured anecdotes from former Jayhawks about some of the rough play on the Missouri's part and tough antics from their fans, notably the notorious "Antlers." The *Star's* feature, "Roots of a rivalry," took a more historical perspective that included vignettes about legendary KU coach Forrest C. "Phog" Allen, former

169

Jayhawk All-American and enforcer Clyde Lovellette, and former Missouri player and longtime coach Norm Stewart.

With that much build-up and attention, something had to give. A national TV audience on ESPN waited to see if Gooden and his crimson-and-blue crew could indeed separate "the Boyz" from "the Men."

The Game of My Life

BY DREW GOODEN
MISSOURI VS. KANSAS, JANUARY 28, 2002

You learn it when you come in: We don't fool with the Tigers. Me, Nick, and Kirk, this was our third year, and we had lost some heartbreakers at the Hearnes Center.

We played the best basketball we could possibly play in the first half. But so did Missouri, and we only led 43-42 at halftime. I was feeling it in the first half. I hit my first six shots and had 17 points.

In the second half, Boschee came out and hit some threes, Kirk hit a three, and I came down and scored an "and-one." We had a big run. Then we opened up a 35-point lead or something. It was crazy.

I think everyone on the floor that night was trying to guard me. I was feeling it; I was on fire. Travon Bryant, Najeeb Echols, Arthur Johnson, and Josh Kroenke were trying to guard me at different times.

I finished with 26 points and 10 rebounds. Coach took me out early. He took me off to the side and said, "I'm taking you out early because I don't want to mess it up."

I said, "Mess what up?"

He said, "This is the best I ever had a player play for me, the perfect game."

It was my night.

Game and Season Results

Kansas steamrolled Missouri in the second half, outscoring the Tigers 62-31 en route to a 105-73 victory, the Jayhawks' fifth straight triumph. Gooden scored 26 points in 28 minutes. He shot 11-for-16 from the floor and was a perfect 4-for-4 from the line. Besides his 10 boards, Gooden also had three steals, two assists, and two blocked shots. The impeccable Hinrich scored 23 points and held Rush to just 13 points on defense.

"We got into their shots in the second half and did a great job," Williams said. "It seemed like in the second half, everything went great for us and bad for them."

Wayne Simien told another reporter that Williams told the team "this was one of the most fun games he'd ever been a part of."

After the game, Gooden showed his comedic side—actually, most of his postgame quotes his junior season were laced with wit and humor, a slight departure from the typically dry comments given by Williams and most of his players—when he grabbed the microphone from a Topeka sports reporter so he could interview his father about the game.

The Jayhawks won their remaining nine conference games to go undefeated in Big 12 play. At times it seemed easy—KU won five of those last nine games by at least 27 points—and other times the 'Hawks were quite fortunate, as in a seven-point overtime road win against Texas, a one-point escape against Nebraska in Lincoln, and a nerve-wracking 95-92 regular season-ending victory vs. the Tigers in Columbia.

In the Big 12 tournament, KU defeated Colorado by 29 and handed coach Bob Knight his biggest loss in a 90-50 shellacking of Texas Tech. In the championship game, Oklahoma ended the top-ranked Jayhawks' 16-game winning streak with a 64-55 decision.

Kansas enjoyed one more winning streak in 2001-02 when it mattered most—the NCAA tournament. The Jayhawks survived Holy Cross in the first round and then dominated Stanford 86-63 in round two. The next game pitted KU against Illinois in a rematch of the 2001 Sweet 16 game. This time the Jayhawks prevailed 73-69 in another defensive battle.

In the Elite Eight game to decide the Midwestern representative in the Final Four, Kansas broke away from Oregon in the second half to win 104-86. Gooden, who scored 18 points and grabbed 20 rebounds, called cutting down the nets afterward his best memory as a Jayhawk.

The next few days provided Gooden with another magical moment. Before the team departed Lawrence for the Final Four in Atlanta, Williams walked Gooden up to the rafters at the south end of Allen Fieldhouse.

MISSOURI VS. KANSAS, JANUARY 28, 2002

Missouri	42 31	–	73
Kansas	43 62	–	105

Missouri (73)

	Min	FG	FT	Reb	PF	TP
Bryant	16	2-2	0-0	2	1	4
Rush	33	6-19	0-0	7	0	13
Johnson	32	3-11	1-1	4	2	7
Gilbert	33	7-15	0-0	5	2	19
Paulding	31	7-14	2-3	3	0	19
Stokes	17	2-4	0-0	1	4	5
Kiernan	1	0-0	0-0	0	0	0
John	2	0-1	0-0	0	2	0
Gage	11	0-1	0-0	2	3	0
Kroenke	6	0-1	2-2	1	0	2
Ferguson	7	1-1	0-0	1	1	2
Echols	11	1-3	0-0	1	2	2
(team)				6		
TOTALS	**200**	**29-72**	**5-6**	**33**	**17**	**73**

Three-point goals: 10-28 (Gilbert 5-9, Paulding 3-8, Stokes 1-2, Rush 1-7, Kroenke 0-1, Echols 0-1); Assists: 11 (Rush 4, Stokes 3, Gilbert 2, Johnson Kroenke); Turnovers: 18 (Bryant 4, Rush 4, Gilbert 2, Stokes 2, Echols 2, Johnson, Paulding, Kroenke, Ferguson); Blocked shots: 5 (Johnson 3, Paulding, John); Steals: 6 (Kiernan 2, Bryant, Rush, Paulding, Gage).

Kansas (105)

	Min	FG	FT	Reb	PF	TP
Gooden	28	11-16	4-4	10	2	26
Collison	30	6-11	1-1	6	2	13
Hinrich	33	8-11	3-3	1	1	23
Miles	28	3-6	1-2	4	1	7
Boschee	29	5-8	0-0	5	2	13
Harrison	1	0-0	0-0	0	0	0
Ballard	3	0-0	0-0	1	1	0
Langford	18	1-4	4-5	0	3	6
Nash	5	1-1	0-0	1	1	3
Carey	3	2-2	0-0	1	0	4
Simien	16	2-2	6-6	1	0	10
Lee	3	0-2	0-0	0	1	0
Zerbe	1	0-0	0-0	2	0	0
Kappelmann	2	0-0	0-0	0	0	0
(team)				3		
TOTALS	**200**	**39-63**	**19-21**	**35**	**14**	**105**

Three-point goals: 8-13 (Hinrich 4-5, Boschee 3-6 , Nash 1-1, Langford 0-1); Assists: 26 (Miles 8, Hinrich 6, Boschee 3, Langford 3, Gooden 2, Collison 2, Simien, Lee); Turnovers: 13 (Gooden 3, Simien 3, Hinrich 2, Langford 2, Collison, Lee, Kappelmann); Blocked shots: 7 (Gooden 2, Collison 2, Simien 2, Langford); Steals: 10 (Gooden 3, Miles 2, Langford 2, Simien 2, Boschee).

Officials: John Clougherty, Mark Whitehead, Rick Hartzell. Attendance: 16,300.

"I was wondering, 'Why is walking me up here?' Gooden says. "I thought I was in trouble or something. He said, 'Drew I want to be the first one to tell you'—then he dropped a tear—'your jersey is going to be up here. You've been voted co-national player of the year by the NABC.'

"I didn't know what to say. I was only a junior. I thought jerseys only got retired when you were a senior. It was breathtaking."

As the season progressed, two separate-yet-connected speculations took rise among Jayhawk fans and the media. The first was whether Kansas was a national title contender, and, if so, who would the Jayhawks play for the championship? The consensus answers were "yes" and "Duke."

The other speculation dealt with whether Gooden would return for his senior season. When you're 6-foot-10, accumulate 25 double-doubles for the season through a combination of power and finesse around the basket, and earn co-player of the year honors while leading your team to the Final Four, that question is bound to come up. While Gooden alluded to turning pro as the season wore on, he always kept his focus on the next game. Now the next game was against Maryland, not Duke (so much for conventional wisdom), in the national semifinals.

The Jayhawks sprinted to an early 13-2 lead before Maryland methodically took control of the game and led 44-37 at halftime. The Terrapins extended their advantage to 20 points in the second half with 6:10 left before Kansas rallied to cut the deficit to five points with 2:10 to play. But Maryland, behind Juan Dixon's 33 points, withstood the Jayhawks' final charge to win 97-88.

Collison scored 21 points, and Boschee contributed 17 points to lead KU. Gooden missed another double-double by one rebound as he scored 15 points and snared nine boards. The game marked Gooden's last in a Kansas uniform. He later declared for the NBA draft as an early entry and was picked fourth overall by the Memphis Grizzlies.

What Became of Drew Gooden?

Gooden had not played quite a month as a professional before learning that the "B" in NBA stood for "business" as much as it did "basketball." Eight games into his career, the winless Grizzlies fired coach Sidney Lowe and replaced him with veteran coach Hubie Brown. As if Gooden needed another reminder about the business side of the NBA, Memphis dealt him to Orlando later that season.

Despite the two shake-ups, Gooden averaged 12.5 points and 6.5 points and was named to the NBA's All-Rookie team. After a full season in Orlando, the Magic traded Gooden to the Cleveland Cavaliers in the summer of 2004. In Cleveland, Gooden is paired with superstar LeBron James. The Cavaliers made the playoffs in 2006 after an eight-year absence from postseason play. Cleveland defeated Washington in the first round before falling to Detroit in seven games in the Eastern Conference semifinals.

In the summer of 2006, Gooden re-signed with the Cavs for three years for $23 million. So, while Gooden's immediate future seems secure in Cleveland, he realizes he has a permanent home in Lawrence thanks to a sensational junior season in 2001-02.

"I know I'll always have my place in Allen Fieldhouse, no matter what happens," Gooden says in reference to his retired uniform. "I'll be right there."

16

BRETT BALLARD

The Life of Young Brett Ballard

The first Kansas basketball game Brett Ballard saw in person represented a game for the ages. On December 9, 1989, Ballard rode with his father from their home in Hutchinson, Kansas, to see the Jayhawks square off against Kentucky. In a game that seems as surreal now as it did that Saturday afternoon, Kansas continually broke the Wildcats' press and throttled Kentucky 150-95. The score remains a record for most points scored by a Jayhawk team nearly 20 years later.

"I think that was one of the greatest experiences of my life," Ballard says. "We'd always been Kansas basketball fans in my family, but that really made me fall in love with KU. As a nine-year-old I was pretty awestruck. That was my most lasting memory as a KU basketball fan before I came up here to play."

Ballard's first experience with basketball occurred a few years earlier on a Nerf hoop in the living room. Then he started playing YMCA basketball when he was all of five.

"You'd practice once a week for an hour, then play on Saturday mornings," Ballard says. "I used to get pretty fired up about those games. The cool thing about being a little kid is that there is no pressure. You can just go play."

The family also enjoyed watching the Hutchinson Blue Dragon junior college basketball team play at the city's Sports Arena. Every March,

Hutchinson hosted the National Junior College Athletic Association's annual men's basketball tournament, another must-attend event for the Ballards.

"Hutchinson is a pretty typical town," Ballard explains. "We had the state fair and a lot of other things going on. I really enjoyed growing up in Hutch."

As he grew up, Ballard played soccer, baseball, and ran AAU track from the fifth through the eighth grades. But basketball remained a constant in part because his father taught high school science and coached basketball at the middle-school level. Ballard often tagged along with his dad to go to his practices and shoot baskets on the side. In the summer, Ballard shot hoops at a full-length playground across the street from their home.

"I was over there three or four times a day shooting just because it was fun," he says. "As I got a little older, I realized there were certain things you needed to work on to become a better player. I went to Hutch Juco summer camp every year. The high school coach started a camp and I attended that. I shot on my own and worked on my own game quite a bit."

Once he reached high school basketball, Ballard harbored no illusions about ever playing for Kansas.

"I understood the level of athletes and the type of players that Coach Williams recruited or any Division I school recruited," he says. "I never considered myself good enough to play at the Division I level, really."

But by his last two seasons at Hutchinson High, Ballard thought he was good enough to play junior college basketball, a prospect that intrigued him—kind of.

"I started getting recruiting letters from jucos in the state," he says. "That was something I wasn't sure I wanted to do. All my friends had come up to KU. I wanted to keep playing basketball, but I didn't know if I wanted to go to a small town and play junior college basketball. I didn't know if I would enjoy that."

Ballard kept his options open and enjoyed a strong senior season, averaging 17 points and five assists. He earned all-league, All-Southwest Kansas, and honorable mention All-State honors, just as he had as a junior. Unfortunately for Ballard, hometown Hutchinson was loaded at the guard position, including a pair of preseason All-Americans. So he chose Cowley County Community College in Arkansas City, Kansas. Ballard started every game for Cowley and played significant minutes for the Tigers.

Notes on Brett Ballard

Years lettered:	2000-01 to 2001-02
Position:	Guard
Height:	6-foot-1
Playing weight:	175 pounds
Hometown:	Hutchinson, Kansas
Current Residence:	Lawrence, Kansas
Occupation:	Administrative assistant for the University of Kansas men's basketball team
Accomplishments:	Co-recipient of the team's "Senior Award" in 2002; All-Academic Big 12 in '02; backed up Kirk Hinrich at point guard for the undefeated Big 12 champions in '02.
The Game:	Iowa State vs. Kansas in Lawrence, Kansas, February 18, 2002

Between Ballard's freshman and sophomore seasons, the Hutchinson Community College coaching staff inquired through his high school coach, Phil Anderson, to see if Ballard would be interested in playing for Hutch his sophomore year. He was torn. He enjoyed Cowley, his teammates, and coaches. But still, the opportunity gave him a chance to play for his hometown team. He made the switch and averaged nine points and six assists for the Blue Dragons in 1999-2000.

When his sophomore season ended, Ballard faced a decision—for the third time in as many years—on where he would go to school next and whether he would continue playing basketball. This time, his options included most of the NAIA-affiliated schools in the Kansas Collegiate Athletic Conference, several Division II programs and Centenary, the smallest university in Division I. Ballard traveled to Shreveport, Louisiana, to check out Centenary, but he didn't want to attend the school. Once again, he was unsure of what he wanted to do.

Another possibility: walking on at KU. Eric Duft, an assistant coach at Hutchinson Community College, had contacted some of KU's assistants about his players. Duff carried credibility with the KU staff because he had worked at a Jayhawk basketball camp in the past. The Kansas staff knew and trusted him.

Kansas assistant Joe Holliday had scouted some of the Kansas two-year team when he attended the Region VI junior college tournament in Salina. By doing so, Holliday had seen Ballard play in his last few games for Hutchinson.

"He must have liked what he saw, because he invited Chris Zerbe, my teammate at the time, and me up to Lawrence to meet with Coach Williams to discuss the possibility of walking on," Ballard says of the exciting development.

The two players met with Williams in April. Williams told them they could come to KU in August and that Zerbe had impressed Holliday to the point that he "for sure" could be a walk-on player. Williams instructed Ballard to lift weights, do conditioning work, and play pick-up games with the team in August. Then Ballard would have to go through walk-on tryouts in October 2000.

"He said that if I did all the right things during August and September there would be a good chance that I could make the team," Ballard says. "After that meeting, I was on 'cloud nine.'"

College Life

When Ballard arrived in Lawrence, he worked as hard as he possibly could and made sure he was always on time. He left nothing to chance.

"The first couple weeks of pick-up games were very interesting because the players didn't know who Chris and I were," Ballard says. "Coach had introduced us, but we were just kids trying to walk on. They were all great to be around, but when it came to getting in pick-up games it was tough to get in. They would choose up sides, and they chose people they knew could play. They didn't know if I could play or not."

With playing time scarce, Ballard made sure he played hard when he did get out on the court. He says he gained confidence from the experiences and from being around players Kirk Hinrich and Jeff Boschee. He also proved himself. Three days before the start of practice, Williams told Ballard he had made the team.

"One person who really helped me out—the former players are always great—was Nick Bradford," Ballard says. "Nick had talked to Coach and put in a good word for me. He said I worked hard and deserved to be on the

Elsa/Getty Images

team. I really appreciated that because Nick didn't have to do that. I was certainly excited knowing that I was going to be part of the team I had grown up watching."

As the newest member of the Jayhawks, Ballard faced just one problem: The team already had been rehearsing for their "Late Night with Roy Williams" skits. Basketball, Ballard could handle. Skits and dancing, well … (gulp).

"I was about three days behind the curve, and I'm not the greatest dancer as it is," Ballard says. "Needless to say, I was nervous. It ended up being great. The game was great. I had never played in front of that many people before. I wasn't nervous about the game. I was so nervous about the skits that the game was a relief."

When practice started, Ballard's role was playing point guard for the Jayhawks' "red" team, which is the second team or practice squad.

"At first it was a little intimidating being at practice with Coach Williams," Ballard says. "KU practice is very demanding. One thing that helped me, about three weeks into practice, was when Coach Holliday pulled me aside and said, 'You belong here and you need to start playing like it. Play with confidence. Don't worry about missing a shot. Just go out and play.'

"So I did. My main goal was to make Kirk and Jeff better every day by pushing them in practice and making our team better."

To improve his game, Ballard says he spent a lot of time in the weight room to get stronger, focused on defense, and worked on his ball-handling skills. Being a walk-on at Kansas, as glamorous as it appears, represents hours and hours of hard work.

The hard work paid off. He began holding his own against some of his teammates at practice. As the season progressed, Ballard earned more playing time, and not just at the end of blowouts. For the season, Ballard played 154 minutes in 24 games, including 23 minutes in two Big 12 tournament games and 40 minutes in three NCAA tournament contests.

"To get in at the end of the game is great, but it has a whole other meaning when you get in crucial minutes. It makes it that much better," Ballard says. "A lot of people might have been surprised to see me in there, but it was great that Coach Williams had the trust to put me in there to be part of those big minutes and big wins."

Ballard also impressed teammate Boschee.

"When you looked at him, you didn't think he'd be a big-time basketball player," Boschee said. "But he got so much better during his first year. Coach Williams had confidence to play him, and that doesn't happen too much with walk-ons.

"He gave us a spark. He came in and did what he was suppose to do, didn't try to do anything special. That's why he got the playing time toward the end of the year and in the tournament."

With Boschee set for his senior year, the consistently improving junior trio of Hinrich, Drew Gooden, and Nick Collison returning, plus a talented crop of incoming freshmen (Wayne Simien, Keith Langford, Aaron Miles, Michael Lee, and Jeff Hawkins), the Kansas Jayhawks 2001-02 basketball season had all the makings of one to remember.

The Setting

Ballard thought the team "had a chance to be pretty good," but he wanted to gauge how good the freshmen would be. He was pleased to see them hold their own against the upperclassmen during the preseason pick-up games.

"Then we went out to Maui and lost to Ball State in the very first game of the year," Ballard says. "I thought, 'Man, we were supposed to be pretty good.' It was a little disappointing."

The disappointment didn't last long. KU won its next 13 games before dropping a 10-point decision to UCLA in Los Angeles. The Jayhawks regrouped and kept winning and winning in Big 12 play. By the end of January, KU was 7-0 in league games. The Jayhawks heated up February for their league opponents by steamrolling Colorado at home, Kansas State on the road, and Texas Tech at Allen Fieldhouse to reach 10-0.

On February 11, Kansas defeated Texas 110-103 in an overtime game in Austin, the Jayhawks' closest call in league competition. The 'Hawks returned home against Baylor on February 16 and won 87-72 to go 12-0. One more victory and Kansas would clinch a tie for the Big 12 regular-season title.

Standing in the way would be Iowa State. KU had already defeated the Cyclones 88-81 in a January road game. But the Cyclones were brash and had won the previous five meetings between the schools before the January game.

"Iowa State really had our number the year before," Ballard says. "Coach [Larry] Eustachy was there, and they really had it rolling."

The Cyclones had won the previous two Big 12 titles but were struggling in 2002 with an overall record of 11-15 and just 3-9 in conference games. Still, ESPN had scheduled the game months before as a "Big Monday" contest. Just what exactly "big" meant in this case remained to be seen. One way or another, though, history would be made.

The Game of My Life

BY BRETT BALLARD
IOWA STATE VS. KANSAS, FEBRUARY 18, 2002

The year before, we played Iowa State in the Fieldhouse and ended up losing by two points. Losing on your home court leaves you with a sick feeling in your stomach. Also, the year before at Ames, they were whipping us when I got into the game. Their great point guard, Jamaal Tinsley, had been "punking" some of our guards. He made some plays and started staring people down. He got in Kirk Hinrich's face. He got into Jeff Boschee's face. So I got in there, and of course I'm this little walk-on, so he got in my face. I didn't say anything—I just stood up to him. As we were walking down the court he got in my face. So there was a little history there for me. I really wanted to win that game at home and clinch a tie for the Big 12 championship.

The game was never close. We led 49-25 at halftime. When you get on a roll, the crowd gets into it more. Then you get in a groove. Our ball movement was great; we were able to make open shots. It seemed that for the other team that no matter what kind of shot they got, they couldn't get it to go in. The crowd sensed that.

One of the great things about KU fans is that they remember the past. They remembered the game the year before. Some of them wanted the win as much as the players did. We have knowledgeable fans.

I didn't really get in that game too much. I got in toward the end. I got open at the top and put up a three and it went in. It was icing on the cake. If I had missed that shot I still would have had great memories about that game. Just to make that shot, though, it's a little redemption for games with them that had gone on in years past. To get in, make a shot, and have the crowd go crazy is a great feeling.

I was excited about getting in and winning the Big 12. I had never won a league championship at any level. To be in there when we won and accomplished one of the goals we worked so hard to attain, it's just another great feeling.

Deep down, it's better to play and win in the close games, to know you fought hard. But for some reason, even though we won big (102-66), this game really meant a lot.

Game and Season Results

Kansas indeed clinched a tie with the victory and cut down the nets to the delight of the team, coaches, and fans. But the players carefully left strands of the net in the rim to signify unfinished business for the rest of the season.

"There is no better feeling in the world than cutting the nets," Ballard says. "You work so hard with that group of guys and the coaching staff since August, and when you accomplish a goal like that it's a great feeling."

Kansas managed to keep its focus and win the remaining four conference games to go undefeated in league play. The 'Hawks then pounded Colorado and Texas Tech in the Big 12 tournament before losing to Oklahoma in the finals.

"Going 16-0 was a great accomplishment," Ballard says. "We were disappointed we didn't win the Big 12 Tournament. Oklahoma had our number. But we got back on track for the NCAA Tournament."

In the first-round game, Hinrich was injured, and the sluggish Jayhawks pulled out a 70-59 victory against Holy Cross. With Hinrich back in the lineup, Kansas took its frustrations out on Stanford 86-63 in the second round.

Kansas faced Illinois, coached by Bill Self, in the Sweet 16 round. Illinois had knocked Kansas from the 2001 tournament the previous year. This time, Kansas returned the favor and defeated the Illini. Next up was Oregon with the winner advancing to the Final Four. KU clicked on all cylinders to throttle the Ducks 104-86 to reach the Final Four for the first time since 1993.

"It was great getting the chance to cut down the nets after beating Oregon in the regional final to go to the Final Four," Ballard says. "I can't

BOX SCORE
IOWA STATE VS. KANSAS, FEBRUARY 18, 2002

Iowa State	25	41 –	66
Kansas	49	53 –	102

Iowa State (66)

	Min	FG	FT	Reb	PF	TP
Bynum	30	5-7	3-6	5	1	13
Pearson	19	1-9	1-2	2	1	3
Sullivan	34	5-12	2-2	0	1	14
Morgan	36	2-7	4-4	3	3	8
Power	35	4-9	2-3	4	1	11
Homan	25	3-4	5-5	5	3	11
Jefferson	9	1-3	0-0	0	1	2
Varley	6	2-3	0-0	1	1	4
Fries	4	0-0	0-0	0	1	0
Nicol	2	0-0	0-0	0	0	0
(team)				5		
TOTALS	**200**	**23-54**	**17-22**	**25**	**13**	**66**

Three-point goals: 3-5 (Sullivan 2-4, Power 1-1); Assists: 6 (Sullivan 2, Power 2, Morgan, Homan); Turnovers: 18 (Morgan 6, Pearson 4, Homan 2, Fries 2, Bynum, Sullivan, Power, Jefferson); Blocked shots: 2 (Homan 2); Steals: 5 (Bynum 3, Power, Sullivan).

Kansas (102)

	Min	FG	FT	Reb	PF	TP
Gooden	26	12-16	2-2	9	2	26
Collison	23	8-12	0-0	7	1	16
Hinrich	29	4-9	0-0	3	2	10
Miles	25	2-5	1-2	0	0	5
Boschee	28	3-5	0-0	3	1	9
Langford	24	4-8	0-0	2	2	8
Simien	15	7-10	1-1	6	3	15
Carey	7	0-0	0-0	2	0	0
Nash	6	0-1	0-0	1	1	0
Kappelmann	5	1-1	1-1	0	1	3
Harrison	4	2-2	0-0	0	2	4
Lee	3	0-1	0-0	0	0	0
Zerbe	3	1-1	1-2	1	0	3
Ballard	2	1-1	0-0	0	0	3
(team)				2		
TOTALS	**200**	**45-72**	**6-8**	**36**	**15**	**102**

Three-point goals: 6-11 (Boschee 3-4, Hinrich 2-5, Ballard 1-1, Gooden 0-1); Assists: 25 (Miles 9, Hinrich 4, Boschee 3, Langford 3, Collison 2, Lee 2, Carey, Nash); Turnovers: 10 (Boschee 3, Collison 2, Miles, Langford, Simien, Nash, Harrison); Blocked shots: 9 (Gooden 3, Collison 2, Simien 2, Carey, Langford); Steals: 12 (Miles 4, Hinrich 2, Langford 2, Carey, Collison, Gooden, Nash).

Officials: Steve Weimer, Ted Hillary, Steve Olson. Attendance: 16,300.

explain it, but I just enjoyed it a little bit more, cutting down the nets in the league title game than I did going to the Final Four. Going to the Final Four was a little like a dream. It happened so quick that maybe I wasn't able to enjoy it as much as I did the game against Iowa State."

Kansas didn't cut down any more nets in 2002. Maryland controlled most of the national semifinal and defeated the 'Hawks 97-88 to end Kansas' season at 33-4. Two nights later, Maryland defeated Indiana in Atlanta's Georgia Dome for the national title and the rights to cut down the last nets of the season.

What Became of Brett Ballard?

Ballard has stayed in sports—particularly basketball—since graduating from KU. First he joined Lawrence radio station KLWN as one of its hosts for the station's afternoon *Hawk Talk* sports show.

"I wasn't planning on doing that, it just kind of happened," he says. "It was a way to make a little money, pay some bills and have some fun. It came pretty easy to me."

In 2003, Self replaced Williams as KU's head coach and hired Ballard as an administrative assistant for men's basketball. His vast duties include video work, film coordination, film exchange, as well as running clinics and camps.

"The thing I enjoy most—by far—is just being around the players. They are funny and fun to be around. I enjoy being around the Kansas basketball atmosphere, especially Allen Fieldhouse. Being part of game day, sitting courtside and getting paid for it; I feel pretty lucky. A lot of people would do it for free."

When he's not working, Ballard relaxes with his wife, Kelly; watches sports on TV; works out; and goes golfing when time allows.

Brett Ballard, the Kansas kid who worked hard to live the dream of thousands of Kansas kids, paused to think about his favorite memories of his student days.

"I enjoyed the professors, walking down Jayhawk Boulevard—especially in the fall when the trees are changing," he says. "It's like what I pictured college was supposed to look like when I was growing up."

That's quite a picture, but then it always is when dreams come true.

17

JEFF
BOSCHEE

The Life of Young Jeff Boschee

Despite an 11-year age difference, Mike Boschee exerted a major, positive influence over his younger brother Jeff. And in doing so, Mike Boschee also impacted the basketball fortunes at the University of Kansas—a school for which he never played—from 1998 to 2002.

Mike had played college basketball at the University of North Dakota in the late 1980s and early 1990s. Jeff says Mike provided him with a set of basketball shooting and dribbling drills from his college days.

"He had all those drills from UND and some other workouts to do," Boschee says. "I did those religiously, four times a week."

But what's an older brother to do? Jeff and he began playing together when Jeff was three or four years old in the family's basement on a small hoop their father had crafted. A rubber soccer ball served as the basketball.

"I was involved in Little League baseball and played football up to eighth grade," Boschee says. "Basketball was always something I loved to do. Even during the summer I was always at the gym shooting around. I got that work ethic from my brother. I was always around him."

The determined, constant play helped Boschee improve as a basketball player. He started for Valley City High School's varsity team as a freshman and averaged 12 points per game. Boschee quickly became known as one of the top players in the conference and state.

"Then North Dakota took an all-star team to Indiana [University]'s team camp that summer," he recalls. "I played well and one of the assistants was watching us play. The next morning he told me that he wanted to do a workout with me—and Coach [Bob] Knight wanted to watch.

"It was intimidating at first. I started off shooting with Ron Fleming, the assistant. About a half hour into it Coach Knight walked in, and that was a little nerve-wracking. He worked with me on my shot a little bit and told me some things he liked about my game."

Boschee's game improved throughout his high school, culminating with his selection to the McDonald's All-American Game his senior year. As a senior, Boschee averaged 26 points and six assists while leading Valley City to a third-place finish in the state's tournament, the school's best showing in 16 years.

During this time, college recruiters started finding Valley City on the map and began contacting Boschee with regularity. He considered schools closer to home such as Minnesota and Iowa State. Nationally, Duke was in the picture along with Arizona—the Wildcats coach, Lute Olson, began relying on his North Dakota ties to make inroads with Boschee.

Then there was Kansas, which was where Boschee wanted to go.

"Watching college basketball growing up, my brother complimented Kansas' style of play and the way Coach Williams treated his players," Boschee explains. "The biggest incident was when Jerod Haase went flying into the crowd after a play in Oklahoma and some of the fans started heckling and touching him. Coach Williams ran over there to protect him. That's special. It showed a lot of class and how much he cared about his players."

Boschee's parents, Floyd and Roseann, told him, 'Anywhere you want to go, we'll be behind you 100 percent,'" Boschee says.

So, Boschee committed to Kansas without taking a visit there. In the fall of 1998, Boschee headed south to Lawrence.

College Life

Although Lawrence is roughly 15 times larger than Valley City, Boschee did not endure any culture shock upon entering the University of Kansas.

"No, not really," he says. "Playing in AAU, I got accustomed to being in bigger cities, being around different cultures. The biggest thing was

Notes on Jeff Boschee

Years lettered:	1998-99 to 2001-02
Position:	Guard
Height:	6-foot-1
Playing weight:	185 pounds
Hometown:	Valley City, North Dakota
Current residence:	Overland Park, Kansas
Occupation:	Volunteer assistant basketball coach and private basketball instructor
Accomplishments:	Co-winner of the "James Naismith Captains" award in 2002; KU's all-time leader in three-point field goals (338); honorable mention All-Big 12 Team (coaches) in 2000 and '02, and All-Big 12 third team (AP) in '02; winner of the "Ted Owens Defensive Player Award" in 2001 and the "Dutch Lonborg Team Free Throw Percentage" award in 2000; winner of the team's "Cedric Hunter/Jacque Vaughn Assists" award in 1999; Big 12 Conference Freshman of the Year, Most Outstanding Player in the Big 12 tournament, and honorable mention All-Big 12 team in '99; McDonalds All-American in 1998 and two-time North Dakota player of the year.
The Game:	Kansas State vs. Kansas in Lawrence, Kansas, February 27, 2002

getting used to being away from home. It was my first time being away from family and friends for a long time. That took a while to get used to and not feel homesick."

Boschee roomed with Marlon London as a freshman, and the two got along famously.

"We were always acting stupid around each other," Boschee says. "We had a big stereo system in our apartment, and we'd throw on music and dance. It was pretty funny."

Boschee also bonded with Nick Bradford and considers him a good friend to this day.

"He's the one I keep in touch with the most," Boschee says.

When practice started, he took on senior Jelani Janisse, which Boschee considered a tough but valuable assignment.

"He was deceptively quick and so much stronger than me," Boschee says. "Going against him the entire year made me a better and stronger player because he was a heck of a defender."

That experience, along with Boschee's skills and the team's need at shooting guard enabled him to start every game as a freshman.

"I was thrown into the mix," he says. "They had Paul Pierce leave; Ryan Robertson was their point guard. T.J. Pugh was hurt. They really didn't have a 'two' guard. This gave me the opportunity to get in there and play right away."

Boschee adjusted to the faster style of college play and averaged 10.9 points for the rebuilding Jayhawks. Against Colorado on January 30 at Allen Fieldhouse, Boschee showed his adaptability by sinking a game-winning three-pointer with :06 left as the Jayhawks won 77-74.

"The funny thing was that was probably my worst game of the whole year," he says. "I hadn't made a shot, maybe two free throws the entire game. Then they called on me. Coach designed a play where we had a couple options and I was fortunate enough to end up with the ball and fortunate to make that shot."

In the Big 12 tournament, Boschee scored a total of 42 points as the Jayhawks improbably won the league trophy at Kemper Arena in Kansas City, Missouri. He was named the tournament's "Most Outstanding Player" for his deft shooting and all-around games.

Over the summer of 1999, Boschee hit the weights to improve his strength and stamina.

"The coaches were always there for us to do workouts—I think the rule was four players per one coach during summer and spring workouts," he says. "They did a good job developing us players and keeping us motivated. We had to lift four times a week. The strength coaches did a great job of working on our athleticism and quickness. From my freshman to sophomore year was when I made my biggest gains in strength."

Boschee endured some ups and downs as a sophomore in 1999-2000. He led the team in scoring in five games for the 24-10 Jayhawks. His shooting percentages improved slightly across the board, but his scoring

average dipped slightly to an even 10 points per game. He twice broke 20 points in a game, both times against Kansas State.

Besides his summer workouts that off-season, Boschee did something quite radical for him – he grew out his hair.

"I had my shaved head since my freshman year in high school," he says. "After my sophomore year, I had a bad second half and I just got sick of shaving my head all the time. I grew it out during the summer and it got to the point where I could do something with it.

"I didn't think it would be that big a stir until I got back to campus. It was all over the school paper and all over the Lawrence paper."

The new look added to Boschee's "matinee idol" status that he enjoyed during his four years on campus.

"I didn't expect it," he says. "The girls kind of took to me. It was flattering. I'd go out on dates with my girlfriend and have females come up to me in bars and restaurants. Girls were calling the house all the time. It was fun. Who wouldn't want to have something like that happen? But sometimes young teen girls would call and that got to be annoying."

Boschee shrugged off the "distraction" and took it in stride, as he tended to do with most everything else in his life. As a junior, he improved his two-point shooting percentage and raised his scoring average to 11.1 points per game in more than 200 more minutes than he played as a sophomore.

The Jayhawks also improved in 2000-01. Kansas sported a 26-7 record and ended a three-year streak of losing in the NCAA tournament's second round by defeating Syracuse before losing to Illinois in a Sweet 16 contest. The overall improvement bode well for KU in 2001-02. But no one could predict just how well the record-setting season would go.

The Setting

Kansas got off to an inauspicious debut in 2001-02, losing to Ball State in the Maui Classic. The Jayhawks quickly made amends by defeating Houston and Seton Hall for third place in the tournament. In the season's fifth game, KU lit up Arizona in Tuscon 105-97.

Game 10 saw the Jayhawks travel to Grand Forks, North Dakota, for Boschee's "home" game. He didn't disappoint the 13,280 fans crammed into

Englestad Arena. Boschee scored a team-high 23 points on 9-for-12 shooting from the field (including 4-for-6 from the three-point range) plus a free throw.

The Jayhawks' winning streak ran to 14 games before No. 1 KU lost to No. 11 UCLA 87-77 in Los Angeles. That loss would be Kansas' last for almost two months. Heading into the team's annual Senior Night festivities, Kansas had won 12 straight conference games. KU won most of the games decisively, until its last game, an 88-87 escape against Nebraska in Lincoln. The 'Hawks were 14-0 in Big 12 games and had regained their No. 1 ranking in the polls the previous week.

Kansas State would be Kansas' Senior Night opponent. The Wildcats were not a formidable foe, but a Roy Williams-coached club never took any team lightly. Beating Kansas on Senior Night and ending its undefeated conference record would be a major coup for the Wildcats. How, exactly, Kansas would respond to the challenge remained to be seen.

The Game of My Life

BY JEFF BOSCHEE
KANSAS STATE VS. KANSAS, FEBRUARY 27, 2002

We were playing our archrival, K-State. It was wonderful getting to see all those guys—Jeff Carey, Chris Zerbe, Lewis Harrison, and Brett Ballard—get to start (a sixth senior, walk-on Todd Kappelmann played later in the game). It's something special to hear your name called at the Fieldhouse. We played really hard. I hit some shots, and we got off to an early lead, 10-2.

When the starters came in, it was a little bit of a letdown. Sometimes you think when you have the bench players start the game, it will be a big downfall. But we worked our tails off and did some real good things.

[The game quickly turned into a rout. Boschee scored 14 points by halftime, and KU led by 20. He finished with 20 points.]

It was great getting to know the other seniors. Chris Zerbe was a good friend of mine who kept me loose. The same goes for Todd and Lewis. I guarded Lewis every day in practice, and he guarded me. They made things a little bit easier for me.

Allen Fieldhouse—what a great place. The biggest thing was coming in every single day at practice, walking through the hall to get to the gym and seeing 500 people there camping out for games. That gives you some extra motivation to practice, knowing those people had to get there at five in the morning to get tickets to see you play.

Running out of the tunnel, you never forget that. You do that so many times, but that last time was special. It gave me goose bumps. Hearing 16,000 people go crazy, to hear your hometown called and your name in the starting lineup. To see everyone throw their newspapers up in the air and the cheerleaders out in front of you ... that's the most special thing about that place: the atmosphere and the way the fans treat the players.

I watched the game when I went back home for Christmas. The senior speech was the thing that made me the most nervous about that night. Having my parents and brother there to watch me. Getting to say thank you to them. Telling Coach Williams how much he meant to my career. Thanking him for letting me come here to play was great. You can't say enough about how much he did for us.

Game and Season Results

Kansas demolished Kansas State 103-68 to go 15-0 in the Big 12. In the regular-season finale, Kansas outlasted Missouri—the last conference team to go undefeated (14-0 in the old Big Eight in 1994)—winning 95-92 in Columbia.

"Going 16-0, that puts a mark on our team as special," Boschee says. "That's pretty hard to do, especially when we played in one of the top two conferences in the nation that year."

Kansas won handily its first two games in the Big 12 tournament before Oklahoma snapped its 16-game winning streak in the championship game. In the NCAA tournament, Kansas' luck ran out in the Final Four against a talented Maryland team. Boschee scored 17 points, including five treys, in his final college game.

"Jeff was the most confident shooter I'd ever been around," said fellow senior Ballard. "He thought every shot he put up was going in. I never saw him get down or get in a slump. He also was great for me off the court. He took the time to help me out early on. Our lockers were next to each other, so we spent a lot of time talking."

BOX SCORE
KANSAS STATE VS. KANSAS, FEBRUARY 27, 2002

Kansas State   30 38 –   68
Kansas   50 53 – 103

Kansas State (68)

	Min	FG	FT	Reb	PF	TP
Siebrandt	27	4-6	2-2	8	4	10
Pasco	31	6-11	8-12	11	3	20
Reid	29	3-9	2-2	0	2	8
Atchison	29	6-12	2-2	3	0	17
Williams	35	0-4	2-2	4	1	2
Buchanan	2	0-0	0-0	0	0	0
Da Barrosa	2	0-1	0-0	1	1	0
Sulic	7	0-1	0-0	0	0	0
DeJesus	26	4-5	0-0	5	2	11
Canby	12	0-0	0-0	1	2	0
(team)				3		
TOTALS	**200**	**23-49**	**16-20**	**36**	**15**	**68**

Three-point goals: 6-11 (Atchison 3-5, DeJesus 3-4, Reid 0-2); Assists: 17 (Reid 7, Williams 6, Siebrandt, Pasco, Atchison, Canby); Turnovers: 28 (Reid 8, Siebrandt 4, Williams 4, Pasco 3, Da Barrosa 2, Sulic 2, DeJesus 2, Atchison, Buchanan, team); Blocked shots: 8 (DeJesus 4, Pasco 3, Williams); Steals: 3 (Williams 2, Reid).

Kansas (103)

	Min	FG	FT	Reb	PF	TP
Carey	8	0-2	2-2	0	1	2
Zerbe	5	2-4	0-0	0	0	4
Harrison	7	0-2	0-0	0	1	0
Ballard	4	1-2	0-0	0	1	2
Boschee	30	8-15	1-2	1	1	22
Gooden	26	7-15	2-3	9	3	16
Collison	22	4-10	4-4	4	4	12
Langford	13	3-5	0-0	1	1	7
Hinrich	34	9-14	3-3	6	0	24
Miles	25	2-3	0-0	1	1	4
Nash	3	0-1	0-0	0	0	0
Simien	14	1-2	8-8	7	3	10
Lee	3	0-0	0-0	1	0	0
Kappelmann	6	0-4	0-0	2	1	0
(team)				4		
TOTALS	**200**	**37-79**	**20-22**	**36**	**17**	**103**

Three-point goals: 9-20 (Boschee 5-9, Hinrich 3-7, Langford 1-1, Zerbe 0-1, Harrison 0-1, Kappelmann 0-1); Assists: 23 (Miles 8, Hinrich 4, Boschee 3, Gooden 2, Zerbe, Harrison, Ballard, Collison, Langford, Kappelmann); Turnovers: 7 (Boschee, Gooden, Collison, Langford, Hinrich, Miles, Kappelmann); Blocked shots 11 (Gooden 5, Simien 4, Collison 2); Steals: 17 (Boschee 4, Collison 3 Gooden 2, Langford 2, Hinrich 2, Ballard, Miles, Nash, Kappelmann).

Officials: Scott Thornley, Eddie Jackson, Kerry Sitton. Attendance: 16,300.

What Became of Jeff Boschee?

If Ballard said he spent a lot of time talking with Boschee, then it happened. But Boschee isn't the most talkative player to ever suit up for KU. He even admits as much as he described the process he went through to write a book about his career titled *Long Shot: Beating the Odds to Live a Jayhawk Dream*.

"It was a hard thing to do," Boschee says. "Mark Horvath, the guy from Chicago who wrote it, made six or seven trips to Lawrence during my last year here. It was hours and hours of interviews. That was the tough part, getting me to open up to him. He was a stranger. I don't open up real easily."

Boschee also continued playing basketball with stints with the Salina Cagerz of the USBL and the Kansas City Knights of the ABA.

"I was only with the Knights for two months," he says. "They had some financial problems, and I bolted for Iceland."

Boschee liked Iceland much more than he originally thought he would. He played for a team in the small town of Grindavik. What made the experience all the more enjoyable was having Nick Bradford playing for Keflavik, Grindavik's archrival, 10 minutes down the road.

Then there was Greece, which was not an enjoyable situation for Boschee.

"We had four or five Americans on the team, but none of us lived together and none of us were close," he says. "Driving anywhere in Athens takes you a half-hour to get there. When I first got there, I didn't have an outlet converter, so none of my stuff worked. I had a TV, but no cable. I couldn't get the American movie channels. I felt isolated and homesick."

Today, Boschee coaches and instructs basketball rather than play it. He is a volunteer assistant coach at Blue Valley Northwest High School in Overland Park, Kansas, and he conducts a basketball academy for children.

"I've done it since August [2005] and worked with about 60 kids third grade and up, boys and girls," Boschee says. "I do private lessons, group lessons, team practices. I like teaching. I never had a younger brother when I was growing up, so I like working with the younger kids."

Now that Boschee is firmly planted back in America, there's no telling what he will accomplish or help others to achieve.

As former Jayhawk teammate Drew Gooden said of Boschee, "When his feet are set, I'll put my life on the line that he's going to make it."

18

NICK COLLISON

The Life of Young Nick Collison

Growing up the son of a high school basketball coach, Nick Collison learned many things about the game at a young age.

Although Dave Collison never forced basketball on his son or ran him through drills, he imparted some of the game's nuances to Nick before he reached high school. These subtle fundamentals, Nick says, included moving without the ball, how to keep track of your man in the post, and playing defense away from the ball. Father and son also watched many games on TV together at home and discussed different game situations as they occurred.

But the most important lesson of all, Nick Collison recalls, came from one of his own observations.

"The biggest thing I picked up having my dad be a coach was how not to be," Collison says. "He had a lot of bad teams over the years and a lot of good teams over the years. When he had the bad teams he would come home and complain about his players, that they were lazy or selfish or didn't work hard over the summer.

"That's when I realized what you needed to do as a player, what coaches wanted from you. That helped me more than anything. I became more prepared than other kids."

Collison's basketball preparation began as a second grader in a YMCA league with 7-foot-tall rims in Fort Dodge, Iowa.

"I didn't really enjoy it," he says. "It was kind of awkward because I was big but not that coordinated. By the time the next year rolled around, I was playing all the time and really into it."

Dave Collison coached baseball as well as basketball at Fort Dodge. Collison went to many of the games and practices during grade school.

"I was always shooting on the side or playing catch," Collison says. "I would watch his basketball practices and they would talk about team defense. And most kids in fourth or fifth grade, you just roll the ball down and play. So I just picked it up."

If he wasn't at one of his dad's practices, Collison often played basketball at outdoor courts three blocks from his home.

"I played against some older kids, and kind of got 'beat down,'" he says. "I think that was good for me. I was surrounded by basketball."

When Collison was 13, his family moved to Iowa Falls when his father took a new coaching job there. Collison went from being one of the best young players in Fort Dodge to being just another player in Iowa Falls.

"They had a really good group of young players there—big, strong kids," Collison says. "I was a late bloomer, so I kind of fell back a little bit. As a freshman, I was not even good enough to play on the junior varsity team, and this was at a school of only 400 students, the second smallest class of schools in Iowa."

Collison may have been a late bloomer as a freshman, but he blossomed as a sophomore. He grew five inches to 6-foot-7 and joined an AAU traveling team after his sophomore season.

"That's when I made big strides," Collison says. "Every week we'd play in Chicago or a tournament in Indiana. It was my first time playing against bigger, stronger, faster kids. It made me accelerate my game. At the end of the summer I was twice as good of a player as when I started."

College coaches quickly took note of Collison's improvement. Iowa and Iowa State offered scholarships to him that summer. At first Collison wondered if he was good enough for Division One competition given his small-town background. When more colleges became interested in him and after another strong showing in AAU ball after his junior year, he no longer doubted his abilities.

What Collison wondered about, however, was where to go to college. He liked coaches Tom Davis at Iowa and Tim Floyd at Iowa State, but both

Notes on Nick Collison

Years lettered:	1999-2000 to 2002-03
Position:	Forward
Height:	6-foot-9
Playing weight:	255 pounds
Hometown:	Iowa Falls, Iowa
Current residence:	Seattle, Washington
Occupation:	NBA player
Accomplishments:	First-round draft pick of the Seattle SuperSonics in 2003; '03 National Association of Basketball Coaches National Player of the Year; consensus first-team All-American in '03; USA Men's Senior National Team in '03 and USA Men's World Championships Team in 2002; Big 12 Conference Male Athlete of the Year in '03; Academic All-Big 12 in 2003; Big 12 Player of the Year (coaches) in '03; All-Big 12 (coaches) in 2001 and '03); ranks second in career scoring at Kansas (2,097 points); McDonald's High School All-American (1999).
The Game:	Texas vs. Kansas in Lawrence, Kansas, January 27, 2003

men would be out of the picture by summer 1998; Davis announced he would retire, and Floyd moved to the Chicago Bulls in the NBA. Kansas caught Collison's eye in part because of Iowa native Raef LaFrentz's success there. Collison appreciated the Jayhawks' style of unselfish play and the raucous atmosphere at Allen Fieldhouse.

"Coach Williams recruited me pretty hard since my junior season," Collison says. "It was one of the best programs and somewhat close to home. My parents could still drive to the games, which was big for me. So, that pretty much was where I was going to go.

"Then Coach K [Mike Krzyzewski] at Duke started recruiting me. Duke has a great program. I visited both schools. I felt like I trusted Coach Williams more, plus it was closer to home. If I had gone to Duke, my parents would fly out maybe once a year.

"It felt a lot better at Kansas. So I made that decision."

College Life

Outside of a little homesickness, Collison found the transition to college life a fairly easy one. He roomed with his former AAU teammate and fellow Iowa native Hinrich, and became better acquainted with Drew Gooden, who Collison had met at a high school all-star game earlier in 1999.

"The first fall I was there, we ended up playing pickup games and conditioning and everyone accepted us right away," Collison says. "With Coach Williams' teams that's always the way it is. He recruits guys he knows are going to get along and are good people. They embrace you from day one, show you the ropes, and show you how things need to be done.

"That's the best part of college for me, all the teammates I got to play with. They became really good friends of mine."

Jeff Boschee, who was a year ahead of Collison and his fellow freshmen, said Collison had "a wonderful sense of humor." He needed it. Collison drove an older model Chrysler minivan, not exactly the wheels of choice of most college students. But what the van lacked in charm, it made up for in function, as more teammates and friends could pile in when Collison and company went out.

Then again, fun took a back seat to learning for Collison, Hinrich, and Gooden. The freshmen had been in Lawrence two months when practice started in mid-October. Collison says Lester Earl introduced Gooden and him to college basketball.

"He was a physical specimen," Collison says of Earl. "That was the one thing I struggled with, physical strength, as a freshman. When you have guys like Lester who are in great shape and play hard all the time, it wore us out. There were a lot of days when he kicked Drew and me all over the court."

Collison realized the value in those lessons.

"It was good for us," Collison says. "And it was good for us to play for Coach Williams, who I think is a genius at getting young guys and making them tougher. He knows exactly how to handle guys in the first year. I think that's a huge part of his success."

Thanks in part to his development as a coach's son, Collison says he picked up on what Williams instructed the team to do rather quickly. Gooden noticed this, too.

"I have to commend Nick for a lot of my post work and my footwork," Gooden says. "He had that coming in from high school and I did not. I think we learned from each other and got better together."

The 1999-2000 season featured a series of ups and downs for the Jayhawks. The team finished 24-10, losing in the second round of the NCAA tournament to Duke. Except for "Senior Night," Collison started every game and averaged 10.5 points (third best on the team) and 6.9 rebounds. Comparatively, Gooden started only eight games and averaged 10.6 points and 7.5 boards while Hinrich started 13 games and averaged 5.5 points.

"It was important for our development that we were thrown into the fire," Collison says. "We took our lumps, lost some games, got killed a couple of times. It was good for us to have that responsibility. We didn't handle it very well at times because we were so young. But it was good to have those bumps in the road."

As sophomores, Collison, Hinrich, and Gooden were part of a team that improved to 26-7. The team broke a three-year hex by winning its second-round game in the NCAA tournament versus Syracuse before losing to the Bill Self-coached Illinois team in the Regional semifinals. Collison averaged 14 points and 6.7 rebounds that season.

The 2001-02 Jayhawks enjoyed a golden season by winning all 16 of their conference games, going 33-4 for the campaign and advancing to the Final Four for the first time since 1993. Collison's stats continued improving as he averaged 15.6 points and 8.3 rebounds per game. By then, Boschee had played three years with Collison and considered him one of the top Jayhawks ever.

"He was one of best players in the post at Kansas," Boschee says. "He struggled a little as a freshman with turnovers, the way I did as a freshman. But when you got him the ball in the post, it was almost guaranteed to go in and you could run back on defense."

The Setting

"The sound."

When the Jayhawks were rolling, Allen Fieldhouse rocked with a joyous noise like few basketball arenas in America. Such was the case in January 2003 when KU roared to a 52-39 halftime lead against No. 1-ranked Arizona.

But in the second half, Arizona went on its own roll, outscoring Kansas 52-35 to capture a 91-74 victory. Kansas blew a 20-point first-half lead, the largest blown lead in Williams' tenure. Salim Stoudamire's 32 points, most coming from three-point range, stunned the Jayhawks and practically silenced their fans that Saturday afternoon.

"The only bad thing about playing in Allen Fieldhouse is that when teams go on a run you hear this groan," Collison says. "The crowd wants to be behind you so much that they get this groan."

That the loss was Kansas' second straight added some despair to the crowd's groan. Earlier in the week, Colorado beat the Jayhawks 60-59 in Boulder, Colorado. The Buffaloes' victory ended KU's 23-game regular-season winning streak in conference play, which extended to 2001.

So, Kansas was 13-5 heading into the game with third-ranked Texas. The Jayhawks were hurting physically, having lost injured sophomore Wayne Simien for the season early in the month, and emotionally, having lost two consecutive games for the second time in the season.

Collison recalls Sunday's practice was "upbeat," an approach that he and the team appreciated and responded to.

"It wasn't that bad," he says. "I think Coach was trying to keep our confidence up because he knew we had a tough game on Monday."

To the media, however, Williams sent a message that the Jayhawks had to toughen up and start hitting shots.

"You've got to shoot the ball in the hole," the 15-year head coach said. "You've got to be tough enough to shoot the sucker in, or don't shoot it."

Despite the two straight setbacks, KU entered the game a seven-point favorite, and coach Rick Barnes of the 13-2 Longhorns paid the 'Hawks the requisite pregame homage.

"I still believe they're a top-five team," he said. "I really respect the schedule that Roy plays. Because of the tough situation he puts them in, they're able to overcome a lot of things."

Toughness. Both coaches recognized that intangible factor, albeit from different perspectives. In turn, the two teams absorbed the lessons of the rigorous season.

"At Kansas, it seems like if you lose then it's the end of the world, especially the way that Arizona game went," Collison says. "The Texas game was a big game for our season. If we had lost that third straight game it would have been tough for us to come back from."

As both teams shot around that night in front of the anxious Allen Fieldhouse fans, and as ESPN readied its broadcast crew—including Dick Vitale—for a national TV audience, no one had any idea just how "big" Big Monday was about to become.

The Game of My Life
BY NICK COLLISON
TEXAS VS. KANSAS, JANUARY 27, 2003

That afternoon, I went over to Allen Fieldhouse with a friend from Iowa who had been living with me. I shot around for a while, which is not what I normally did before a home game.

Despite the change in routine, I wasn't feeling any different than usual before a game. I knew I would be in for a tough game dealing with James Thomas and Brad Buckman. Thomas was one of the toughest guys for me to play against in college. He was big and strong and rebounded so well.

I had good games against Texas, but they were one of the tougher teams to play. I really felt worn out after playing them because our frontline had to play so hard to keep Thomas, Buckman, and later Brian Boddicker off the boards.

The first half was rough. We got down by 12 points early, but we cut their lead to five by halftime (48-43). We made a little run and got back into it. That was huge for us.

I had 13 points and 11 rebounds by halftime. I knew the team needed me to be aggressive. I probably took some bad shots or forced the issue a couple times (four-for-13 from the field). I was really trying to get the ball and go play, not necessarily be so patient and get the perfect shot. Just trying to force the issue a little bit and get myself going.

I think rebounding helped me a lot. I was able to get in a "zone" rebounding by anticipating where the ball was going and being quick to the ball. Some games you had it and some games you wouldn't. Coach Williams used to call it "Losing yourself into the game." I totally did in that game.

In the second half, I hit a three-point shot with 6:12 left that put us ahead (79-78) for good. The pass came in high, I let the ball go without thinking about it, and it went in. The rhythm I got into in the first half just kept going the whole game.

I fouled out with 1:18 left in the game. Many KU fans watching on TV remember this because Dick Vitale gave me a standing ovation when I went to the bench—so I'm told. The thing is, I didn't see Vitale stand up. All I remember was being upset that I fouled out. I was worried that we weren't going to win the game, because I felt like when I was in there I could get every rebound.

Everyone talks about me in that game, but Kirk was huge. He had 25 points and hit big shots right when we needed them. Aaron Miles also played well. Everyone stepped up and wouldn't let us lose the game. You could tell we played our best to not lose the game.

After the game, Texas' coach, Rick Barnes, visited our locker room. It was kind of weird at first, because it had never happened to me. He just wanted to come over and say how much he appreciated how everybody played. That was a real classy move by him. Both coaches and all the players had so much fun playing the game, because both teams played so hard and played so well.

Game and Season Results

With Michael Lee hitting a pair of free throws in the final minute, KU withstood Collison's absence and Texas' final run to defeat the Longhorns 90-87. Collison finished the game with 24 points on nine-for-20 shooting and an astounding 23 rebounds, the most by a Kansas player in 33 years, since Dave Robisch collected 26 rebounds versus Iowa State in 1970.

Vitale's effusive standing ovation delighted Jayhawk viewers across the country when Collison fouled out late in the game. Surprisingly for a showman such as Vitale, it was only the second time he had stood at press row—generally considered a no-no given impartial media decorum standards—and applauded a player for his efforts. The previous time had been for David Robinson when he scored 45 points for Navy versus Kentucky in the mid-1980s.

Coach Williams joined the chorus of applause for Collison's performance.

"I don't know if I have seen a person as relentless on the backboards," Williams said. "Twenty-four points and 23 rebounds, that's a heck of a line."

BOX SCORE
TEXAS VS. KANSAS, JANUARY 27, 2003

Texas	48 38	– 87
Kansas	43 47	– 90

Texas (87)

	Min	FG	FT	Reb	PF	TP
Thomas	19	1-4	8-10	14	4	10
Buckman	12	2-4	0-1	3	3	4
Mouton	37	6-14	2-2	5	1	14
Ford	36	8-23	8-11	7	1	25
Ivey	28	3-6	0-0	4	2	6
Harris	15	0-2	0-0	1	1	0
Klotz	26	4-8	0-2	5	4	8
Ross	4	0-0	0-0	1	1	0
Boddicker	23	6-9	2-2	3	4	20
(team)				2		
TOTALS	200	30-70	20-28	45	21	87

Three-point goals: 7-16 (Boddicker 6-9, Ford 1-4, Harris 0-2, Mouton 0-1); Assists: 17 (Ford 10, Mouton 2, Buckman, Ross, Boddicker); Turnovers: 15 (Mouton 5, Thomas 3, Ford 2, Buckman, Klotz, Ross, Boddicker); Blocked shots: 9 (Klotz 3, Buckman 2, Ivey); Steals: 7 (Mouton 2, Ford 2, Boddicker 2, Thomas).

Kansas (90)

	Min	FG	FT	Reb	PF	TP
Collison	36	9-20	5-6	23	5	24
Graves	18	1-4	3-3	5	5	5
Langford	36	5-13	0-2	2	2	10
Hinrich	39	7-14	8-11	2	2	25
Miles	30	7-14	0-0	5	3	15
Hawkins	3	0-0	0-0	0	2	0
Lee	14	1-1	2-2	1	2	4
Nash	16	2-2	2-3	3	1	7
Niang	8	0-0	0-1	0	1	0
(team)				2		
TOTALS	200	32-68	20-28	43	23	90

Three-point goals: 4-8 (Miles 2-3, Langford 1-1, Lee 1-2, Giddens 0-2); Assists: 18 (Miles 6, Langford 5, Giddens 3, Lee 2, Simien, Moody); Turnovers: 10 (Simien 3, Langford 2, Giddens 2, Moody, Miles, Kaun); Blocked shots: 1 (Simien); Steals: 4 (Giddens 2, Miles, Lee).

Officials: Ted Hillary, John Clougherty, Mike Whitehead. Attendance: 16,300.

The number "24" also represented the number of NBA scouts attending the game. Collison barely noticed.

"We always had a lot of scouts the game, with Drew the year before, Kirk and me, so I didn't pay too much attention to that," he says. "T.J. Ford [of Texas] also was playing in that game. It was a big enough game already. I knew the scouts would see me regardless."

Besides the scouts and the usual 16,300 frenzied fans (150 of whom uncharacteristically stormed James Naismith Court after the game), former Jayhawk great and Jo Jo White also attended the game. The university honored him by retiring his number 15 jersey at halftime. Ted Owens, White's coach from the 1960s, introduced the two-time All-American.

Perhaps the most out-of-place fan in Allen Field House that evening was former long-time Missouri coach Norm Stewart. Williams invited Stewart to Lawrence for the game in recognition of his tireless work for "Coaches vs. Cancer." No doubt Stewart also stood and saluted Collison for his tremendous game, which would have marked the first time in more than 30 visits to the venerable fieldhouse that the Kansas faithful did not chide Stewart to "Sit down, Norm!"

The Jayhawks won six straight league games after defeating Texas until a late-season loss to Oklahoma in Norman. Kansas won the regular-season Big 12 title with a 14-2 record, one game ahead of Texas and two better than Oklahoma. Texas joined the Jayhawks in the Final Four in New Orleans that season, and Oklahoma reached the Elite Eight.

In Collison's last 15 college games, including the six-game run during the NCAA tournament, he accomplished 10 double-doubles, including a 33-point, 19-rebound game against Duke in the Regional semifinals, and a 19-point, 21-rebound effort versus Syracuse in the national championship game. He holds the Kansas record for most rebounds (181) in 16 NCAA tournament games.

Collison's list of superlatives and accomplishments goes on and on, but after a while the statistics meld into the cacophony of a great collegiate career. The annual Kansas basketball media guides teem with this kind of information, which when examined closely, is staggering in its breadth and depth of noteworthy accomplishments for a program as a whole and an individual player as successful as Nick Collison.

Collison is used to the din, obviously, having played four years in the choreographed noise box that Allen Fieldhouse becomes from mid-November to early March every basketball season since 1955 and caused the decibel level to rise with his stellar play.

"There were only five or six games where it sounded like that," Collison says recalling that late January night in 2003. "When it sounds like that, there isn't a better place to play. It's so loud, it can't get any louder and you can't hear anything. It's a lot of fun to play that way."

What Became of Nick Collison?

The year 2003 was one of the best in Collison's life: national player of the year honors, recognition as a consensus first-team All-American, helping to lead the Jayhawks to a national championship game appearance and topped off by being selected in the first round of the NBA draft by the Seattle SuperSonics, the 12th player picked overall.

Then, as he started his pro career, an old nemesis—shoulder injury—returned.

"All four years of school, my left shoulder would slip from time to time. It would be painful, but I just played through it," Collison says. "I got an MRI once and they said there was nothing structurally wrong. The ligaments got stretched and it was unstable, so I just learned to play through it."

On the third day of the Sonics training camp, Collison's left shoulder popped out of joint three times on three straight plays. This time "playing through it" was not an option and surgery followed. Collison missed the entire 2003-04 season but actively rehabilitated first his left shoulder and then his right shoulder, which was operated on in February 2004.

"I didn't look at it too negatively. That whole year I realized I was very fortunate to be in the NBA and still have an opportunity to get healthy," Collison says. "Everyone told me I could make a full recovery if I did the work.

"I kept a positive mind-set when it was really pretty boring. I didn't get down and depressed. It was long and monotonous, but I focused on the rehab and was excited by my progress. Every week, I was able to do something more. I got through it and had a pretty decent rookie year [in 2004-05]."

Indeed, Collison appeared in all 82 games that season, averaging 5.6 points and 4.6 rebounds. He improved those numbers in 11 playoff games, averaging 8.4 points and five rebounds. A foot injury cost Collison 16 games in 2005-06, but he improved his regular season statistics to 7.5 points and 5.6 rebounds in almost 22 minutes of playing time per game.

Not surprisingly, Collison enjoys his NBA experience.

"It's a fun life. The best part about it is that you just have to play basketball and don't have to do much else," he says. "Every two or three days you have a game, get to travel the country and play against the best players in the world."

Still, Collison realizes how much he enjoyed himself at Kansas.

"Besides the Texas game, beating Missouri at Columbia my junior year to finish the conference season undefeated, then my senior year to win the conference, going to two Final Fours, all were great memories," he says. "Then there was just hanging out with the guys on the team—times after practice, we'd be in the locker room for an hour watching TV and messing around. Those were probably the most fun times. Or going out on the weekend, everybody piling into my minivan and going out to party.

"We were a real close-knit group. It was a great way to go to college: playing basketball."

19

KEITH LANGFORD

The Life of Young Keith Langford

In the summer growing up, Keith Langford always had game. Trouble was, Langford's game was football. But he spent his summers in The Bronx where his father, André Langford, lived.

"I used to love football, but during the summer there was no place to play," Langford explains. "So, we'd go to the playground and play basketball."

The times Langford spent on the courts of the New York borough would pay off for him back in his native Fort Worth. As an eighth grader, Langford's friends tried out for their school's team. They asked Langford if he'd like to do the same. The decision was not as automatic as people might think.

"I took the permission slip home to my mom [Charlene Taylor], and she said I was going to have to get a lot better if I was gong to play basketball," he says. "It all started from there."

Langford kept playing basketball. His game improved from the steady practice and play. As a sophomore, he grew a couple of inches and played the post.

"I really started to see the benefits you could get out of basketball," Langford says. "It was one of the ways that I could go to college."

He and his mother discussed his future. They decided if Langford couldn't go to college, he would join the U.S. Army. Of the two choices, both preferred college. So Langford further focused his efforts on basketball that summer with an eye toward playing basketball at a junior college or small Division I program.

Around that time, one of Langford's high school teammates attended an AAU basketball tryout. Langford went along and played well. This series of events led him to meet Wes Grandstaff, his AAU coach for Team Texas.

"He helped a lot with rides to practice, times I couldn't depend on family members to do things or be at events, he was there for me," Langford says. "My family really took a liking to him. He came to a ton of college games. I still call him now. He's more of a family member than a mentor."

Between playing for North Crowley High School in Fort Worth and the Team Texas AAU squad, Langford had a steady diet of hoops to help elevate his game. A left-hander, Langford modeled his game after fellow southpaw Jalen Rose of the NBA.

"I enjoyed how easy he made things look, and I have that same kind of demeanor in my play," Langford says.

Langford's demeanor on the court represented pure drive and determination. He explains that his drive came from growing up on Fort Worth's south side.

"A lot of guys from there just don't make it," Langford says. "A lot of guys don't have a familiar face or anything positive that they can see, like a guy they know graduating from college.

"For every person who says, 'You can do well,' there are just as many thinking negatively about you. I always had those people in the back of mind. They continue to drive me to be successful. A lot of it comes from my family, too. I want them to enjoy my success as much as I do."

Langford enjoyed plenty of success at North Crowley. As a senior, he averaged 25.7 points, 8.6 rebounds, and 4.2 assists per game. He led the Panthers to a 29-5 record and helped them win a district, bi-district, and area championship.

With the success came the recruiting. Most players tire of the incessant sales pitches, but not Langford.

"It was one of the best times of my life," he says. "You hear a lot of people complain that 'this coach called me or sent me a letter every day.' I was the guy coming home looking for letters in the mail every day. There's nothing like being wanted.

"Some of the letters might be form letters, and some are hand-written. Then you have guys coming up to the school to watch you play. It was incredible. I really enjoyed that process."

Notes on Keith Langford

Years lettered:	2001-02 to 2004-05
Position:	Guard
Height:	6-foot-4
Playing weight:	205 pounds
Hometown:	Fort Worth, Texas
Current residence:	Fort Worth, Texas
Occupation:	Professional basketball player in Italy
Accomplishments:	All-Big 12 second team (AP and coaches) in 2005; co-winner of the team's "James Naismith Captains" award in '05; Preseason and Midseason Wooden Award Watch List and Preseason Naismith Award Watch List in '05; second-team All-Big 12 in 2004; Wooden Award finalist in '04; NCAA All-Final Four Team in 2003; honorable mention All Big 12 and Big 12 All-Underrated Team in '03; winner of the team's "Clyde Lovellette Most Improved Player" award in 2002.
Nickname:	"Freeze"
The Game:	Kansas vs. Marquette in New Orleans, Louisiana, April 5, 2003

As a junior, Langford verbally committed to the University of Mississippi. The SEC school attracted him because of its size and the level of competition—such as the storied program of Kentucky—the league offered.

In the summer of 2000 between his junior and senior years, Langford had a change of heart after a strong showing at a Nike camp. Many more coaches showed interest in him and he wavered. Finally, he decided he did not want to go to Ole Miss.

"My mom and I sat down and we called the Mississippi coaches," Langford says. "It was one of the toughest things I've ever had to do, to tell them I wasn't going there. We had developed a great relationship."

Langford appreciated how Kansas coach Roy Williams handled the delicate situation during Langford's reconsideration.

"Coach Williams was real classy about the whole thing," Langford says. "He said we won't recruit you, much less discuss anything with you, until I publicly rescinded my commitment. We went through that whole process.

"My mom was gung-ho. Kansas was the Big 12, and played a lot of games in Texas, plus, the Big 12 tournament was going to Dallas."

The following sentence may shock many Jayhawk fans, but Langford insists that Kansas "is not a big name" where he comes from. His first exposure to KU occurred in 1998 when the Jayhawks met Prairie View A&M in the first round of the NCAA tournament. Langford caught the game on TV because he knew a couple of Prairie View's players from his neighborhood. Two years later, Langford became a Jayhawk.

"So, it was a big thing to have Coach Williams come to my neighborhood and be in my school," he says.

If one were to ask Williams, no doubt he'd say it was a big deal to have Langford come to his school, too.

College Life

Langford arrived in Lawrence in the summer of 2001 as one-fifth of the highly regarded freshman class that also featured Wayne Simien, Aaron Miles, Michael Lee, and Jeff Hawkins, who would take a redshirt that first season.

"They were all really good guys," Langford says. "It was all about winning rather than individual goals. Coach Williams and his staff did a good job explaining to us what our roles would be and what we would need to do for the team to win.

"They brought a bunch of guys together who didn't have personality conflicts. They knew what they really wanted, and that's what they ended up with."

Langford admits that he went through some culture shock adjusting to Lawrence. He adds that he didn't mind one bit.

"I don't want to seem brash, but I had always been around more black people," he says. "But [coming to KU] helped me in everything from how I carried myself, to the way I talked to people, to how I act, being able to articulate and communicate. I'd make the same decision 100 times if I could."

A lesser form of culture shock occurred for Langford when the annual "Late Night" skits and scrimmage rolled around in mid-October.

"It was incredibly nerve-wracking," he recalls. "I hadn't played in front of more than 2,000 people, and I probably knew half of them because they were from Fort Worth.

"I didn't even want the ball. I didn't want it to come my way. I knew that first shot was going over the goal or I'd lose it off my leg.

"The only way I got over it was to tell myself, 'These people want you to do good. You don't have to be nervous. They don't want you to fail, they want the team to win.'"

In practice, Langford usually went up against Bryant Nash, who he had seen play in high school in Texas.

"When I first got there, it was tough to keep him off the boards," Langford says. "He was a high jumper. Coach would really get on me about blocking out. Bryant knew the ropes, so he would take advantage of me sometimes."

When the season started, Langford experienced what many former high school stars go through as college freshmen: the bench. Williams told the reserves to "help us by not hurting us." He emphasized defense, penetrating to the basket when possible, rebounding, and running the floor.

"It was kind of tough at first," Langford says. "You come from high school, averaging 27.5 points per game, everything is going through you, you're bringing the ball up, posting up, all kinds of freedom, then you have to become a role player. But it was easy for me to adapt."

Langford's first game as a Jayhawk ended in defeat to Ball State in the Maui Invitational. By the team's third game in Hawaii, Langford drove the lane for a basket and was fouled.

"I remember that I got caught up in the moment and stuck my tongue out at the camera," he says. "I got in the groove of the game. I was having fun playing. I remember a lot of my homeboys calling me after that saying, 'Man, you were on ESPN.'

"Knowing that I was involved got me over the hump. I still had slumps and times when I lost confidence, but playing in that game and ... being able to compete against them and be successful helped me."

For the season, Langford averaged 7.9 points in 19 minutes of playing time per game. He scored his season high of 20 points versus Oregon in the Elite Eight game that sent Kansas to the Final Four.

"As a freshman, he was quiet and didn't say much," says former teammate Jeff Boschee. "As he got older and became one of the team leaders, it was funny to see how verbal he was with his leadership. He was the best person I've ever seen getting to the basket. It was so easy for him. He just slithered around defenders."

The Setting

Langford started all 38 games as a sophomore and doubled his scoring average to 15.9 points. He scored in double-figures in all but two games and helped lead the Jayhawks back to the Final Four. In the first-round game against Utah State, Langford led the 'Hawks with 22 points as KU edged the Aggies 64-61. He contributed 19 in the rout of Arizona State and scored 13 against both Duke and Arizona in the West Regional.

In the Midwest Regional Finals, Marquette dismantled Kentucky 83-69 to advance to its first Final Four since 1977. Guard Dwyane Wade led the Golden Eagles resurgence, and he became Langford's focal point heading into the national semifinals in New Orleans.

"We watched film on Marquette," Langford says. "Dwyane Wade was having an incredible NCAA Tournament. We watched him play Kentucky, and Wade had the only triple-double in tournament history."

Williams said the day before the game that he wasn't letting the team watch any more film of the Marquette-Kentucky game "because it was scary." Kansas' game plan called for the 6-foot-3 Hinrich to guard the 6-foot-5 Wade. Meanwhile, Langford drew the assignment of guarding a taller player in 6-foot-7 Todd Townsend and also his back-up, 6-foot-10 Steve Novak.

Langford said at the time that he had guarded bigger players during the year, including Arizona's 6-foot-8 forward Luke Walton. "There's advantages both ways. A bigger guy trying to guard me probably doesn't move his feet as well."

Meanwhile, Williams said, "My guess is that we'll guard Marquette's perimeter players and change matchups quite a bit to make sure that we do give them a different look and at the same time stay out of foul trouble."

Translation: Langford would get his fair share of times guarding Wade and his backcourt mate, Travis Diener. In 2006, Dwyane Wade became likened to "the next Jordan" for his play and ability to take over a game—

especially an NBA playoff game—in the final minutes. Wade led the Miami Heat (including former Jayhawk Wayne Simien) to the NBA title in six games against the Dallas Mavericks.

But in 2003, while Wade was still an excellent collegiate player who presented challenges for KU, it should be noted that the Jayhawks of Collison, Hinrich, Langford, Miles, and Jeff Graves presented some match-up problems for the Golden Eagles as well.

The Game of My Life

BY KEITH LANGFORD
KANSAS VS. MARQUETTE, APRIL 5, 2003

I was definitely nervous. That was our second time in the Final Four, but this time my role on the team was a lot different. I was one of the main components to the team, especially with Wayne going down early in the year.

The coaches made a big deal about Wade's game against Kentucky. There was everything in the press about it. I knew it was going to be a tough game. Playing in front of all those people, I was soaking it all in.

About Wade, you have a game plan. You know you're going to have help, because it's impossible to guard a good college player one-on-one, let alone someone as good as he is. You can go all out on defense, because you know you're going to switch out and someone else will guard him the next few possessions.

So, you give him some different looks and hope you can contain him. He ended up with 19 points, but I think we accomplished what we wanted to on him.

People talk about watching film and other ways to prepare, but the only way to get a feel for what it's going to take against a great player like that is to get out there guard him for a possession or two. Being out there on the court, you could tell that his talent level was a notch above a lot of the other guys on the floor, but I don't mean compared with Nick and Kirk.

The first couple of possessions of the game, I dropped baseline and had a relatively basic drive that ended up a two-handed dunk, and from that point I got into an incredible rhythm and I felt great. After I made a play, or someone else made a play, I got fired up looking at our bench and seeing the

218

guys get excited. After that dunk, I saw the coaches get excited. When I saw that, you could see how much everyone wanted to win—it was a boost. From there, the aggressiveness just sort of kicked in. I started dong the things I'd been doing all year: complementing Nick and Kirk and driving.

We led 59-30 at the half, and I had scored 17 points. But if you had been in that locker room, no one was smiling, no one was high-fiving and no one was "hoopla-ing." If anything, it was as if we were in a deadlocked game or were down… we walked in there focused.

Everyone knew that we had been here the year before. We were like, "Let's play the second half, let's not get anyone injured, let's do the things we have been doing. Let's hit it the same way." We came out and everyone was incredibly focused.

In the second half, Travis Diener tried to do a bounce pass to Scott Merritt. I got the jump on it. I saw it early and intercepted it in the middle of the bounce. Then I took it down for a fast-break dunk to give us a 67-30 lead.

Later on an out-of-bounds play, I came through the middle of the lane—there was a picture of it in the paper—with Wade and Robert Jackson trying to block the shot, and I scooped it underneath them.

Game and Season Results

The Jayhawks annihilated Marquette 94-61 to advance to the championship game. Langford's line for the game was 11-for-14 from the field, including a missed three-point attempt, and 1-for-3 from the line for 23 points. He also added five rebounds and four assists.

"They just did what they could and tried to take it all away, which they pretty much did," Wade said afterward.

As a team, Kansas shot 53.5 percent from the field and 42.1 percent beyond the arc while holding Marquette to 31.1 percent on all field-goal attempts.

"Some people could say we reached the pinnacle of our game today," Williams said. "I hope there's still something left in us."

Unfortunately, KU's "something" was still there on Monday night, but they did not have enough of it against Syracuse. The 'Hawks went cold from the field and the free-throw line in the championship game and lost 81-78 to Syracuse.

BOX SCORE
KANSAS VS. MARQUETTE, APRIL 5, 2003

Marquette	30 31	–	61
Kansas	59 35	–	94

Marquette (61)

	Min	FG	FT	Reb	PF	TP
Townsend	22	0-3	1-2	2	3	1
Merritt	24	5-14	2-2	11	1	12
Jackson	30	6-12	3-4	9	1	15
Wade	29	7-15	4-8	6	3	19
Diener	35	1-11	2-2	1	2	5
Bradley	14	1-7	0-0	1	1	3
Sichting	1	0-0	0-0	0	0	0
Novak	18	1-7	0-0	3	2	2
Gries	1	0-0	0-0	0	0	0
Chapman	10	0-3	0-0	0	1	0
Grimm	5	1-1	0-0	1	0	2
Sanders	11	1-1	0-0	4	3	2
(team)				1		
TOTALS	**200**	**23-74**	**12-18**	**39**	**17**	**61**

Three-point goals: 3-16 (Wade 1-1, Diener 1-5, Bradley 1-3, Novak 0-5, Townsend 0-1, Chapman 0-1); Assists: 7 (Wade 4, Diener 2, Bradley); Turnovers: 11 (Diener 8, Merritt, Wade, Sanders); Blocked shots: 3 (Merritt, Jackson, Wade); Steals: 7 (Wade 2, Diener 2, Townsend, Jackson, Bradley).

Kansas (94)

	Min	FG	FT	Reb	PF	TP
Collison	26	6-7	0-0	15	2	12
Langford	32	11-14	1-3	5	1	23
Graves	27	2-4	1-4	9	4	5
Hinrich	25	6-13	3-4	1	1	18
Miles	29	7-12	2-3	5	2	18
Hawkins	6	0-3	0-0	0	0	0
Olson	3	0-1	0-0	2	0	0
Vinson	5	0-2	0-0	1	1	0
Lee	22	4-8	2-2	6	1	13
Nash	18	1-4	1-1	4	3	3
Moody	3	0-0	0-0	2	0	0
Niang	4	1-3	0-0	1	0	2
(team)				1		
TOTALS	**200**	**38-71**	**10-17**	**52**	**15**	**94**

Three-point goals: 8-19 (Hinrich 3-7, Lee 3-3, Miles 2-4, Langford 0-1, Hawkins 0-2, Vinson 0-1, Nash 0-1); Assists: 22 (Collison 5, Langford 4, Miles 4, Lee 4, Hinrich 3, Graves, Vinson); Turnovers: 12 (Langford 3, Collison 2, Miles 2, Graves, Hinrich, Hawkins, Lee, Nash); Blocked shots: 5 (Graves 2, Collison, Langford, Miles); Steals: 8 (Graves 2, Hinrich 2, Lee 2, Langford, Nash).

Officials: Mike Kitts, Karl Hess, Tom Lopes. Attendance: 54,432.

The championship game marked Williams' last as Jayhawk coach. A week later he resigned to return to North Carolina, his alma mater and the program he had left as an assistant coach in 1988 to take the Kansas job.

What Became of Keith Langford?

The Marquette game provided Langford with a glimpse of his possible future.

"After that game was the first time I had agents contact me about playing at the next level," he says. "It was a game that propelled me to a different mind frame."

In time, Langford dismissed the idea of leaving school and returned for his junior and senior seasons under new coach Bill Self. The Jayhawks record slipped slightly to 24-9 in 2003-04, but KU reached the Elite Eight before Georgia Tech knocked them out of the tournament in overtime. Langford averaged 15.5 points that season.

As a senior, a hyper-extended elbow injury early in the conference campaign and a sprained ankle in the last regular-season game hampered Langford's effectiveness. Plus, he was hit with the flu during his convalescence from his ankle injury. When Langford returned to play in Kansas' first-round NCAA tournament game against Bucknell, he was less than 100 percent.

In a shocking upset, Bucknell defeated Kansas, the Jayhawks' first loss in the tournament's first round since 1978. Langford made no excuses for his play despite his injury. He finished his career as KU's sixth-leading all-time scorer with 1,812 points.

Langford also graduated in May 2005, earning a strategic communications degree through the school of journalism.

"I wanted a major that would keep my interest, something that I would enjoy," he says.

Collison calls Langford "a deep thinker, a deep person. He didn't always accept things just because that's the way it was done. I think that says a lot about him. Maybe he thought about things more than the rest of us. Maybe that's why he's a good writer. Maybe he's a little more intellectual than the rest of us."

Langford went undrafted in the 2005 NBA draft but tried out for the Houston Rockets in preseason. The Rockets cut him, so Langford joined his hometown Fort Worth Flyers of the NBA's Developmental League.

Midway through the season, Aaron Miles joined him after the Golden State Warriors cut him. The two ex-Jayhawks helped the Flyers reach the league's championship game, which they lost to Albuquerque. Langford scored 39 points in the loss and averaged 11.5 points per game for the Flyers.

For the 2006-07 season, he is playing for Vanoli Soresina in Italy's A-2 division

When asked about his KU experience, Langford speaks fondly of fame and his alma mater.

"I loved being recognized," he says. "I loved going to Kansas City and people doing a double-take because they couldn't believe that was Keith Langford walking by. I enjoyed watching a little kid walking around with a Keith Langford jersey, wearing number 5, the whole concept of everyone enjoying so much what we were doing. How genuine it was for everyone.

"Kansas is second to none for atmosphere. It's a special place. I'd go back now if I could. I'd encourage anyone to go there. Not just for sports. It's so diverse. It's a good place to mature."

20

WAYNE SIMIEN

The Life of Young Wayne Simien

Basketball nets took a back seat to fishing nets for a very young Wayne Simien.

"I had a fishing pole in my hands before I had a basketball in my hands," says Simien. "My dad was a big outdoorsmen, so when I was with him we'd go camping, hunting, and fishing."

The fishing trips for bass, crappie, and catfish often took dad and son to various farm ponds, Perry and Clinton Lakes in Kansas, along with Smithville, Table Rock, and Truman Lakes in Missouri.

Simien started playing competitive hoops in the third or fourth grade. Basketball camps became a common summer activity for him two or three years after that. Simien also enjoyed playing football and baseball as well as running track. In middle school, however, basketball quickly became Simien's primary game.

"By sixth, seventh, eighth grade, I was so much bigger than a lot of the other kids that I ended up playing with the high school kids," Simien says. "I was the last one to get picked and got knocked on my butt a lot, but I wanted to play with the older guys for the competition. It really made me tough."

Tough enough to endure missing his freshman season with a knee injury. Tough enough to come back strong as a sophomore and begin traveling nationally with an area AAU team.

"When I started competing against the big-city guys, people thought no good players were going to come from small-town Kansas," Simien says. "When I was competing against guys from L.A., New York, Chicago, Dallas—areas that are known for producing basketball players—my confidence was up. I also had a few Roy Williams camps under my belt by then."

As a junior, Simien led the Leavenworth High Pioneers to a 23-2 record and the Kansas 6A state championship in 2000. He was named Kansas player of the year by a slew of media outlets in 2001 after averaging 19.3 points and 10 rebounds as a senior.

In an Army town where change is a constant, "consistency" could best describe Simien, thanks to the gentle-but-firm guidance from his parents, Wayne Sr. and Margaret. Simien and his family lived in the same house all 18 years in Leavenworth. He played with the same kids. His father, a former college basketball player at Avila (Missouri), first taught Simien the game. His high school coach, Larry Hogan, coached Simien "for years, almost as long as my dad has."

Simien says his parents enjoyed his basketball experiences as long as he did.

"I didn't have a training regime, I just played the game and went to all the camps I could, but they were always on me to make sure I was still having fun and I wasn't being pushed," he says. "They didn't want me to get burned out. Knowing they were there to support me was great."

Recruiting was "a good feeling," Simien recalls, especially when some of the big schools got involved. A big-picture thinker, he deeply appreciated that recruiting meant getting his education paid for.

"I was excited to go to college without that burden on my parents," Simien says. "I had dreams of being good enough to make it to the next level, but I really wanted to get an education, graduate, and come back and perhaps work in a local business."

Simien set that plan in motion when he verbally committed to the University of Kansas during high school and signed with the Jayhawks in the early signing period in the fall of 2000.

"It was a no-brainer, being in the backyard of one of the great schools," he says.

Notes on Wayne Simien

Years lettered:	2001-02 to 2004-05
Position:	Forward
Height:	6-foot-9
Playing weight:	255 pounds
Hometown:	Leavenworth, Kansas
Current residence:	Miami, Florida
Occupation:	NBA player with the Miami Heat
Accomplishments:	2005 first-round draft pick of the Miami Heat; consensus first-team All-American in '05; Big 12 Conference Player of the Year and Big 12 All-Tournament Team in '05; winner of the team's "Dr. Forrest C. 'Phog' Allen Most Valuable Player Award," the "James Naismith Captains" award, and the "Bill Bridges Rebounding" award in 2004 and '05; Naismith Award and John R. Wooden Award finalist in '04 and '05; third-team AP All-American in '04; first-team All Big 12 Conference in '04; Big 12 All-Reserve Team in 2002; McDonald's High School All-American and Gatorade Player of the Year in Kansas in 2001.
Nickname:	"Big Dub"
The Game:	Oklahoma State vs. Kansas in Lawrence, Kansas, February 27, 2005

College Life

Roy Williams' 2001 recruiting class possessed quality and quantity. Simien was one of five players in that class, which featured high school teammates Michael Lee and Aaron Miles from Portland, Oregon; Keith Langford from Fort Worth, Texas; and Jeff Hawkins from Kansas City, Kansas.

"I was the only one with a car," Simien says. "That was quite an experience, being a taxi driver and getting in trouble with those guys. I think that made the entire situation better, going through it with those guys."

225

Simien roomed with Langford. The two got along well except for an initial language barrier.

"He has that little Texas drawl," Simien says of his roomie. "It took me about a week to understand what he was talking about. It tailed off after that. But he went home from Christmas and he picked it back up again. So we started over from scratch."

All five freshmen formed a tight bond, Simien says, so they left their doors open to make visiting easier. This "open-door" policy worked well for the most part, except Simien's refrigerator—stocked with genuine home cooking—sometimes caused problems.

"It got to where the guys would come straight into my room, walk right past me, not say anything and head straight to the refrigerator," Simien says with a laugh. "I had to lay down the law, especially with Mike Lee. I got into a few wrestling matches with him. My mom would make my favorite dessert, and he thought it was his."

When practice began in October, Simien was pitted against juniors Nick Collison and Drew Gooden. Simien enjoyed the challenge.

"When you go up against two All-Americans every day in practice, you can't help but get better," he says. "I just played 'follow the leader,' mimicked them, and played hard. That was a great part of my development during my first year. It got me ready to step in to start my sophomore year after Drew had left. Those guys helped me out tremendously."

As a freshman, Simien played with a 33-4 Final Four team that lost to eventual champion Maryland in the 2002 national semifinals. He averaged 8.1 points, 5.3 rebounds, and 15 minutes off the bench in 32 games. Simien missed Kansas' first five games recovering from arthroscopic knee surgery.

Simien's play quickly earned the respect of his teammates.

"He's everything you could hope for in a college player: size, strength, athleticism, unselfish, wanted nothing other than to win the games," Collison said. "He was a great teammate to have."

Simien became a starter as a sophomore, producing six double-doubles in first 11 games. But he dislocated his right shoulder in the 12th game of the season vs. the University of Missouri-Kansas City on January 4, 2003, at Kemper Arena in Kansas City, Missouri. Simien missed the next 11 games before playing in four more contests in late February. He played well but was

hurting. After playing only one painful minute against Texas A&M, he left the game and did not return for the season, undergoing surgery in late March. In the 16 games he played in 2002-03, Simien averaged 14.8 points and 8.2 rebounds

Kansas persevered, winning the Big 12 regular-season championship with a 14-2 mark. The Jayhawks continued their valiant play in the NCAA tournament despite Simien's absence, defeating Duke and Arizona in the West Regional to reach the Final Four in New Orleans, where KU destroyed Marquette in the national semifinal game.

"I felt bad for Wayne when he got injured his sophomore year, because he was playing great. We needed him on the floor," Collison said. "I had to sit out a year in the NBA, but hopefully I can play for 10 years. In college you only get four years. I really felt for Wayne that year, but it's the way life goes sometimes."

Simien, who called his injury "a tough situation," accompanied the team to New Orleans. Wayne Sr. visited his son's room at the team's hotel before the championship game to help his son, whose arm was in a sling, get ready.

"The hardest part was sitting out the national championship game," Simien says. "My dad was helping me put on my suit and tying my tie for me. Our eyes met for a split second, and that was all it took. We both broke down in tears. He gave me a big hug because he knew how much I wanted to be out there playing, and I knew how much he wanted me to be out there playing. But it just wasn't the time for me."

Unfortunately, it "wasn't the time" for Kansas, either. Syracuse took an early lead and withstood a determined Kansas rally to defeat the Jayhawks 81-78.

"Looking back on it now, I wouldn't trade that time for anything because of the growth that came about, personally, spiritually, and as a basketball player," Simien says.

"Spiritually" is the key word in the previous quote. In the summer of 2003, Simien became a born-again Christian after dealing with the pain of missing the season's exciting ending and the loss of coach Roy Williams to North Carolina.

"[My spirituality] means the world to me. It's the most important thing to me in my life now, and before it wasn't," Simien says. "It was a transformation of 'What am I really living for?'

"At the time I was really living for myself and basketball. Being a high-profile college athlete, a 'big man on campus,' I had everything that the world says will make you happy on a college campus. I had the spotlight and the attention, but none of it fulfilled me. I was looking for something greater to live for. I found that in Jesus Christ and the Kingdom of God.

"I remember there was a time I was so fired up about that that I didn't even want to play basketball. I really considered hanging it up because basketball had been such an idol in my life. I asked God, 'If you want me to give this up, I will.' But He told me to use my talent as a platform, that He could use me to reach a lot of people.

"In my last two years at Kansas, that's really what my main focus was. It wasn't as much to play basketball or to achieve and graduate, but it was to really use a platform that God had given me to share with other people about how Jesus Christ had changed my life."

Simien entered his junior year in 2003-04 with his newfound purpose and a new coach, Bill Self, directing the Jayhawks. With a new system in place and minus stars Collison and Kirk Hinrich, the Jayhawks "slipped" a little, going 24-9 overall and tying for second in the Big 12 with a 12-4 record. Simien missed only one game due to injury and led the team in scoring with 17.8 points and rebounding (9.3 per game).

A fourth seed in the St. Louis Regional, Kansas jelled in the NCAA tournament. The Jayhawks routed their first three opponents—Illinois-Chicago, Pacific, and the University of Alabama-Birmingham—before losing to Georgia Tech in overtime in an Elite Eight game.

The Jayhawks rocketed to a 14-0 start in the 2004-05, the senior year for Simien, Langford, Miles, and Lee (Hawkins was a redshirt junior). Key victories during the streak included a pulsating 70-68 overtime defeat of Georgia Tech on New Year's Day in Allen Fieldhouse and a hard-nosed 65-59 road triumph (both minus Simien, who missed four games due to a thumb injury) over Kentucky in Rupp Arena.

Villanova ended the perfect start, defeating KU 83-62 on January 22 in Philadelphia. The 'Hawks bounced back to win six straight conference games to improve their record to 20-1 and 10-0 in Big 12 play before hitting a rough three-game stretch in one long week during the year's shortest month.

The Setting

Kansas took its perfect conference record to Lubbock, Texas, on Valentine's Day. The Big Monday game on ESPN against Texas Tech nearly extended into early Tuesday as the game went double-overtime with Tech prevailing 80-79. The Jayhawks appeared to have the game won, leading by two with 7.9 seconds left when Miles rebounded a missed Red Raider shot. Replays indicated Miles was fouled on the play, and a puffy eye after the game confirmed it. However, Miles was called for traveling and Tech got the ball back. Seconds later Tech's Darryl Dora sank a trey to defeat the Jayhawks.

Back home on Saturday, KU went ice cold from the floor and lost to Iowa State 63-61 in overtime. The 'Hawks had little time to regroup. A quick turnaround sent the team to Norman, Oklahoma, two days later for another ESPN Big Monday contest. Emblematic of Kansas' string of bad luck, a fire alarm at the team's motel went off in the middle of the night and sent the team and the other guests into the parking lot for more than an hour while the Norman Fire Department attended to a clothes dryer fire.

Later that night, Oklahoma jumped to a 19-point lead on Kansas in the first half. To the 'Hawks credit, the team cut the deficit to one point in the second half before bowing 71-63 to the Sooners. The three-game losing streak was Kansas' first in 11 seasons.

In a week's time, Kansas tumbled from second to eighth in the polls and worse, lost its lead in conference play. Joy turned to doubt in many Jayhawks fans' minds, and Self used his radio show to ask fans to criticize the coaches and not the players. In turn, the players decided to focus solely on their next game, Sunday, February 27, at home against Oklahoma State. The Jayhawk players essentially entered "blackout" mode during the week – no media interviews, no cell phones, and no outside engagements. Excluding classes, the game came first, second, and third.

It needed to. The Cowboys arrived in Lawrence with an identical record as the Jayhawks (20-4, 10-3 in conference play). The Cowboys also were coming off an upset loss to Nebraska. Finally, Oklahoma State had drilled Kansas 80-60 in Stillwater the previous season.

Redemption. Revenge. High-caliber talent. Evenly matched teams. Senior pride. All of the elements of a great college basketball game converged that afternoon in Allen Fieldhouse. And two highly focused teams were not about to disappoint the 16,300 fans and national television audience with anything less than a terrific showing.

The Game of My Life

BY WAYNE SIMIEN
OKLAHOMA STATE VS. KANSAS, FEBRUARY 27, 2005

Most games are just a blur to me, especially afterward. But I remember being fired up. We went down there [Stillwater] the previous year and were blown out, annihilated. It was a tough moment for Coach Self because he had both played and coached at Oklahoma State. That game meant a lot to him personally. I had a burden in my heart for Coach that game, how poorly we had performed going down there that year and wanting to do well for him this year.

Both teams were tops in the Big 12. It was a championship game in the regular season. I was going head-to-head against Joey Graham, who was going for Big 12 Player of the Year. And it was on CBS. So it was like a heavyweight title match. Allen Fieldhouse was rockin' and I knew time was winding down for me. We had K-State for Senior Night and that was it at home. There was a lot on the line.

I hit a couple of shots early and we played well in the first half. But so did Oklahoma State. We had a seven-point lead, but they tied us a minute later. Later we led by five and they tied us again. They even got ahead of us, but Michael [Lee] hit a three and later Ivan McFarlin got a dunk to tie the score at 39 going into halftime.

Things went our way to start the second half. Most of my shots were falling and we got ahead by eight [with 12:47 remaining in the game] when Keith got a fast-break lay-up.

We knew what kind of team Oklahoma State was—a veteran team and an athletic team capable of a big run. But at no time did we think they would get a 27-12 run on us. We went cold for a little spell and we weren't getting stops, and the next thing you know we're fighting for our lives against them and the clock [OSU led 76-69 with 5:01 to play].

Then Aaron hit a three and JamesOn Curry made a two for OSU. They led 78-72 when Terrence Crawford fouled me with 3:59 left. I made both free throws and later tied the game at 78 on two more free throws with 1:31 to go.

I've always been a solid free-throw shooter. But they really had trouble stopping me that day. Aaron, Keith, and Mike all did a great job that day getting me the ball. Getting to the goal, getting fouled, knocking them down when it counts was tough.

The fans were just magnificent that game.

Game and Season Results

With the scored tied at 78, Lucas missed a shot with 1:10 to play that Hawkins rebounded. Kansas worked the shot clock down, and Miles converted a lay-up with 38 seconds left to give KU an 80-78 lead. With 25 seconds remaining, Christian Moody fouled Curry, who missed the first free throw but made the second to cut the Jayhawk lead to one. After KU inbounded the ball, OSU fouled Miles. The senior point guard missed the first attempt but sank the second. KU led 81-79 with 20 seconds to play.

Oklahoma State worked the ball for a good shot. KU thwarted an attempt to get the ball to Joey Graham for a three, so John Lucas took a 23-foot three-point shot with :04 left. Lee defended him closely and the shot missed. The Cowboys' Ivan McFarlin rebounded but his shot also failed as the horn sounded. KU won 81-79.

Simien finished with a career-high 32 points on 11-for-17 shooting from the field plus 10-for-11 from the line.

"Wayne just made himself Big 12 player of the year today," Langford said. "He is player of the year, hands down. We rode his back."

Basketball doesn't offer the equivalent of a "perfect game" as does baseball when a pitcher retires all 27 batters he faces without any of them reaching base. But on that afternoon, Kansas and Oklahoma State came close to perfection. The Jayhawks shot 66 percent from the field compared with the Cowboys' 58.5 percent. The two teams combined to shoot 62 percent (62-for-100) from the field.

"Twenty-five years from now, 50,000 people will be saying they were here," Self said.

As his former teammate Collison said of Simien's season-ending injury in 2003, "It's the way life goes sometimes." That comment serves

BOX SCORE
OKLAHOMA STATE VS. KANSAS, FEBRUARY 27, 2005

Oklahoma State	39 40	– 79
Kansas	39 42	– 81

Oklahoma State (79)

	Min	FG	FT	Reb	PF	TP
J. Graham	33	9-17	0-0	4	4	19
McFarlin	33	1-4	6-6	5	3	8
Lucas	40	9-11	0-0	2	1	22
Bobik	27	2-4	0-0	0	3	5
Curry	36	6-8	1-2	5	2	15
S. Graham	17	4-7	1-1	0	4	10
Crawford	14	0-2	0-0	3	3	0
(team)				1		
TOTALS	200	31-53	8-9	20	20	79

Three-point goals: 9-19 (Lucas 4-5, Curry 2-3, Bobik 1-3, S. Graham 1-3, J. Graham 1-5); Assists: 14 (McFarlin 3, Lucas 3, J. Graham 2, Bobik 2, Curry 2, S. Graham 2); Turnovers: 9 (Bobik 3, J. Graham 2, McFarlin 2, Curry, S. Graham); Blocked shots: 2 (McFarlin 2); Steals: 4 (Lucas, Curry, S. Graham, Crawford).

Kansas (81)

	Min	FG	FT	Reb	PF	TP
Simien	34	11-17	10-11	12	2	32
Moody	34	5-6	1-2	0	2	11
Langford	34	6-8	1-2	3	2	14
Miles	35	5-7	1-4	1	1	13
Giddens	18	0-3	0-1	1	0	0
Lee	22	3-4	0-1	1	2	7
Hawkins	11	0-0	2-2	2	2	2
Jackson	7	1-1	0-0	2	1	2
Kaun	5	0-1	0-0	0	1	0
(team)				1		
TOTALS	200	31-47	15-23	23	13	81

Three-point goals: 4-8 (Miles 2-3, Langford 1-1, Lee 1-2, Giddens 0-2); Assists: 18 (Miles 6, Langford 5, Giddens 3, Lee 2, Simien, Moody); Turnovers: 10 (Simien 3, Langford 2, Giddens 2, Moody, Miles, Kaun); Blocked shots: 1 (Simien); Steals: 4 (Giddens 2, Miles, Lee).

Officials: Ted Hillary, John Clougherty, Mike Whitehead. Attendance: 16,300.

as a fitting summation for the final five games of Kansas' 2004-05 season.

Donning retro uniforms, the Jayhawks defeated Kansas State 72-65 in a Senior Night game that also celebrated Allen Fieldhouse's 50th anniversary. Simien scored 25 points and had 20 rebounds in the victory and gave a lengthy, emotional speech afterward.

The Jayhawks' season finale in Columbia, Missouri, turned out to be emotional as well, but for entirely different reasons. Missouri upset the Jayhawks 72-68, and Langford sprained his ankle. The senior also had endured a hyperextended elbow earlier in conference play.

In the Big 12 conference tournament, Kansas defeated Kansas State but then lost to Oklahoma State 78-75 in the semifinals. Langford missed both games, not only because of his ankle injury but also due to being dehydrated from a bad case of the flu.

Kansas entered the NCAA tournament as a three-seed against unheralded Bucknell in Oklahoma City's Ford Center. In one of the biggest first-round upsets in NCAA tournament history, Bucknell edged Kansas 64-63. The Jayhawks led 31-28 at halftime, but the Bisons hung tough with the cold-shooting 'Hawks (1-for-11 beyond the arc and no field goals in the final eight minutes) in the second half to capture a shocking victory. Simien led the team with 24 points and 10 rebounds. He caught a near-80-foot in-bound pass from Lee but missed a difficult, twisting turnaround jumper from near the free-throw line as the game ended.

"It was a great opportunity," Simien said after the game. "The ball was in my hands. It didn't work out."

Thus ended the gallant college careers of Simien, Langford, Lee, and Miles as the Jayhawks lost their first first-round tournament game since 1978, a few years before any of the seniors were born.

What Became of Wayne Simien?

When the Miami Heat picked Simien as the next-to-last first-round pick of the NBA draft in June 2005, the selection took him about as far away from Kansas geographically and culturally as possible.

It didn't change him, though. Simien remains the same well-grounded Kansas guy he's always been.

"I definitely know that every time I step out on the court, in college and especially now, that I represent something more than myself: my family, my hometown, the whole state of Kansas, the university, all the people who helped me get here," he says. "I use that as a motivation to go out and work hard every day and go out just be a man of character and integrity."

The integrity showed during a lengthy season that extended almost nine months long. From college All-American to NBA benchwarmer, Simien never pouted or complained while playing in only 43 regular-season games in which he averaged 3.4 points and two rebounds in slightly less than 10 minutes per game. He saw limited action during the 2006 playoffs and did not play at all during the veteran-laden Heat's come-from-behind world championship run versus the Dallas Mavericks in the NBA finals.

Simien also continues sharing his spirituality as a professional athlete.

"It's been amazing," he says. "I want to see other people's lives change like my life changed a few years ago."

His life further changed in the summer of 2006 when he married Katie Allen, a Florida State graduate whom he met through church. And the summer before that, his life of fishing with his father came full circle when the two explored Florida's Lake Okeechobee before training camp started. Dad and son caught some large-mouth bass and reeled in a 17-pound tarpon.

"It was probably the best fishing day we ever had together to this point," Simien says.

The phrase "to this point" summarizes well the accomplishments and promise of Wayne Simien. After all, with the Big Guy on his side (and we don't mean Shaquille O'Neal), how can Simien do anything but succeed?

ACKNOWLEDGMENTS

Thank you to the University of Kansas men's basketball office, head coach Bill Self, and secretary Joanie Stephens for their invaluable assistance. Thank you to Chris Theisen, assistant athletics director for media relations at the University of Kansas, and his staff—especially office manager Candace Dunback (now director of KU's Booth Family Hall of Athletics) and assistant media relations director Beau White—for opening their office and vast number of files to me.

Thank you to Barry Bunch, assistant archivist, University of Kansas Archives; Bill Crowe; and the staff at the Spencer Research Library for excellent and thorough record keeping and prompt, helpful service.

Thank you to media relations specialists Michael Lissack of the Miami Heat, Semaj Marsh of the Houston Rockets, Jeff McCoy of the Indiana Pacers, Garin Narain of the Cleveland Cavaliers, and Mark Rosenberg of the Seattle Supersonics for their time and effort in helping me secure interviews with our Jayhawks playing professionally. Gentlemen, you are the pros' pros.

Thank you to area sportswriters and columnists Gary Bedore and Chuck Woodling of the *Lawrence Journal-World;* Ric Anderson, Kurt Caywood, Rick Dean, Pete Goering, and the late Bob Hentzen of the *Topeka Capital-Journal;* Blair Kerkhoff of the *Kansas City Star;* and Rick Plumlee of the *Wichita Eagle* for their consistently fine and entertaining work that supplied background information and accuracy for this book. You serve your readers extremely well.

Thank you to my instructors and editors through the years, including Dave Torbett and the late Dick Hardy from my hometown of Independence, Kansas; the late Harold Keith, Johnny Keith, and Mike Treps from the University of Oklahoma; and Tim Bengtson, Tom Eblen, Ted Frederickson, Paul Jess, and the late Bob Rhodes from the University of Kansas.

Thank you to Doug Hoepker, my editor at Sports Publishing, for your patience, understanding, and guidance.

Thank you to my good friend, Phil Wilke, for serving as a sounding board, transcribing many lengthy taped interviews, and direction.

And thank you to my lovely wife, Tammy, for her infinite patience regarding the numerous "So how does this sound?" questions and enduring, loving support.

CREDITS

Lawrence Journal-World:
Ch. 3 quotes 20 (April 5, 1988), 25 (April 1, 1988), 26 (April 6, 1988)
Ch. 4 quotes 11 and 12 (Nov. 21, 1989)
Ch. 5 quotes 16 and 17 (March 23, 1991)
Ch. 6 quote 19 (April 2, 1991)
Ch. 7 quote 20 (March 21, 1993)
Ch. 8 quote 19 (Dec. 22, 1993)
Ch. 9 quote 15 (Jan. 25, 1994)
Ch. 10 quote 13 (Dec. 7, 1996)
Ch. 12 quote 14 (Jan. 10, 1998)
Ch. 13 quotes 13 (March 14, 1999), 14 (March 16, 1999)
Ch. 14 quotes 13 (March 6, 2000), 14 (March 5, 2000)
Ch. 18 quote 23 (Jan. 28, 2003)
Ch. 20 quotes 16 and 17 (Feb. 28, 2005), 18 (March 19, 2005)

Topeka Capital-Journal:
Ch. 15 quote 12 (Jan. 29, 2002)
Ch. 18 quotes 20 and 21 (both Jan. 27, 2003)
Ch. 19 quotes 19 and 20 (April 5, 2003), 21 (April 6, 2003)

Kansas City Star:
Ch. 11 quote 11 (Feb. 23, 1997)
Ch. 14 quote 10 (March 5, 2000)
Ch. 15 quote 11 (Jan. 29, 2002)

Wichita Eagle:
Ch. 10 quote 12 (Dec. 6, 1996)
Ch. 13 quote 12 (March 14, 1999)

Associated Press:
Ch. 12 quote 19 (Jan. 21, 2005)

Daily Oklahoman:
Ch. 3 quote 22 (April 5, 1988)

NCAA (post-game statistics and quotes):
Ch. 3 quote 23 (April 4, 1988)
Ch. 6 quote 18 (April 1, 1991)

New York Times:
Ch. 1 quote 7 (March 26, 1986)

University Daily Kansan :
Ch. 14 quotes 11 and 12 (March 3, 2000)

University of Kansas Sports Information Office:
Ch. 9 quotes 16 and 17 (Jan. 26, 1994)

USA Today :
Ch. 1 quote 9 (March 28, 1986)
Ch. 19 quote 22 (April 7, 2003)

Celebrate the Heroes of Kansas Sports
in These Other Releases from Sports Publishing!

Beware of the Phog: 50 Years of Allen Fieldhouse

The history of the facility that houses Kansas basketball gives unique insight into the epic battles that have occurred in the legendary building from the coaches, players, fans, and administrators who lived them.

ISBN: 1-58261-718-X
$29.95 hardcover

Crowning the Kansas City Royals: Remembering the 1985 World Series Champs

Crowning the Kansas City Royals celebrates the Royals' 1985 World Series victory with profiles of stars from that team, including George Brett, Frank White, and Bret Saberhagen; and details on the comeback victory in Game Six of the World Series.

ISBN: 1-58261-826-7
$19.95 hardcover

Tales from the Jayhawks Hardwood: Second Edition

This updated and revised collection of first-hand memories from the players and coaches who have made history at Kansas includes stories about Wilt Chamberlain, Jo Jo White, Danny Manning, Drew Gooden, and others.

ISBN: 1-58261-890-9
$14.95 softcover

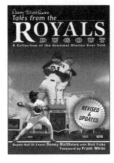

Denny Matthews' Tales from the Royals Dugout (updated edition)

The Royals' longtime radio announcer relives the club's greatest moments and proud tradition with tales about the team's great rivalries with the Yankees and A's, and the remarkable players who have become heroes in Kansas City.

ISBN: 1-59670-039-4
$14.95 softcover

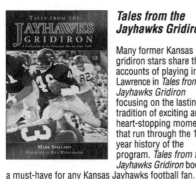

Tales from the Jayhawks Gridiron

Many former Kansas gridiron stars share their accounts of playing in Lawrence in *Tales from the Jayhawks Gridiron* focusing on the lasting tradition of exciting and heart-stopping moments that run through the 100+ year history of the program. *Tales from the Jayhawks Gridiron* book is a must-have for any Kansas Jayhawks football fan.

ISBN: 1-58261-791-0
$19.95 hardcover

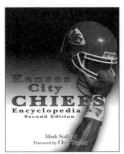

Kansas City Chiefs Encyclopedia: Second Edition

Kansas City Chiefs Encyclopedia chronicles the history of the Kansas City Chiefs franchise – from its beginning in Dallas with head coach Hank Stram, the great 1962 AFL championship game, the move to Kansas City, and much more.

ISBN: 1-58261-834-8
$39.95 hardcover